M000238269

The Morality of Radical Economics

Ron P. Baiman

The Morality of Radical Economics

Ghost Curve Ideology and the Value Neutral
Aspect of Neoclassical Economics

palgrave
macmillan

Ron P. Baiman
Benedictine University
Illinois, USA

ISBN 978-1-137-45558-1   ISBN 978-1-137-45559-8   (eBook)
DOI 10.1057/978-1-137-45559-8

Library of Congress Control Number: 2016940311

Cover image © edie raff / Alamy Stock Photo

Printed on acid-free paper

This Palgrave Macmillan imprint is published by Springer Nature
The registered company is Nature America Inc. New York

To my lifelong partner, Michelle, and children, Jeremy, Rachel, and Rebecca, for their unwavering support of my radical economics journey, and to my mother, Sydney, and late father and brother Jerome Giora and Jonathan, for starting and accompanying me on my path.

ACKNOWLEDGEMENTS

I would like to acknowledge the help of my son, Jeremy Baiman, and student assistants Caitlyn Prosapio and Yalin Wang, who reviewed earlier drafts of some of the chapters and performed miracles by producing, at very short notice, many of the figures in this book.

I would also like to thank present and past Chicago Political Economy Group (CPEG) friends and colleagues Bill Barclay, Peter Dorman, Luis Diaz-Perez, Mehrene Larudee, Joe Persky, Mel Rothenberg, Sidney Hollander, Bruce Parry, Sharon Post, and many others; Democratic Socialists of America (DSA) friends and colleagues Michael Baker, Tom Broderick, Nurtan Esmen, Alec Hudson, Bob Roman, Jan Sansone, Joe Schwartz, Peg Strobel, and many others; Ethical Humanist and Ethical Culture friends Tom Hoeppner, Steve Julstrom, Alan Kimmel, Yafim and Lena Kotlyar, Oliver Pergams, Jim White, and many others; and my too-numerous-to-enumerate past work colleagues and friends and Union for Radical Political Economy (URPE) and New School for Social Research friends, colleagues, teachers, and class-mates for their support and encouragement along the path that led to this book. A special thanks goes to fellow radical economist Vince Snowberger who found an error in my first progressive pricing paper that induced me to publish the second corrected paper cited in Part III of this book.

Finally I would like to acknowledge the support of past and present Palgrave Macmillan editors Leila Campoli, Sarah Lawrence, and Allison Neuburger and my indexer Suzanne. Sherman Aboulfadl for their faith, encouragement, and patience in allowing me to initiate and complete this project, and the financial support of the Benedictine University Faculty Development Fund and the encouragement and support of my Benedictine University colleagues for my work on this book.

CONTENTS

LIST OF FIGURES

LIST OF TABLES

Economics as a Moral Science: The Philosophy and Science of Morality

Are people atoms or molecules? Are societies solar systems? Or insect colonies? Can a social science be value-free? Is not morality or empathy for our fellow humans and other living beings, a core part of being human?

Should social science attempt to be value-free? Can it do this? What are values or morals? Do they have meaning outside of specific cultures, religions, and histories? Are there universal values and can they be reasonably debated based on empirical evidence?

Can economics be value-free? Should it? Are there economic schools of thought that are openly values-based? Is there a choice? Is it not time to expose the value neutral pretense of mainstream or Neoclassical (NC) and economics as a status-quo supporting ideological construct, and acknowledge that economic thinking is always values-based and that the real issue is *what* values?

Part I is an exploration of these questions.

CHAPTER 1

Introduction

INTRODUCTION

A 2013 Oxfam report estimates that the richest 85 people in the world own as much wealth as the entire bottom half of the world's population (Oxfam 2014).[1] Another recent report indicates that 23.1 % of children in the USA live in poverty, the highest percentage among 35 developed countries—surpassed only by Romania,[2] even as the country hosts, at 5.9 % of households, the highest share of millionaire households, with over a million dollars in private financial wealth, of any large country in the world.[3] A widely disseminated "political economy book of the century"[4] documents in devastating empirical and historical detail the increasing "patrimonial" nature of twenty-first-century capitalism showing that it is well on its way to resurrecting a nineteenth-century class system based on inherited wealth that violates even the most basic notions of meritocracy (Piketty 2014).

---

[1] http://www.oxfam.org/sites/www.oxfam.org/files/bp-working-for-few-political-capture-economic-inequality-200114-summ-en.pdf

[2] http://www.unicef-irc.org/publications/pdf/rc10_eng.pdf

[3] According to the 2012 Boston Consulting Group estimates of private financial wealth, the USA has the 7th highest per-capita share of millionaires of any country in the world, after Qatar, Switzerland, Singapore, Hong Kong, Kuwait, and Bahrain, see: http://www.bcg.de/documents/file135355.pdf. The US millionaire household share is more than twice as high as that of the only other large country in the top 15—Canada in 15th place with 2.9 %.

[4] "It's been half a century since a book of economic history broke out of its academic silo with such fireworks." Giles Whitell, *The Times*, May 7, 2014.

© The Editor(s) (if applicable) and The Author(s) 2016
R.P. Baiman, *The Morality of Radical Economics*,
DOI 10.1057/978-1-137-45559-8_1

The direct causes of these extreme concentrations of poverty and wealth are obvious for any who cares to look. A marquee example is Walmart, the largest private employer in the world.

Walmart has what is euphemistically called "a low-wage business model."[5] In 2012, a leaked document detailing Walmart's official compensation policy revealed that its "sales associates" typically start at or near minimum wage ($7.25 an hour for states without higher state minimums) and received raises of only 20–40 cents an hour in incremental promotions. A worker with consistently "flawless performance evaluations" who started at $8.00 an hour could, after 6 years, expect a maximum hourly wage of $10.60.[6] Walmart workers are paid so poorly that they are eligible for numerous US means tested public subsidies such as food stamps, Medicaid payments, and earned-income tax credits.[7] A 2013 report for the Democratic staff of a US Congressional Committee estimated that the average Walmart store costs US taxpayers $904,000 a year or roughly $5000 per employee.[8] Walmart is also notoriously antiunion and a pioneer and leader in low-wage outsourcing from China (Workplace Fairness 2014)[9] (Scott 2007).[10]

At the same time, Walmart made $17 billion in profits in 2013, paid its CEO in excess of $20 million, and provided an estimated $3.16 billion in dividends to entities controlled by three Walmart heirs.[11] In 2014, the six Walmart heirs were estimated to be worth at least $ 150 billion.[12] In 2010, they were estimated to own more wealth than the bottom 42 % of US families combined.[13] With this enormous concentrated economic power,

[5] In 2012 Walmart had 2.1 million employees worldwide, and (in 2013) 1.6 million in the USA, see: http://www.bbc.com/news/magazine-17429786 and http://www.economist.com/blogs/dailychart/2011/09/employment?fsrc=scn/tw/te/dc/defending

[6] See: http://www.huffingtonpost.com/2012/11/16/walmarts-internal-compensation-plan_n_2145086.html

[7] The USA had the 8th lowest social spending as a share of GDP among the 35 OECD countries in 2013, see: http://www.oecd-ilibrary.org/social-issues-migration-health/government-social-spending_20743904-table1

[8] See report for the Democratic staff of the House Committee on Education and the Workforce, May 2013: http://democrats.edworkforce.house.gov/sites/democrats.edworkforce.house.gov/files/documents/WalMartReport-May2013.pdf

[9] http://www.workplacefairness.org/reports/good-bad-wal-mart/wal-mart.php

[10] See: http://www.epi.org/publication/ib235/

[11] http://walmart1percent.org/why-the-waltons/

[12] http://www.forbes.com/billionaires/list/#tab:overall

[13] http://walmart1percent.org/2012/07/17/new-data-waltons-richer-america-poorer/ and http://www.forbes.com/billionaires/list/#tab:overall

the Walmart heirs are actively supporting numerous conservative political causes (Rich 2014).[14] These six passive investors, by virtue of their inheritance, are sitting on and controlling a $150 billion pile of claims to resources, resources that allow them to extract billions in further claims from the work of a veritable army of low-paid workers who can barely survive, even as they toil to generate more wealth for their passive billionaire owner-employers.[15]

In the advanced capitalist countries, Walmart has increasingly become the rule rather than the exception. As noted above, using the most detailed and exhaustive data on individual income ever assembled, Piketty (2014) has shown that inherited privilege has become a dominant "law of motion" of modern capitalism. Does this make any sense to anyone? Are these enormous levels of wealth inequality functional or justifiable?

Even if the initial accumulation was "earned" through a combination of talent, education, luck, and ruthless monopolistic business strategies, as for example, in the case of Bill Gates, does it make sense for one person to be, in the words of American Federation of Teachers President Randy Weingarten, "richer than God" with an estimated $80 billion in wealth? (Sorkin 2014).[16]

When a single individual has this much personal economic power, anything they do is almost sure to swamp the political and democratic process. For example, Gates and his philanthropic Foundation are (arguably, unlike the Waltons) trying to do good things for drug and vaccine development and public education, but his brute economic power renders even the most well-intentioned initiatives controversial. For example, Gates' Foundation staff reportedly "don't talk about drug patents," a critical barrier to drug

---

[14] http://mobile.nytimes.com/2014/04/26/us/a-walmart-fortune-spreading-charter-schools.html?referrer=&_r=0

[15] The term "rentier" comes from the French and designates persons who derive income from "rentes" or state bonds. In political economy, it refers to persons or entities who derive income from "economic rents" or ownership of property, such as real estate or income-generating financial assets, which confers passive income for which no labor is necessary. Classical political economists, such as Smith, Ricardo, and Marx, routinely railed against rentiers, mostly landlords at the time, who were considered to be an unproductive parasitical class. Keynes similarly called for the "euthanasia" of the rentier (Keynes 1936, Chap. 24), and, at least in theory, "economic rent" is considered an undeserved and unproductive use of economic resources in both modern NC and radical economics.

[16] http://www.nytimes.com/2014/09/07/magazine/so-bill-gates-has-this-idea-for-a-history-class.html?_r=0 and http://www.america.aljazeera.com/opinions/2014/10/bill-gates-thomaspikettycapitalwealthinequality.html

and vaccine dissemination, because it is a source of Gates' wealth,[17] and as prominent education scholar Diane Ravitch points out, in reference to a Gates' "Big History Project" education initiative: "I wonder how Bill Gates would treat the robber barons. I wonder how Bill Gates would deal with issues of extremes of wealth and poverty."[18]

Does anybody think that these conditions are the mark of a successful economic system? Neoclassical (NC) economics[19] legitimizes these, intolerable by every major religious and philosophical moral standard, absolute and relative disparities of income and wealth by claiming to be *value neutral*[20] with regard to *socially preferred* wealth and income distribution.[21] Is there an economics school of thought that robustly condemns this outcome as the moral, political, and economic failure that it is and that bases its theoretical and policy analysis on this understanding? This book argues that so-called radical economics in the USA, and progressive "heterodox economics" or "political economy" in other countries, is based on this understanding—an understanding that should be shared by *all* economic schools of thought.

This is not just a matter of a destructive economic model.[22] It is a moral outrage. Economists should not eschew their moral responsibility to condemn these grossly unjust and undemocratic arrangements by

---

[17] Op. cit.

[18] Op. cit.

[19] The label Neoclassical economics designates the standard economics taught today in 99 % of formal economics courses in the USA and most other parts of the world. The term is meant to differentiate the founders of this school of thought, Marshall, Jevons, Menger, Walras, Clark, Pareto, and others who came to dominate academic economics in the late nineteenth and early twentieth centuries, from the earlier eighteenth to mid-nineteenth century "classical" political economic thinking of Smith, Malthus, Ricardo, Marx, and others.

[20] As is discussed in detail later on in the text, the NC value neutral position assumes that the "science" of economics must eschew any concern about morality or other forms of prescriptive thinking about good or bad economic outcomes in its "core" theoretical apparatus. In their professional scientific role, economists must exclusively focus on "how" questions and these questions can be entirely separated from "ought" questions having to do with politics and values.

[21] Many individual NC economists are political liberals who personally oppose growing economic inequality but, as is discussed in detail in this book, the "scientific" position of NC economics is that these kinds of value judgments lie outside the proper domain of economics as a social science.

[22] The massive US low-wage service sector increases poverty, increases trade and public and private debt, increases trade deficits, undermines the middle-class and general prosperity, and supports parasitical and destructive rentiers (Baiman et al. 2011; Baiman 2014).

pretending to be value-free and amoral, and they should surely not be in the business of justifying these economic systems out of some misguided conception of impartiality. Silence on these and the many other profoundly immoral outcomes of modern capitalism is complicity. If it is to be relevant to people and to society, economics must be based on moral values. There is no excuse for not condemning economic arrangements that violate the most universally shared moral imperatives to help and support the poor and destitute and to condemn wealthy exploiters of the poor. Economic theory needs to be based on these broadly accepted moral values and should not hide behind an indecisive, misplaced, and effectively apologetic amorality, or moral relativism.

We have accepted a status quo in which billions of human beings are reduced to mass deprivation, exploitation, and abuse. A good part of this is due to economic arrangements that place property rights above human needs by, for example, sanctioning the rights of rentiers, or passive investors, to accumulate unfathomable wealth even as the billions of humans who produce this wealth are reduced to hopelessness and misery. This includes both abysmally low-paid workers and the millions who are languishing without employment,[23] all without a public response to create well-paid employment and minimal guaranteed income (Baiman et al. 2011). The hegemonic economic school of thought, NC economics, bases its core theoretical analysis on hypothetically *fully employed* labor markets and the *optimal welfare efficiency* of capitalist market economies (Weeks 2014, Introduction; Taylor 2004). Economics should not be at the forefront of justifying this illegitimate system as an unavoidable outcome of markets and sacrosanct property rights but, rather, should be leading efforts to expose the immorality of this kind of economic arrangement and proposing and advocating policy solutions for it.

This does not mean that economists need to be wild-eyed utopians. Realistic and politically popular policy options, such as the "Robin Hood" tax on financial speculation, to fund large-scale living-wage job programs in green energy, social services, and infrastructure are perfectly plausible

---

[23] The International Labor Organization (ILO) has estimated that 203 million people were unemployed—that is, they were in the labor force desiring a job but could not get one—in 2013: http://www.ilo.org/global/research/global-reports/global-employment-trends/2014/WCMS_234107/lang–en/index.htm. And this is undoubtedly a gross underestimate of the massive armies of unemployed workers, especially in developing countries, who have no hope of ever getting a full-time wage or salaried job in the formal sector of the economy and are not counted as officially unemployed.

(Baiman et al. 2012).[24] Piketty (2014, Chap. 14) has suggested a global tax on capital. Many other perfectly realistic proposals have been offered (Hartmann 2014). Hill (2010), Huber and Stephens (2001), and Baiman (2014) and many countries, particularly in northern Europe, have made tremendous progress toward building more just, sustainable, and democratic economies by removing a large proportion of economic activity completely or partially out of the private for-profit production sector.

Why can we not "euthanize the rentier" as Keynes famously advocated (in their economic function, not as people) (Keynes 1936, Chap. 24)? The answer, of course, is political; but a major source of political legitimation for this manifestly inequitable and increasingly dysfunctional global economic system is NC economics—a theory based on the presumption that the natural and normal way for national and world economies to function is as capitalist market economies with minimal constraints on capital. And this argument continues to be made even as rentierism, a fundamental and increasingly dominant characteristic of these economies, undermines their ability to generate real production and living-wage employment and avoid a planetary crisis (Klein 2014).

Karl Polanyi (1944) pointed out at the end of the previous round of debate over what were then liberal, and now neoliberal, free-market policies, that markets are fundamentally creatures of society. There is no such thing as markets acting in isolation. Rather markets act, or should act, as they have been constructed to act by social policy. Properly regulated competitive markets, especially under conditions of relative income and wealth equality, can promote innovation and efficiency in production. Low markups in mature competitive markets, can keep prices close to production costs for consumers. But left on their own, unregulated markets under capitalism become vehicles for increasingly concentrated and polarized economic and political power that leads to a growing abrogation of liberty and democracy. Contrary to the most basic tenets of NC economic ideology taught in mainstream introductory textbooks, market outcomes, especially with regard to distribution, employment, and growth, have no inherent normative value. Their morality or immorality is a function of the social and political system within which they are embedded.

---

[24] See: http://www.cpegonline.org/reports/jobs.pdf for earlier 2009 version.

The Mainstream or NC Economics Position

Mainstream, or NC, economics professes to be a value neutral positivist scientific discipline that describes how the economy works and can be made to work better, or more efficiently, that is strictly separable from normative value judgments. This stance allows NC economics to position itself as The Science of Economics and claim superiority over economic schools of thought that, in the NC view, are theories based on ideology as they include normative judgments. The latter, in the NC view, are the proper subject matter of politics and other "softer" social sciences like political science, sociology, and anthropology. This position has led to a persistent institutional repression by NC economics of non-NC schools of thought causing isolation and marginalization of heterodox economics schools of thought within economics departments, academic publications, and general economics conferences (Lee 2009).[25]

The NC wall of separation of values, or politics, from economics is premised on the assumption that the economy is fundamentally a realm of free and voluntary equal exchanges among individuals that is separable from the realm of government or politics. Politics, in the NC view, involves coercion and, in particular, the use of state power and direct bureaucratic authority to implement social choice. As will be explained in this book, NC economists believe that, subject to government enforcement of contracts and property rights and appropriate measures to correct for market failures, the economy is a realm of freedom, and the proper role of economics is to enhance this freedom by reducing "deadweight" (politically neutral) loss from these exchanges. Economics should restrict itself to finding ways in which one or more individuals can improve their (self-defined) economic welfare without harming the economic welfare of any other individual.

In a canonical treatment of this issue, Bowles and Gintis (1987) have described this critical liberal partitioning of society into public and private domains, the former subject to principles of liberty *and* democracy and the latter subject only to principles of liberty, as key to "making the power of capital invisible" and the labor market and the economy "a realm of private voluntary exchange" in liberal political theory, rather than its more accurate characterization as "a structure of command" and "system of control" (p. 64–65). They claim that though standard texts in political

---

[25] For example among 235 economics journals in the worldwide "Social Science Citation Index" (SSCI) only 8 are "heterodox," and there are only 22 "heterodox" accredited economics PhD programs among the 359 worldwide. See: http://heterodoxnews.com/hed/graduate/ and http://www.gradschools.com/search-programs/economics.

theory do not generally offer a clearly articulated rationale for this assumption that "socially consequential power" that based on democratic principles should be subject to democratic accountability is irrelevant to the private economy, the implicit NC argument appears to rest on two central propositions: (a) a "labor commodity" proposition, which asserts that "the employer has no more power over the worker than the shopper has over the grocer, or any other buyer over a seller," and (b) an "asset neutrality" proposition, which asserts that competitive capital markets "divorce the substantial control of economic activity in business and finance from the ownership of assets" (p. 67–68). The later is the assumption that anyone can organize a company and hire anyone else to work for them and that markets will impartially support the most efficient and beneficial companies and managers.

Bowles and Gintis present a detailed critique of the NC view by noting the numerous ways in which profit for owners, and engineering or organizational efficiency of production, are not the same given the surveillance and monitoring costs that are necessary when "capital hires labor." They also point out the many reasons why "democratic labor-organized" firms do not have equal access to capital. These include little collateral, no hierarchical system of power allowing lenders to easily influence and control production, and no ability to summarily fire and hire workers in the interests of greater profits.[26] These examples illustrate the commonsense understanding that *ownership is power* or, in the words of Thomas Hobbes, "to have servants is to have power."[27] An understanding that anyone who has had to keep a job with an abusive employer because they cannot seamlessly exit a work place and find another comparable job (as the NC textbook mythology of a full-employment competitive labor market based on voluntary contracts between agents of equal power implies) can readily see.[28]

---

[26] Among other things, the NC position is based on a presumption that the market will determine a single, unique equilibrium point, which, as is discussed in later chapters, is highly unlikely even under the most stringent NC initial assumptions.

[27] The neutral term 'employee' did come into general use until the full development of capitalism in the nineteenth century (Bowles and Gintis 1987, p. 72).

[28] To be fair, there is a strand of NC theory, initiated by Coase (1937), that recognizes that the existence of the firm is an indication that non-market intra-firm planned coordination is a key component of even the most free-market capitalist economies. But the focus of this analysis is on "transaction cost" savings and other efficiencies captured by the firm (or its owners), rather than on the internal hierarchical command structure that workers are subjected to within the firm.

Research showing the increasing limits of social mobility between classes, with the USA having the least mobility of advanced capitalist countries,[29] along with Piketty's finding, alluded to above, that capitalism is reverting to its historic patrimonial inherited-wealth-based class structure, serve to reinforce this commonsense understanding. Piketty's exhaustive empirical analysis showing that the returns to wealth have historically been higher than real economic growth provides authoritative empirical support for Marx's point that, left on its own, capitalism will bury "living" earned income under a mountain of "dead," accumulated, and increasingly oppressive wealth, is refreshing in its candor and forthright demystification and condemnation of the carefully constructed NC mythology of merit and risk-based rewards (Piketty 2014, Chaps. 11 and 12).[30] But all this is invisible in liberal political theory, an invisibility that is aided and abetted by a similar glaring lacuna in NC economics.

In effect, the NC argument is that competitive markets will determine an optimal equilibrium point for technology, and labor and capital, for every possible initial allocation of wealth, so that individual or social power plays no significant role in the economy. In the standard NC treatment, inherent self-interest (*individual preferences*), labor force growth (*biology*), and natural human inventiveness (*technology*) interact through voluntary exchanges in a value neutral market to set economic outcomes so that social choice, values, or politics play no significant role in economic outcomes. This view stands in stark contrast to neo-Marxist and neo-Keynesian

[29] See for example this 2010 OECD report: http://www.oecd.org/tax/public-finance/chapter%205%20gfg%202010.pdf and this earlier PEW/Brookings report based on 1998–2001 data from the International Social Survey Program by Julia Isaacs: http://www.brookings.edu/~/media/research/files/reports/2008/2/economic%20mobility%20sawhill/02_economic_mobility_sawhill_ch3.pdf

[30] Though Marx would probably go farther and point out that the key problem with returns on wealth being higher than real economic growth (r > g) is not really that r is greater than g but the highly unequal functional distribution of income based on wealth and labor and the pretense that wealth in itself generates value and deserves a return, instead of being a surplus that ultimately comes from the work and inventions of real people that needs to be allocated for the benefit of humans and not to prior wealth. However, Piketty is correct that the extraordinarily unequal accumulation of these claims on real assets (that confer real power even if they cannot possibly all be redeemed for real goods, services, and property due to their inflated values) is a threat to the very foundations of democracy and an economy that is supposed to deliver sustainable *mass* prosperity. His wealth tax proposal may also be the most politically viable way to deal with this (short of simply de-legitimating the idea that wealth deserves a return). Reallocating these dangerously large concentrations of wealth to public funds would also serve to increase the power of collective (governmental) action that is critical if we are to save ourselves from planetary disaster (Klein 2014).

(or post-Keynesian) models in which class struggle over wages and profits and investor confidence and decisions play key social choice roles in setting broad economic outcomes (Marglin 1984, Chap. 2).

Thus in the NC view, economists should exclusively engage in the study of objective (market-mediated) relationships between economic variables in order to advise political leaders on how to achieve particular socially chosen economic outcomes through these market processes. But as scientists, economists should refrain, as much as possible, from being influenced by subjective values and politics and use economic science to provide purely value neutral descriptive advice on the most efficient means for reaching the chosen political goals, whatever these goals may be. The NC definition of efficiency is directed toward reducing or eliminating "deadweight loss" ensuring that no agent can be better off without harming another agent and that aggregate "consumer and producer surplus" or benefit is maximized. Both of these controversial definitions of efficiency are discussed extensively in later chapters. These chapters also discuss how closely linked these definitions of efficiency and, indeed, this entire frame of reference are to the basic, but fundamentally erroneous, supply and demand model (SDM) of the NC economic meme. The key point in this context is, however, that neither of these forms of efficiency includes any consideration of equity or fairness in distribution.

Hill and Myatt (2010) offer this succinct summary of NC economic ideology[31]:

> What is the ideological perspective with which Neoclassical economics is infused? .... The roots of neo-classical economics go back through Adam Smith to the classical liberals – to John Locke and then later to John Stuart Mill – and their fundamental values of individual responsibility, freedom of choice, the sanctity of private property, and minimal government interference. In other words, neoclassical economics is aligned with a political philosophy that in the eighteenth and nineteenth centuries was called classical liberalism and today would be called conservative. (p. 42).

---

[31] See (Linder and Julius, 1977) for an earlier critique of this kind.

THE RADICAL OR PROGRESSIVE HETERODOX
ECONOMICS POSITION

Radical, or progressive heterodox, economics critics believe that the value-neutral positivist understanding of NC economics masks a version of economic theory and practice that is neither value-free nor politically neutral. Rather, They believe that NC economics is an elaborately formalized theoretical apparatus based on classical liberal values and ideology that is explicitly constructed to show that market capitalism is the best of all possible economic arrangements. In this view, the positivist view of NC economics described above is simply a sophisticated veil that facilitates uncritical dissemination and support for NC economic ideology—an ideology that, in turn, derives much of its power and influence from its broadly promoted self-description as a value-free objective science.

Though a more detailed discussion of *radical* economics will have to wait until Chap. 3, a general characterization is in order here. Radical economists reject the NC value-neutral separability hypothesis, which asserts that values can be strictly separated from economic science and the associated NC claim of exclusive scientific status within economics. They believe that economists, or more properly, political economists, should explicitly base their economic thinking on values and politics and recognize that understandings of the economy cannot be divorced from prescriptive thinking about economic problems.

In this book, I employ a big-tent definition of radical economics that includes all versions of politically progressive economics that reject NC assumptions and associated methodology including radical, post-Keynesian, Marxist, institutionalist, structuralist, and evolutionary, as well as (non-NC) feminist and environmental, economic schools of thought. All of these schools reject many or most of the core NC assumptions. They all explicitly address the role of unequal power relationships within the economy and support policies that seek to improve both the sustainable efficiency *and* the fairness of the economy.

In contrast to NC economics, these schools do not generally have a history of repressing alternative schools of thought in economics (Lee 2009).[32] Radical schools of economics tend to, at least publicly, profess a

---

[32] The institutional history of economics departments in the USA suggests unstable cohabitation of heterodox and NC economists, as NCs in mixed departments are often able to marginalize their radical colleagues by exploiting the overall institutional power of NC economics via journal and department rankings, and in the perceptions of (non-economist) administrators, to marginalize and close down radical offerings and programs in these

belief in a pluralism of economic theories that reflects the divergent values and political views of their supporters (Bowles et al. 2005, Chap. 3). Radical economists have stridently argued for a broad and pluralistic approach to economics by, for example, pointing out the way in which the dogmatic adherence of NC economics to a narrow methodology and scope of inquiry has caused it to fail to foresee major economic events such as the Great Recession (or Lesser Depression) that started in 2007, in spite of warnings by numerous heterodox economists that, in some cases, included accurate near-term forecasts of imminent macroeconomic collapse (Keen 2011).

THE GOAL OF THIS BOOK

This book is based on the premise that the ultimate goal of social science is to improve society. The word "improve" includes a teleology—a moving forward toward something better. The something better does not have to be a complete utopian blueprint but it does imply that at least some aspects of current social arrangements can be improved upon. Most social scientists would probably agree with this. However, this simple statement does not address the *fine print* of how a social science will best serve the goal of generally *improving* society.

Three positions on this may be succinctly summarized:

(a) Should a social science position itself as a source of purely techno-cratic *value-free* expert advice of use to all members of society regardless of political persuasion or personal values? Is this even possible?

(b) Or should social science schools of thought accept that they will inevitably be values-based ideological constructions that are most relevant to those who share their values and view themselves in a pluralistic fashion as reflecting one of many different theories of society, all *equally* valid but based on different sets of values?

departments. Examples of this include the now defunct graduate political economy programs at Notre Dame and University of California Riverside (Lee 2009). The few radical departments that have survived long-term have tended to be those that are dominated by heterodox economists. See: http://heterodoxnews.com/hed/graduate/ for a complete list of Ph.D. granting heterodox economics departments in the USA and worldwide.

(c) Or, finally, is there a third position of a values-based social science that attempts to scientifically (with evidence and reasoned argument) justify its theoretical constructions and policy recommendations *and* its values not as one of many possible approaches, but as the most valid (to be argued for, not ideologically imposed) approach that best conforms to broadly based universal human values?

Though attractive as a tolerant big-tent view of economic theory, the common heterodox pluralistic view of economic schools of thought (position (b) above) is problematic as it ends up according more or less equal legitimacy and value to all schools of thought in economics, making it difficult to advise students or political leaders on best decisions. If economic thought depends on values, and divergent values are to be accorded equal respect in a pluralistic society, how is one to decide between the often conflicting policy positions advocated by different economic theories? Moreover, I think this position can be fairly critiqued as being insincere, as in practice schools of heterodox economics, like the NC school, believe in the correctness and validity of their views as being the best understandings and recommendations, and not simply as one of many equally valid approaches.[33]

I also find the variation of (a), which appears to be the view of some post-Keynesian economists, that though NC economics *correctly* asserts that economics should be a value-free positivist social science, it does not live up to its own methodology because of unrealistic basic assumptions and faulty methodology, equally implausible. In this view, though NC economics is, at its core, hopelessly ideological, apologetics, a value-neutral science of economics can be constructed by starting with more realistic basic assumptions and methodology.[34] In contrast to this position, I hope to convincingly demonstrate in this book, that economic theory *cannot*, no matter how astutely constructed, separate itself from underlying values.

A key goal of this book is thus to provide support for position (c) above, held by a large number of radical economists, that the problem with mainstream or NC economics is *not* that it is based on a particular set of values, even though it clearly is, but rather that these are the *wrong*

---

[33] This is abundantly clear from the very critical stance taken by heterodox texts toward NC economics. See for example (Bowles et al. 2005; Keen 2011).

[34] Keen (2011) and Lee (1998), for example, appear to have this view.

values—at least in the sense that they exclude fairness and democracy—
and that NC theory is able to uphold these wrong values only by

(a) rejecting all *self-awareness* of its own ideological bias by professing
value neutrality and cloaking itself in a mantle of *scientific objectivity* including the awarding of natural science-like pseudo "Nobel"
prizes in economics (Weeks 2014, p. 16); and

(b) engaging in heavy-handed institutional and intellectual repression of
alternative economic thinking (Lee 2009) instead of acknowledging
that, as a social science, economic thinking will inevitably be based on
values and participating in reasoned debate with other schools of economic thought over alternative economic theories *and* values.

Note that this does not preclude debate among social scientists. It
rather enlarges the scope of this debate to include the *values* upon which
the theories and policy recommendations of social science are based. The
claim is that, at least for economics, it makes sense to assess the degree to
which the theoretical approaches and policy outcomes of different schools
of thought conform to broadly shared ideals of a morally justifiable and
sustainable economy (Klein 2014).

In this view, economists need to drop the pretenses of either positivist
value neutrality or pluralist value relativity and forthrightly return to their
roots as moral philosophers who study and work to make the economy, not
just more efficient or in greater accord with a particular set of values, but
better in a broad moral sense. I use the term pretense because, as discussed in
this book, I do not believe that either of the first two positions are sincerely
held by many of their practitioners. The world cries out for economic guidance that relates directly to moral values because the most basic problems
with current economic arrangements are fundamentally *moral* problems.

Basic economic policy viewpoints, such as the degree of useful public
funding and involvement in the economy, are not merely theoretical disputes over data and theory but are also fundamentally related to economic
policy prescriptions that cannot be separated from the values that underpin them. An example of this, as discussed extensively in later chapters,
relates to the question of the appropriate level of public funding and social
choice versus individual for-profit market-based allocation in the economy. Most economists would agree that both of these economic coordination methods have a role to play in any economy, but the underlying
values that are most closely associated with these contrasting systems are
often unacknowledged in economic policy debates. Instead of residing in

the background, this book argues that these underlying *values* should be forthrightly and explicitly in the *foreground* of these debates.

By opening up this inquiry I hope to lend support to reasoned debate over values as legitimate and inevitable components of social science, without compromising the need for any social theory to be also based as much as possible on *scientifically grounded* fact and logical inference.

My argument will be threefold:

(a) There exists a set of broad universal values affecting economic policy that are common to the world's largest and most important religious, cultural, and philosophical traditions, so that it makes sense to ask whether the underlying values and policy recommendations of a particular economics school of thought conforms to these broadly accepted "universal human values." Moreover, it is increasingly possible to base these generally accepted values, in particular, those that are relevant to economic policy, on scientific research (Harris 2010).

(b) As many have pointed out (Hill and Myatt 2010; Meek 1967), far from being value neutral, NC economics is based on classical liberal values that, though once progressive in the sense of furthering efforts for a more inclusive nonfeudal capitalist industrial economy (Acemoglu and Robinson 2013), now from the basis for a theory that indirectly and directly supports regressive distribution and undemocratic extraction and concentration of power—a concentration of power that constitutes a major barrier to social and environmental progress; and

(c) To the extent that broadly defined (in the USA) radical economics, which includes all branches of progressive political economy, is based on widely accepted universal values of relevance to economic policy, radical economists are more likely to produce policy recommendations that are aligned with these generally accepted values, and thus, more likely to foster human progress that leads to wide spread sustainable prosperity and greater democracy. In particular, I argue that the Kaleckian (or Structuralist) post-Keynesian and Analytical (or Roemerian) Marxist schools of radical economics are most relevant to solving many of our current political economic problems (Palley 2013; Lavoie 2009; Godley and Lavoie 2006; Taylor 2004).

My hope is that the best way to induce NC economists to own up to the underlying values basis of NC economics and its implications is to acknowledge the underlying values basis of radical or progressive political economy and forthrightly argue that a key reason to support these schools of thought and their resultant policy recommendations, to the extent that they are based on evidence and reason and not on arbitrary and unjustifiable methodological and values exclusion, is that they *are*, unlike NC economics based on broadly shared universal human values and thus more likely to foster, rather than stand as a major obstacle to, the realization of these age-old (at least since the late seventeenth-century Enlightenment) aspirations for "liberty, equality, and solidarity" in human societies.[35]

A SHORT OUTLINE OF THE BOOK

This book includes three parts. "Part I: Economics as a Moral Science: the Philosophy and Science of Morality," includes three chapters that provide a general overview of the central argument that economics can and should be a moral science through a broad discussion of economics, morality, philosophy, and politics, including proposals for opening up the meme of introductory economics to moral considerations. "Part II: Textbook Fables Support Immoral Policies: Economics is not About Supply and Demand or Aggregate Supply and Demand" includes five chapters that offer a detailed critique of textbook introductory economics, including jettisoning *supply and demand* analysis that depends on the mostly *nonexistent ghost supply curve* and replacing it with more realistic *demand and cost* analysis and proposals to introduce morality and heterodox economic thinking in introductory economics courses.

"Part III: The Morality of Radical Economics: Investigating the Value Neutral Aspect of Neoclassical Economics" includes three chapters that provide a detailed technical critique of the value neutral and amoral positions of both theoretical and applied NC economics, showing that applied NC microeconomics, in particular, has led to immoral outcomes. The section concludes with a final call for all economics to be based, like radical economics, on widely shared moral values. This last section is a direct outcome of the personal experiences related below.

---

[35] A paraphrasing of the well-known French revolutionary motto: "Liberté, égalité, fraternité."

My Own Encounters with NC Economics

Finally, a personal story, demonstrating how NC economic ideology has provided critical support for the implementation of catastrophic public policy even in the hands of presumably well-intentioned progressive non-economist public policy leaders.

From 1987 to 1993, while working as a modeling manager at AT&T in New Jersey, I was able to complete a dissertation for a PhD in (hetero-dox) economics at the New School for Social Research in New York City, entitled "Non-Neoclassical Microeconomics: A Nominal Total Bill Approach to Residential Telephone Usage Demand Estimation" (Baiman 1993). This topic came out of first-hand experience working in a large unit of, mostly neoclassically trained, economists at AT&T dedicated to telecommunications demand forecasting, and becoming aware of the way in which graduate train-ing in NC economics was capable of undermining common sense, even for something as practical and nonideological as telephone demand forecasting.

The central problem was my NC colleague's insistence, following NC textbook theory but against all evidence, that telephone users responded to specific changes in rates for different times of day, days of the week, and call distances, and seamlessly *passed through* inflation effects. Luckily, I found that my *noneconomist* boss was more receptive to a commonsense "total bill" approach that assumed that customers responded to changes in the value of their *total* bill regardless of what specific pricing tariffs may have caused them.[36] Though I did not have the power to redirect company resources away from the unrealistic NC *ideological* modeling exercises of my colleagues, I was able to convince my boss to give me time at work to develop an alternative more realistic *total bill* approach, which became my PhD dissertation.

After receiving my degree in 1993, I started a public policy job at the New York State Department of Economic Development (NYDED) as associate director of the Telecommunications Exchange. As the group I was working with at NYDED included a number of New School alums and other progressives and was headed by a progressive deputy commis-sioner who reported to a liberal governor (Mario Cuomo), I was hopeful that my new colleagues and the generally progressive public policy folks that I interacted with would be more open to paying critical attention to

---

[36] It is not coincidental that I am now working in a business school and not in an econom-ics department.

the assumptions underlying standard NC economic modeling exercises than my generally apolitical NC economist colleagues at AT&T had.

I was right about my immediate colleagues but wrong about the more general public policy community that I was working with, even though most of them were indeed self-identified liberals and progressives. At NYDED I quickly realized that even progressive senior public policy leaders, in this case mostly lawyers and engineers working on telecommunications regulation issues or, at this point in time, deregulation issues, in one of the most liberal state governments in the country *had been taken in by NC economic ideology to the point of undermining basic commonsense public policy principles* (Baiman 1995). Though there were many factors at play, including the degree to which regulatory agencies had been captured by the industries they were regulating (not a problem at the time in New York state where the Public Service Commission was perceived as one of the most independent and proconsumer utility regulation commissions in the country) and the effort to support private investment in new broadband, and eventually Internet and world-wide-web technologies as much as possible, a key argument of the dominant pro-deregulation faction was that *market pricing* would *increase social welfare* due to the core NC doctrine that efficiency is optimized when "price = marginal costs."

Thus, I was again confronted with the pervasive and pernicious influence of NC economic ideology on well-meaning and otherwise (at least publicly) progressive public policy leaders. The dominant view was *not* that we needed to expand and improve regulatory capacity to take into account the new developments in telecommunications and strengthen civil-service codes and other "revolving door" measures to prevent "regulatory capture," but rather that we needed to extensively *deregulate* and rely primarily on *market forces* as these would cause prices to move closer to *marginal costs* thus minimizing market distortions away from the above mentioned "rule of allocative efficiency." As is extensively documented and discussed in Part III, the regulators were in this regard following the explicit policy recommendations of leading NC economists (including self-described liberals).

When I tried to explain that the regulatory principle that marginal cost should equal, or be as close as possible, to marginal price, was a result of NC assumptions that ignored distribution effects (as is discussed at length later in this book), I was told to "take it up with other economists." The price equal marginal cost principle, which is included in virtually all introductory economics textbooks, was also a core principle in Alfred Kahn's canonical book on regulatory economics (Kahn 1970), and Kahn, who taught at Cornell and had played a major role in the now infamous Carter

Administration deregulation push as Chair of the federal Civil Aeronautics Board, was a key member of the Telecommunications Exchange that I staffed.

In mid-1994, partly due to not wanting to work under the new conservative incoming Republican Governor George Pataki but also with the hope that I could play a more effective role confronting NC economic ideology in academia, I left NYDED for a teaching job at Roosevelt University in Chicago.

Two years later, in 1996, an electric utility deregulation bill was, with the assistance of many of these same prominent NC economists, passed by the California legislature and signed into law by the Republican Governor Pete Wilson. And a few years after that, in 2000–2001, a California electricity crisis led to massive rate hikes, rolling blackouts across the state, effective bankruptcy for the state's two largest regulated utilities, Pacific Gas and Electric and Southern California Edison (both had to be bailed out by the state), enormous windfall profits for a little-known (at the time) energy trading company called Enron Corporation, and the eventual recall of the sitting Democratic Governor Gray Davis and election of a new Republican Governor, Arnold Schwarzenegger, in 2001 (Sweeny 2002).[37]

One final incident. Since the official, November 2007, beginning of the Lesser Depression, heterodox economists have pointed out that professional economists can be divided into those who foresaw and warned of the coming worldwide economic crash and those who did not (Keen 2011, Chap. 2). Prominently visible in the latter camp were the so-called Bezemer 12 including Keen, and in the USA, Baker, Godley, Roubini, Shiller, Schiff, Janszen, and Hudson (highlighted in Bezemer (2009)). In addition, most, if not all, radical political economists (in the USA, members of the Union for Radical Political Economics (URPE), such as Baker) had no doubt that it was just a matter of time before the collapse of the financial bubble.

For example, my Chicago Political Economics Group (CPEG) colleague, Mel Rothenberg, and I were leading seminars at the University of Illinois at Chicago's Center for Urban Economic Development from 2001 to 2004 on Wynne Godley's predictions of a US macroeconomic collapse and developed a close relationship with Alex Izurieta who worked with Godley at the Levy Institute at the time.[38] We also, with fellow Illinois Committee for

[37] Sweeny, James L. (Summer 2002). "The California Electricity Crisis: Lessons for the Future," *The Bridge* 32 (2). Published by the National Academy of Engineering.
[38] See http://www.levyinstitute.org/pubs/sa_nov_07.pdf and http://www.levyinstitute.org/pubs/sa_dec_08.pdf and http://www.levyinstitute.org/pubs/stratan-jul-04b.pdf

New Priorities (CNP) Board members including Joe Persky, organized a speaking engagement to promote Godley's analysis in a broadly advertised public panel in 2004 at which I very explicitly warned about the impending macroeconomic collapse.[39] Rothenberg and I then submitted a paper warning that the current macroeconomic configuration was not sustainable and I presented this paper as part of the URPE at the Allied Social Science Association panel in January 2007 (Baiman and Rothenberg 2008).[40]

Finally, in February of 2008, while working for the Illinois Department of Employment Security (IDES), I got into serious trouble with senior administrators for circulating a confidential paper to the deputy director of IDES and the director of research at the Illinois Department of Revenue. I also sent the paper to Joe Persky, another CPEG colleague, who was then serving on the Illinois Governor's Council of Economic Advisors. The paper analyzed historical and contemporary patterns of unemployment claims data to show *that Illinois was already in a recession.* It was titled: "Composite Co-Incident Indicator Gives 93 % Probability of Illinois Economic Recession Beginning in 2007:Q3." I later learned that the reaction to my report was influenced by the position of a prominent NC economist at the University of Illinois at Urbana Champaign, a specialist in regional and state economics, who was claiming at the time that the Illinois economy was on sound footing with no danger of a recession. I expect that many other non-NC economists in the USA and other countries have similar stories to tell about that period.

These repeated experiences of the failure and damaging influence of NC economic ideology on private practice and public policy were a key motivation to write the journal articles (Baiman 2001, 2002), the CPEG working paper (Baiman 2012),[41] and finally, this book.

---

[39] My presentation was titled "'Three by Two' Macroeconomics," CNP Forum, May 4, 2004. I was part of a panel that also included Jared Bernstein from the Economic Policy Institute who spoke on other issues. The CNP by the way was also a key organizer of the public anti-war presentation at which then Illinois state senator Barak Obama came out against the Iraq war. This talk got a lot more publicity subsequently!

[40] The paper "Rentier-Based Finance-Led Macroeconomies: Keynesian or Classical in the Short-Run, but Unsustainably Debt Dependent and Minskyan in the Long-Run," was also (before the crash) submitted to (and rejected by) by a number of economics journals. The presentation was entitled "Accumulation Through Dispossessing: Modeling the New U.S. Rentier Capitalism" at the URPE sessions of the American Economic Association meetings in Chicago in January 2007.

[41] http://www.cpegonline.org/workingpapers/CPEGWP2012-2.pdf

BIBLIOGRAPHY

Acemouglu, Daron and James A. Robinson. (2013). *Economic Origins of Dictatorship and Democracy.* Cambridge University Press.

Baiman, Ron. (1993). *Connecting to the Future: Greater Access, Services, and Competition in Telecommunications,* co-author with other core staff, report of the New York Telecommunications Exchange, Published by the Office of Economic Development and Department of Public Service of New York State, Dec. 1993.

Baiman, Ron. (1995). Neoclassical Economics and the End of Equitable, Open, and Universal Telecommunications Services in the United States. *Review of Radical Political Economics.* 27(3), 95–103.

Baiman, R. (2001). Why equity cannot be separated from efficiency: The welfare economics of progressive social pricing. *Review of Radical Political Economics, 33,* 203–221.

Baiman, R. (2002). Why equity cannot be separated from efficiency II: When should social pricing be progressive. *Review of Radical Political Economics, 34,* 311–317.

Baiman, Ron and Mel Rothenberg. (2008). Rentier-Based Finance-Led Macroeconomies: Keynesian or Classical in the Short-run, but Unsustainably Debt Dependent and Minskyan in the Long-Run. CPEG Working Paper 2007-1. Retrieved March 2016 from: http://www.cpegonline.org/working-papers/CPEGWP2007-1.pdf.

Baiman, Ron, Bill Barclay, Sidney Hollander, Haydar Kurban, Joseph Persky, Elce Redmond, Mel Rothenberg. (2012). A Permanent Jobs Program for the U.S.: Economic Restructuring to Meet Human Needs. *The Review of Black Political Economy.* 39(1), 29–41.

Baiman, R. (2012). *Self-adjusting "free trade": A generally mathematically impossible outcome.* Available from author, submitted for publication.

Baiman, Ron. 2014. Unequal Exchange and the Rentier Economy. *Review of Radical Political Economics.* 46(4), 536–557.

Bezemer, Dirk. (2009). Why some economists could see the crisis coming. September 7. *Financial Times.*

Bowles, Samuel and Herbert Gintis. (1987). *Democracy and Capitalism: Property, Community, and the Contradictions of Modern Social Thought.* New York: Basic Books.

Bowles, S., Edwards, R., & Roosevelt Jr., F. (2005). *Understanding capitalism: Competition, command, and change.* New York: Oxford University Press.

Coase, Ronald H. *The Nature of the Firm. Economica.* 4(16), 386–405.

Godley, Wynne and Marc Lavoie. (2006). *Monetary Economics: An Integrated Approach to Credit, Money, Income, Production and Wealth.* New York: Palgrave Macmillan.

Harris, S. (2010). *The moral landscape: How science can determine human values.* New York: Free Press.

Hartmann, Tom. 2014. The Crash of (2016): The Plot to Destroy America. *New York: Grand Central Publishing.*

Hill, S. (2010). *Europe's promise: Why the European way is the best hope in an insecure age.* Berkeley: University of California Press.

Hill, R., & Myatt, T. (2010). *The economics anti-textbook: A critical thinkers guide to micro-economics.* Halifax and London: Fernwood Publishing and Zed Books.

Huber, E., & Stephens, J. (2001). *Development and crisis of the welfare state: Parties and policies in global markets.* Chicago: University of Chicago Press.

Kahn, Alfred E. 1970. *The Economics of Regulation.* MIT Press.

Keen, S. (2011). *Debunking economics* (2nd ed.,). London: Pluto Press.

Keynes, J. M. (1936). *The general theory of employment, interest, and money.* London: Macmillan/Cambridge University Press.

Klein, N. (2014). *This changes everything.* New York: Simon & Schuster.

Lavoie, M. (2009). *Introduction to post-Keynesian economics.* New York: Palgrave Macmillan.

Lee, Fredric. (2009). A History of Heterodox Economics: *Challenging the mainstream in the twentieth century.* Abingdon-on-Thames, UK: Routledge.

Linder, Mark. (1977). The anti-Samuelson. *Volume One.* Macroeconomics: basic problems of the capitalist economy. New York: Urizen Books, 1977.

Linder, Marc and Sensat, Julius. (1977). *The anti-Samuelson. Volume One.* Macroeconomics: basic problems of the capitalist economy. New York: Urizen Books.

Marglin, S. (1984). *Growth, distribution, and prices.* Cambridge: Harvard University Press.

Meek, Ronald L. (1967). *Economics and Ideology and Other Essays.* London: Chapman and Hall.

Oxfam. (2014). *Working for the few: Political Capture and Economic Inequality.* 178 OXFAM Briefing Paper Summary. January 20. Retrieved March 2016 from: https://www.oxfam.org/sites/www.oxfam.org/files/bp-working-for-few-political-capture-economic-inequality-200114-summ-en.pdf.

Palley, T. I. (2013). *Money, fiscal policy, and interest rates: A critique of Modern Monetary Theory.* Author's working paper. Retrieved January, from http://www.thomaspalley.com/docs/articles/macro_theory/mmt.pdf

Piketty, T. (2014). *Capital in the twenty-first century.* Cambridge, MA: The Belknap Press of Harvard University Press.

Polanyi, K. (1944). *The great transformation.* New York: Beacon.

Rich, Motoko. (2014). A Walmart Fortune, Spreading Charter Schools. April 25. *New York Times.*

Scott, Robert E. (2007). *The Wal-Mart effect: Its Chinese imports have displaced nearly 200,000 U.S. jobs.* June 25. Issue Brief #235. Economic Policy Institute. Washington D.C., USA.

Sorkin, Andrew Ross. (2014). So Bill Gates Has This Idea for a History Class ... September 5. *New York Times.*

Sweeny, James L. (2002). The California Electricity Crisis: Lessons for the Future. *The Bridge 32*(2), 23–31.

Taylor, Q. P. (2004, Winter). An original omission? Property in Rawls's political thought. *The Independent Review, VII*(3), 387–400.

Weeks, J. (2014). *Economics of the 1 %: How mainstream economics serves the rich, obscures reality and distorts policy.* London: Anthem Press.

Workplace Fairness. (2014). *The Good, the Bad, and Walmart: The Year in Workplace Fairness.* Written by Timothy Brantner with help from colleagues. Retrieved March 2016 from: http://www.workplacefairness.org/reports/good-bad-wal-mart/textonly/credits.php.

CHAPTER 2

The Philosophy and Science of Morality

Historically there have been two diametrically opposed positions on morality. Harris (2010) puts it well:

> [P]eople who draw their worldview from religion generally believe that moral truth exists, but only because God has woven it into the very fabric of reality; while those who lack such faith tend to think that notions of "good" and "evil" must be the products of evolutionary pressure and cultural invention. On the first account, to speak of "moral truth" is, of necessity, to invoke God; on the second, it is merely to give voice to one's apish urges, cultural biases, and philosophical confusion. (p. 2)

Harris goes on to write that his purpose is "to persuade you that both sides of this debate are wrong," and that the goal of his book is to "begin a conversation about how moral truth can be understood in the context of science" (p. 2).

The goal of *this* book is in effect to apply this insight to economics. It is to persuade economists and others interested in political economy that morality is an essential and unavoidable part of economics and that this morality can be based on broad economic moral principles that are widely shared by all major religious, philosophical, and cultural traditions and increasingly informed by crossnational scientific investigation of both human brains, as Harris shows, and of human societies, as this book will show.

© The Editor(s) (if applicable) and The Author(s) 2016
R.P. Baiman, *The Morality of Radical Economics*,
DOI 10.1057/978-1-137-45559-8_2

These moral principles may be considered to be almost universal in the sense that they are widely shared at any given point in time, but they are not absolute as they are subject, even when initially informed by liberal religion or tradition, to evolving evidence and research on the causes and sources of human well-being. These principles of economic morality that can and should serve as the basis of any economic and social science that professes to be relevant to human affairs will be subject to evolution and change, as has occurred throughout history (with some major setbacks), based on reason, evidence, and increasing human capacity and proclivity toward moral empathy.

As noted in the introduction, my essential purpose is to demonstrate that both the supposed amoral objectivity of NC economics and the purely relativist "let all flowers bloom depending on your personal values" professed view of many heterodox texts and departments are erroneous positions. Rather, my contention is that economics and other social sciences are inescapably moral and political endeavors that are based on moral values, and should be, as much as possible, based on an evolving universal morality as described above.

The basic morality upon which meaningful forms of economic research and theory can be grounded need not be excessively esoteric or nuanced to fit every possible moral or collective action dilemma, or exigency in economics.[1] The basic goal should be to support human dignity or well-being as much as possible for all people. This means eliminating mass poverty and economic misery across the globe to the extent that planetary resources, production capacity, and knowledge allow. It also means, as President Franklin Delano Roosevelt (FDR) stated in his famous "Four Freedoms" speech, that a basic right to economic security and opportunity or "freedom from want" must be an integral part of economic thinking.[2] Beyond

---

[1] Though some economists have ventured deeply into the intricate dilemmas of moral and democratic collective action—see for example Sen (1987) and Arrow (1951), I do not believe that this is necessary for all economists attempting to develop the broad principles of a moral economic thinking.

[2] FDR 1/6/1941 "State of the Union" address to Congress, see: http://www.fdrlibrary. marist.edu/pdfs/fftext.pdf. In FDR's own words:

(a) The first is freedom of speech and expression—everywhere in the world.

(b) The second is freedom of every person to worship God in his own way—everywhere in the world.

(c) The third is freedom from want which, translated into world terms, means economic understandings which will secure to every nation a healthy peacetime life for its inhabitants—everywhere in the world.

this, economic morality implies that resources should be allocated in a way that serves to facilitate and motivate all humans to develop and employ their capabilities and talents to benefit society and enrich (in the fulfillment, not monetary, sense) and empower their own lives, as much as possible.

It does not take great insight to see that economic arrangements that produce extreme wealth and income from inheritance alongside extreme poverty and deprivation, are immoral, dysfunctional, and do not motivate socially productive contribution, but rather quite the opposite. "Bad lives" (see below) rightfully engender resentment, envy, anger, social conflict, and massive human suffering.

Obscene multi-billion dollar payoffs for marketable innovations and new products (or to monopolistic positions facilitated by these innovations (Baker 2014)[3]), even to folks who contributed to (usually the final step) of their realization, are also not justifiable by even the most elementary social value calculus as economic history leaves little doubt that multi-billion dollar incentives are *not* necessary to stimulate socially valuable inventions or entrepreneurship. Entrepreneurship in applied business innovation has in the past been robust at inequality scales much below those prevalent today.[4] There is no justification for the CEO-to-average-worker compensation ratio in the USA, for example, to skyrocket from 20.1 to 1 in 1965 to 273 to 1 in 2012.[5] Much smaller and less disruptive to broad economic and political equality material incentives would be sufficient. In fact, many, if not most, of the most brilliant and far-reaching contributions in science, technology, and culture, have been motivated not by material wealth but by social recognition and appreciation by colleagues, and the natural human joy of discovery.[6]

(d) The fourth is freedom from fear, which, translated into world terms, means a worldwide reduction of armaments to such a point and in such a thorough fashion that no nation will be in a position to commit an act of physical aggression against any neighbor—anywhere in the world.

[3] Dean Baker, "World's Richest Man Tries to Defend Wealth Inequality," Oct. 16, 2014, Al Jazeera America.

[4] See for example (Gordon 2012) who argues that (in spite of levels of inequality that are unprecedented in the post-war period (Piketty 2014)) current and future innovation is declining.

[5] "The CEO-to-Worker Compensation Ratio in 2012 of 273 Was Far Above That of the Late 1990s and 14 Times the Ratio of 20.1 in 1965," Larry Michel, Economic Policy Institute (EPI) 9/24/2013, see: http://www.epi.org/publication/the-ceo-to-worker-compensation-ratio-in-2012-of-273/

[6] Genetics, the transistor, and the theory of relativity, for example were all discovered by monks or salaried scientists: Mendel working at St. Thomas Abby, Shockley and Pearson at

And, in a deeper sense, there is no excuse for economic arrangements that consign vast shares of the population to disempowered wage labor with few if any democratic rights or influence over the product of their labor, other than an often inadequate, and much smaller than the value of their contribution, pay check. Dignity, empowerment, and nonalienated work for all are goals that all economic systems should aspire to. I touch on these deep moral issues even as most of my focus will be on the easier to reach low hanging fruit of the socially perverse and highly inefficient and wasteful distribution of resources increasingly sanctioned by capitalist market economics that adhere most closely to NC economic principles.

From this perspective it makes no sense to legitimate a theory that professes to support any market outcome subject to an initial distribution of endowments that happens to occur by claiming that an objective and scientific (NC) economics can have nothing to say about its morality so long as the markets themselves are efficient. Where "efficiency" exculsively is defined as eliminating deadweight loss that would allow more resources to be distributed to some parties without taking away resources from any other party.[7] Or to claim that it is always best to, as much as possible, favor market distribution and guidance of the economy on the basis of insupportable demonstrations that market outcomes are generally optimal. Rather, as will be shown in Chapter 11, comparative national economic evidence quite clearly shows that economies that produce and distribute a large share of resources *outside* of the market, achieve morally superior economic and social well-being outcomes based on multiple international comparisons.

THE GENERAL CASE FOR AVOIDING SOCIALLY "BAD" OUTCOMES

Again, as few have put this more clearly than Harris (2010) whose work on the general question of morality was, as noted above, a key inspiration for undertaking this effort to clarify and apply these insights to economics, the remarks below will closely follow and extend Harris' arguments to economics (Harris 2010, Chap. 1).

Bell Labs (indirectly publicly funded through regulated utility pricing), and of course Einstein at a Swiss patent office and subsequent non-profit universities and research institutes.

[7] This is the "Pareto Optimality" standard championed by NC high theory to be discussed in later chapters.

Following and partially paraphrasing Harris (2010, p. 15–16), imagine two different lives.

A Bad Life

You are a young widow who had to witness the rape and brutal murder of her 7-year-old daughter by her 14-year-old son who was forced to do this at the point of a machete by a gang of drugged up soldiers. Moreover, you have scarcely had a day in your life without experiencing misery, torture and cruelty as your society has been in a perpetual state of civil war and economic deprivation since you were born. You have never had an education, experienced modern plumbing, or been able to get away from the village of your birth. Everyone that you know has had a similar life, though your life has been singularly unlucky even relative to your society, and it is about to end.

Your country and culture is a failed nation with enormous economic inequality and political repression that has almost no infrastructure, education, or health care. The constant terror and brutality described above is a result of constant feuding between competing horrifically brutal war lords and fanatic religious and ideological zealots who demand on pain of torture and death absolute conformity to their power and precepts.

The Good Life

You are married to someone whom you dearly love and who dearly loves you. You have very close friends with whom you are able to share your life on a regular basis. You have children who are doing very well in life and appear happy and love their parents (you and your partner). Both you and your partner have been able to pursue work that has been personally meaningful and rewarding, and of great benefit to others. Both you and your partner's work has been widely praised by others and provided you with a very comfortable living that has allowed you to have the leisure to travel and enjoy cultural and natural beauty around the world, and the means to pursue your own musical, artistic, sports, culinary, and other leisure activities for pure personal enjoyment, in a balance that enhances your commitment to your work activities and fulfillment from them. You are also very fortunate to live in a social democratic country and society, say Denmark,[8] that based on numerous social indicators[9] affords among the world's highest overall level of health care, education, housing, wages, leisure, democracy, gender and social equality, broad opportunity for social mobility, as well as commitment to supporting families and children, the local and planetary environment, and developing countries, and that is ranked highest of 156 countries on the 2013 world United Nations (UN) Sustainable Development Solutions Network's World Happiness index.[10]

A Comparison

To claim moral indifference between these two kinds of lives, is to postulate that experience of terror, fear, hunger, illness, love of children, family and friends, good food, cleanliness, peace and rest, leisure, sport, art and music, meaningful work, social status, material wealth, political empowerment and so on are so radically different between humans that there is no objective way to judge human well-being. On the other hand, any concession to the ability to objectively judge between "bad" and "good" lives, for example through measurements tied to physical changes in the human brain—that are sometimes possible now and likely to be much more so in the future—essentially admits that there is a range of human experience of well-being that can be universally applied across all cultures and societies.

This is, in fact, explicitly acknowledged in the UN Declaration of Human Rights[11] and in various global campaigns for greater political and economic opportunity for: women, nutrition, health care, disease eradication, education, peace, security, democracy, help for the disabled, worker rights, and greater social and economic opportunity and mobility not tied to gender or birth status. If universal morality were a non sequitur, none of this would make any sense. We make these efforts precisely because we believe that the "Good Life" is better for our fellow humans than the "Bad Life."

---

[8] I have never been to Denmark. However I am sure that it, like every other country in the world, has its downsides: Excessive drinking? Cold climate? Homogenous and xenophobic small country and culture? However, based on every broad measure of social and economic well-being that I have encountered, Denmark appears to excel, and large scale economic outcomes are, of necessity, best measured by broad indicators.

[9] See for example OECD data presented in (Baiman 2014) and similar data presented in this book.

[10] http://unsdsn.org/resources/publications/world-happiness-report-2013/

[11] See: http://www.un.org/en/documents/udhr/

Though one can envision many different "good lives" and "good societies" suitable to different individuals, cultures, and natural and constructed environments, there is considerable agreement among humans and major human cultures regarding the evils that societies and economies should avoid. And there should be no question that this commonsense morality should be an integral part of meaningful social science rather than a taboo values consideration that is artificially presumed to be *separable* from objective economic and social science.

OK, you may say. But you are looking at the most extreme examples that no major human religious or philosophical moral system would contest. What about areas of economic and social policy where moral consensus breaks down?

Good question. There are, and probably always will be, differences of opinion between humans and human cultures on *some* values issues. However, the deeper point of this book is to argue that in cases where there are moral or religious differences but scientific clarity on values issues, social science should base its underlying morality on evidence and reason. For example, though all of the major religions and philosophical moral systems support help for the poor, the disabled, and others such as single mothers with young children who are constrained in their ability to earn an income adequate to support themselves and their families, and denounce excessive accumulation of wealth and economic oppression and exploitation of other humans for self-enrichment, this common sense moral consensus breaks down on other major political economic issues like population growth, women's empowerment, and global warming.

Orthodox Christians, Muslims, Hindus, Budhists, and Jews, for example, all believe that having a large family is a moral virtue. Catholics and Orthodox Jews are also opposed to birth control. These positions make sense if one wants to grow one's religion, but run directly counter to the critically necessary need to reduce human population growth, which is evident if one looks at the scientific evidence on the planet's carrying capacity, including the potentially catastrophic impact of continued large increases in human population on carbon emissions. Indeed, heterodox economists, such as Georgescu-Roegen (1999) and Daly (1997), have been warning of the unsustainability of growth-based capitalist industrial economies for years, even before the current disastrous effects of global warming were evident. In the course of human history, the need for collective action has never been more obvious if we are to avoid planetary disaster.[12] As Naomi Klein has aptly put it: "[T] his changes everything" (Klein 2014). The need for economic theory which is a core legitimation theory of modern society to offer collective action alternatives to individual self-interest as the basis for economic behavior and organization has never been more urgent. Human survival will depend on an economics of cooperation, fairness, and sustainability. The pretense of an objective and scientific (NC) economic theory based on a misguided notion of efficiency is, now more than ever, wholly inadequate.

Similarly, most, if not all, traditional religions are highly patriarchal, and the most orthodox continue to prescribe a limited reproductive and domestic caring role for women as family home makers. This results in continued lack of opportunity and outright restrictions on women's education and empowerment with regard to social, political, and household decisions such as family planning. It also reduces political support for government programs to assist single mothers and care for the elderly, disabled, and infirm, all of which are deemed to be family responsibilities largely to be borne by women.

This traditional patriarchy clearly conflicts with much of the universal moral agenda described above, particularly as it relates to the empowerment of women. Family planning advocates note that the empowerment of women is the single most important factor supporting family planning and population control, more important than simply disseminating contraceptives or raising family incomes, for example.[13] The need for reduced growth and eventual stabilization of the number of humans on earth if we are to sustain life on this planet is a *scientific fact*. It, therefore, makes no sense for economists to profess neutrality with regard to the social, economic, and political empowerment of women. No economy can be efficient in any real sense, if economic, social and political opportunity for

---

[12] For example, though it flies in the face of Western valuation of "individual liberty," China's "one child" policy may be one of the single most important "collective action" steps to support the planetary sustainability of life that has ever been taken.Of course, this was not a *democratic* decision, which would have been much more difficult, if not impossible, in current "liberal capitalist" democracies, highlighting again the need for a more "collective" and "social choice" based morality in economics and other social sciences that would support these kinds of decisions should they be scientifically necessary.

[13] See for example Susan Ehler on Thom Hartmann RT TV 8/8/2014 and interviewed by Annushay Hossain in *Forbes Magazine*, "Women's Rights and World Population: A Conversation with Suzanne Ehler," June 20, 2013. See also Susan Ehler Interview on Thom Hartmann's "Big Picture" RT TV 8/8/2014.

half the population is arbitrarily limited. Again, an alternative economics, a radical economics that demonstrates how discrimination in employment often serves profit motives, why social policy measures are necessary to address institutionalized gender, race, and class oppression in market economies, is necessary (Arrow and Bowles 2000).

Finally, among wealthy countries, the USA stands out as being one of the weakest supporters of measures to curb global warming. Not coincidentally, the USA is the most religious of the wealthy countries, and the most evangelical of US religious groups (Evangelical Protestants) are in greatest denial regarding global warming and a host of other "secular scientific" findings that conflict with literal interpretations of religious doctrine.[14]

Again, as human survival and current and future economic prosperity depend on finding a solution to global warming, economics cannot afford to be neutral on this issue. The political or *values* issue of combating global warming is an economic issue (Klein 2014). Real efficiency includes environmental sustainability. A narrow Pareto Optimal definition of efficiency as a value that can be separated from other values such as global economic sustainability and equity, is counter productive and dellusionary.

On all three of these critical global issues—family planning, women's education and political and social empowerment, and global warming—some versions of traditional morality *are factually the wrong morality* as they directly oppose measures that are critically necessary for future human and planetary well-being. In all of these cases, the need for science, that is the investigation of the natural and socially constructed worlds based on evidence and reason, to increasingly influence and guide morality could not be more obvious.

Again, you may think that this is too simplistic. Are there not deep philosophical problems and great dangers that arise when *values* are conflated with *facts* or when science attempts to prescribe *morality?* Let us take up some of these issues.

---

[14] Hickman, April 17, 2009, "Just what is it with evangelical Christians and global warming?" report on poll conducted by the Pew Forum on Religion and Public Life: http://www.theguardian.com/environment/blog/2009/apr/17/climate-change-religion.

A SHORT EXCURSION INTO THE PHILOSOPHY AND SCIENCE OF MORALITY

Hume's Law

The eighteenth-century Scottish philosopher David Hume, a member of the Scottish Enlightenment like Adam Smith whom he profoundly influenced, famously stated in his *Treatise on Human Nature* (1738, Book 3) that systems of moral philosophy that derive "ought" conclusions from "is" premises are making deductions that are "altogether inconceivable" and that attention to this problem would "subvert all the vulgar systems of morality, and let us see, that the distinction of vice and virtue is not founded merely on the relations of objects, nor is perceiv'd by reason" (1.1.27).[15]

Though there is some controversy about what Hume actually meant by this,[16] one interpretation, consistent with Hume (and Smith's) view that morals are grounded in "human sentiments," is that "ought" or value statements cannot be derived from deductive reasoning alone. This is basically the view taken by Harris and applied in this book to economics, with a more modern empirical twist that human sentiments can increasingly be studied and measured scientifically. In this view, since morality seeks to enhance human well-being and human well-being can increasingly be studied and measured, rules of morality cannot be based purely on reason but must at some level refer to *facts* about what is and what is not conducive to human well-being. In other words, morality should, as much as possible, be *scientifically* (in the broadest sense of this term) grounded.

However, a more common interpretation sometimes referred to as "Hume's Law" is a reversal of this point. According to this interpretation, Hume's point was that no *ethical* conclusions can be derived from any set of purely *factual* premises.[17] But if morality is ultimately about the well-being of humans, which it must be (though some may argue that the definition is circular, tautological, or inadequately defined—a point that will be taken up below), this cannot be true.

---

[15] Cited in *Stanford Encyclopedia of Philosophy* (2010), section 5. on "Is and Ought," see: http://plato.stanford.edu/entries/hume-moral/
[16] Ibid.
[17] Ibid.

To take one easy example raised by Harris (2010, p. 3). As of 2008 twenty one US states permitted corporal punishment in public schools.[18] In these states, the number of reported incidents of corporal punishment went from a low of 8 and 16 in Colorado and Arizona to a high of 49,197 (1.1 % of all public school students) in Texas and 38,131 (7.5 %) in Mississippi. The states with the highest *percentages* of public school students that have received corporal punishment were Mississippi (7.5 %), Arkansas (4.5 %), Oklahoma (2.3 %), Louisiana (1.7 %), Tennessee (1.5 %), Texas, and Georgia (1.1 %).

US readers will recognize these as Bible belt states with disproportionate shares of fundamentalist religious believers. In particular, these states have disproportionately high shares (31 % or above) of Evangelical Protestants relative to their proportion in the USA as a whole (26 %).[19] Of the major religious groupings in the USA, Evangelical Protestants are most likely to be religious fundamentalists who base their morality on a literal interpretation of the bible. For many, this includes a belief in corporal punishment that has historically been supported by citing Proverbs 13:24: "He that spareth his rod hateth his son: but he that loveth him chasteneth him betimes" (King James Bible). This, in spite of the fact that scientific studies of the effects of corporal punishment on child development and human well-being directly contradict the biblical citation above. There is abundant carefully researched empirical evidence demonstrating the ill-effects of corporal punishment on children. For example, a 2002 meta-analysis of 88 studies found links between corporal punishment and ten negative outcomes (Gershoff 2002).[20]

Also, in contradiction with Proverbs (13:24), there is clear scientific evidence supporting the more general moral proposition that kindness is more effective than cruelty for child development. For example, emotional deprivation has been shown to have negative effects on brain development, negatively affecting parenting, social attachment, and stress

---

[18] http://www.infoplease.com/ipa/A0934191.html. Source: The Center for Effective Discipline, Columbus, Ohio: www.stophitting.com
[19] See http://religions.pewforum.org/maps "Evangelical Protestants" map of US state shares.
[20] For more recent evidence see: http://www.endcorporalpunishment.org/pages/pdfs/Summary%20of%20research%20on%20the%20effects%20of%20corporal%20punishment%20April%202013.pdf which claims that: "more than 150 studies show associations between corporal punishment and a wide range of negative outcomes, while no studies have found evidence of any benefits." (p. 2).

regulation among rats in controlled experiments. It has also been shown to have negative effects among children raised in institutional settings. For example, levels of the hormones oxytocin and vasopressin in the brain have been shown to be correlated with parental care among rodents. These hormones have been shown to *not* show normal surges in response to physical contact with adoptive mothers among children who spend the earlier part of their lives in state institutions without normal levels of parental nurturing (Harris 2010, p. 9).

Tolerance of Intolerance

On the other side of the moral divide, liberal "let all flowers bloom" pluralistic culture-based moral relativism stumbles badly when it leads to accepting religious or social *intolerance* as a valid moral principle for some cultures. Opposition to efforts by religious conservatives to enact antiblasphemy laws at the UN have been hampered by liberal notions of moral relativism that, in direct contradiction to pluralists own belief in the equal validity of many different "moralities," validate the rights of some moralities over those of others. For example, "fatwas" that prohibit and punish on pain of death, critique or depiction of sacred images in an unflattering manner.[21]

This is clearly logically and politically untenable and self-destructive of human society at large, as perhaps the most fundamental requirement of any morality is that it support *society*—the ability of humans to live together in peace and happiness, which a sanctioning of objectively unnecessary and avoidable intolerance obviously precludes. Ultimately both negative and positive, individual and democratic, *freedom* must be an essential part of any morality as without it, some moralities cannot coexist, and one individual's or society's morality becomes another individual's or society's oppression. Moral relativists cannot be relativist about intolerance without undermining their own stance that diverse moralities must be accepted as equally valid. In this sense, moral relativism is an infeasible and illogical position that undermines itself. It is logically

---

[21] Though as far as I know, there is no support even among "moral pluralists" for the Islamic State of Iraq and Syria (ISIS) beheadings of infidels, or Saudi Arabian beheadings of witches. This suggests that even those who believe in culture-based moral diversity have underlying moral redlines, supporting the notion that there *are* "universal" moral precepts that are widely shared among humans.

impossible to accept both intolerance and diverse moralities, and drawing a line in the sand at intolerance contradicts the notion that there are no universal moral principles.

"Moore's Open Question Argument and Well-Being"

Hume's "is and ought" dichotomy was extended and embellished around the turn of the century by Moore (1903) and accepted by modern philosophers like Karl Popper (2002) furthering the notion in current intellectual circles that *facts and values* are strictly separable.

Moore's claim was that any attempt at a factual naturalistic definition of *good* must fail as it will result in an "open question" that a conceptually competent speaker can question. Moore's argument was that any attempt to define "good" will result in an infinite and unresolved conceptual regress without resolution. Any attempt to factually ground the notion of goodness or morality on anything, say happiness or human well-being, must founder on the question of whether happiness or human well-being is good.

But again, this is clearly not the case, as the factual or scientific examples above and below illustrate. Increasingly, factual measurements can be made of human well-being. Violence causes human suffering that can be measured in its effect on human physiology. For example, as noted above, factual or scientific research has demonstrated that the administration of corporal punishment to children leads to an increase in violent behavior that objectively causes more human suffering and that emotional depravation causes suffering among humans, and this can be objectively measured by looking at hormone response in human bodies.

To take a few more well-known examples cited by Harris, I know of no contemporary moral tradition that sanctions "foot-binding" among young girls, or "sati"- the self-immolation of wives upon their husband's death, as these traditions clearly and directly cause extreme suffering by some individuals ostensibly for the benefit of others (in both cases, men) that violates the basic moral principle of all major moral traditions that all humans should enjoy basic dignity and a right to self-fulfillment and happiness. A principle that necessarily includes the command not to inflict unnecessary suffering upon other humans. The suffering imposed by foot-binding is measurable. It is not an infinite linguistic regress.

Additional examples are the Amish prohibition against college education on pain of being banished from the community and Christian Science prohibitions against medical treatment. The former expressly limits the exposure of youth to alternative ideas and views of the world and thus limits their ability to draw on human wisdom at large to make decisions about their own lives, and the latter leads to unnecessary suffering from illness and sometimes early death directly causing current suffering and sometimes affecting any chance of future well-being.

Again, let me again quote from Sam Harris (2010, p. 20):

> Many social scientists incorrectly believe that all long-standing human practices must be evolutionarily adoptive: for how else could they persist? Thus even the most bizarre and unproductive behaviors – female genital excision, blood feuds, infanticide, the torture of animals, scarification, foot binding, cannibalism, ceremonial rape, human sacrifice, dangerous male initiations, slavery, potlatch, the killing of the elderly, sati, irrational dietary and agricultural taboos attended by chronic hunger and malnourishment, the use of heavy metals to treat illness, etc. – have been rationalized, or even idealized in the fire-lit scribblings of one or another dazzled ethnographer. But the mere endurance of a belief system does not suggest that it is adaptive, much less wise. It merely suggests that it hasn't [yet] led directly to a society's collapse or killed its practitioners outright. [brackets mine].

And to elaborate on one more concrete example (echoing inner-city gang subculture in Chicago, substitute "gang member" for "male relative") that overlaps closely with the "bad" society example offered above:

> The people of Albania have a venerable tradition of vendetta called Kanun: if a man commits a murder his family can kill any one of his male relatives in reprisal. If a boy has the misfortune of being the son or brother of a murderer, he must spend his days and nights in hiding, forgoing a proper education, adequate health care, and the pleasures of a normal life. Untold numbers of Albanian men and boys live as prisoners of their homes even now. (Harris 2010, p. 1; Bilefsky 2008; Mottiner and Toader 2005).

Such forms of *traditional morality* clearly are not conducive to human well-being and thus cannot be considered moral based on widely held and scientifically supported general human moral principles.

Rawls and the New Contractarian Approach

Much of the basis for western *liberal* political theory stems from "social contract theorists" such as Hobbes, Locke, Kant, and Rousseau, and most recently John Rawls. However, though undoubtedly fundamental to the history of the development of political democracy, strict philosophical "contractarianism" cannot be the basis for a universal economic morality. This issue has been well studied and discussed by numerous commentators, including Hahnel and Albert (1990). They note that the "original position" or "state of nature" assumption of contract theorists in which principles of social justice are negotiated either through *self-interest* in the Hobbesian line of social contract theory, or from *respect for persons* following the Kantian "categorical imperative" that one should treat other humans as ends and never as means, ignore the way in which economic relationships and institutions, once in place, condition and promote particular preferences and types of individual behavior, whether sanctioned or not by the *original position* contractors (Hahnel and Albert 1990, Chap. 1; Cudd 2013).[22]

For example the emphasis of social contract theorists on *distribution*, as exhibited in the Rawlsian "maximin" or "difference" principle stating that inequalities in the distribution of "basic" economic goods are justified only if they increase the amount of "basics" available to the materially worst-off members of society, leads to critical inattention to overriding issues of *production* and the impact of production relations and the institutional structure of the economy on human development and well-being as highlighted by Marx.[23] Rather, social contract theorists accept the liberal political illusion that market relationships are a powerless arena of private contracts between equals if: property rights are well secured, market information is widely disseminated, monopolization is preempted or broken up, and other externalities and market failures appropriately addressed though regulation, taxes, and spending.

Thus, though Rawls, in particular, is strongly supportive of the commonsense distributive economic morality discussed above, a purely a priori

---

[22] Cudd, Ann, "Contractarianism," *The Stanford Encyclopedia of Philosophy* (Winter 2013 Edition), Edward N. Zalta, Ed.

[23] The classic quote from Marx on this is:

In the social production of their existence, men inevitably enter into definite relations, which are independent of their will, namely relations of production appropriate to a given stage in the development of their material forces of production. The totality of these relations of production constitutes the economic structure of society, the real foundation, on which arises a legal and political superstructure and to which correspond definite forms of social consciousness. The mode of production of material life conditions the general process of social, political and intellectual life. It is not the consciousness of men that determines their existence, but their social existence that determines their consciousness (Marx 1859, Preface, p. 1).

philosophical approach to morality, while less arbitrary and historically conditioned than purely religious approaches, is again an inherently inadequate basis for developing a functional, sustainable, and evolving human morality. Such a morality must instead be informed by an increasing *factual* understanding of the causes and impediments of sustainable "human well-being."

Contractarians, and liberal political philosophy more generally, emphasize the need for individual civil and human rights to protect individual "liberties" from potential state tyranny (the so-called negative liberties). These rights are designed to allow individuals to act on their own volition as much as possible without reducing the scope of action of others, as in Rawls' "liberty principle" of maximum individual liberty consistent with equal liberty for all (Hahnel and Albert 1990, Chap. 1). This has been a historically important political principle essential to the development and survival of democracy, particularly with regard to the necessary protection of "minority rights" that allows democracy to continue and to the general protection of individuals from abuse of state power. But in their sanctioning of the principle of private property and capitalism, liberal contractarians have ignored the direct authority and power of owners to exploit other humans for their own benefit through the labor market, which is, as has been discussed in the introduction, a key, and over time increasing, source of concentrated power and oppression within capitalist market economies.

For example, Kant's "second categorical imperative" referred to above states that one should:

> "[a]ct in such a way that you always treat humanity, whether in your own person or in the person of any other, never simply as a means, but always at the same time as an end" (Kant 1785). But this imperative fails to recognize that production in modern societies and economies is largely carried out by hierarchical social organizations that are dependent on the managerial authority of some people to direct the work of others to achieve the goals of the organization so that the entire economy and society are based on "using others as means to achieve ends." The key issue is *not* the means–end relationship but *democracy*. Are the leaders, those who have the power to use others as "ends," democratically accountable? Do they have the consent of the "governed" to lead on their behalf? (Archer 1995). Worker co-ops like the Mondragon in Spain have managers who are vested with the authority to direct the work of others, but they are hired and annually reviewed by elected representatives of the workers and must pursue

overall goals that are set by representatives of the workers that they manage (Whyte and Whyte 1991).

Rawls leaves open the question whether his principles are best real-ized by some form of property-owning democracy or by a liberal socialist regime (Rawls [1971] 1999, xv). Rawls' theory does not address the links between economic institutions and democracy and dignity in production (242) (Taylor 2004b). Moreover, as is well known, Locke postulated a natural right to *private property* that has been interpreted as enshrining the sanctity of corporate, or social, property in *rented* human labor, in all democratic liberal capitalist constitutions, with important variations (Tuckness 2008).

Historically, this injustice has been somewhat mitigated by unions and social democratic governments that recognize the importance of "posi-tive liberty" or the need for an equitable distribution of basic goods like education, health care, housing, and relatively equal access to property and material resources for a democracy to work. Ultimately, however, the *wage–labor* relationship has to be recognized as inherently undemo-cratic and immoral as it is (even with worker representatives on Board of Directors) a direct abrogation of "democratic liberty" or the principle that all should have influence, relative to the degree to which they are affected, over the major decisions that impact their lives now and in the future (Archer 1995). This is because generally most Directors (at least in theory) represent shareholders. But shareholders, who can easily change their portfolio, are generally the least impacted, relative to workers, suppli-ers, customers, and the local community, by corporate decisions.

The underlying claim here is that basing morality on sacred or a priori principles reverses the true and only test of morality, which is whether or not it engenders human well-being. If we are honest with ourselves, we evaluate, and sometimes pick and choose, among traditional religious and philosophical principles to arrive at a morality that is relevant to the mod-ern world and to historically evolved social and economic institutions and *not* the other way around. Like Marx "turning Hegel upside down," it is time to turn the basis of morality "upside down" and anchor it in the real world of facts and measurable human outcomes.

I had an opportunity to outline the principles of a *democratic social-ist* constitution more in alignment with economic and political morality than the currently dominant *liberal democratic* constitutions, in a 1997 visit to Cuba. In addition to establishing the need for basic human, civil, and democratic rights of belief, expression, assembly, movement, person and family, law and judicial process, voting, and so on, such a constitution would establish: "Socialist Property rights," establishing an ultimate democratic collective jurisdiction over *social choices* in the economy; "socialist free speech rights," establishing democratic control and ownership of media with strong guaranties for, and support of, minority and dissenting view points; "socialist free and fair election rights," setting up public financing for all elections to public office, with a strict prohibition on private (domestic or foreign) funding of election activities; "socialist rights to equal economic and social opportunity," which would include work, health care, child care, elder care, housing, and other basic human rights already largely provided in Cuba; "socialist rights to an independent and non-commercial cultural environment," which would establish principles for democratic control and use of culture, including democratically elected and politically independent commissions of artists and nonartists to provide grants, and allocate media exposure, public venues, and space, for cultural production; and a "socialist right to sustainable and life supporting natural environment," which would establish principles for communal environmental protection and stewardship (Baiman 1997).

Though one may obviously quibble with the details of this particular outline, the basic principle of such a constitution would be to take away the blanket right to individual ownership of large-scale, and essentially social, property enshrined in liberal democratic constitutions and to establish rights to *positive liberties* such as health care, education, housing, social services for the young, elderly, disabled, and infirm, as well as an ultimate right to democratic media, culture, and environment.

Designing and structuring economies and societies to produce greater human well-being can and should be based on evidence and reasoned evaluation of best practices, and this must be the basis of any meaningful economic (and social) science. Ancient religious or philosophical ideological taboos for and against underlying sacred or a priori principles of morality are neither necessary nor useful in this kind of scientific evaluation of sustainable nurturing of human well-being.

MORALITY AND ECONOMICS

The moral issues that are, or should be, the major concerns of economics are particularly easy to measure and assess. Though all major ethical and religious traditions view helping the poor and destitute as good, there is no need for a religious or philosophical back stop to make this assertion. The fact that poverty is bad for humans has been demonstrated in a myriad of ways through scientific research.

Poverty causes impeded cognitive function (Vohs 2013). Poverty increases childhood stress, which leads to a greater incidence of Adverse Childhood Events (ACEs) such as "abuse, neglect, exposure to domestic violence, and household dysfunction such as parental substance use, mental illness, incarceration, or divorce that cause the body to bathe in stress hormones," which have a direct dose response relationship to health outcomes (Harris 2014).

Furthermore "A person with four or more ACEs has a relative risk of chronic obstructive pulmonary disease that is an astonishing 260 % of the risk for someone with no ACEs—more than two-and-a-half times the risk. For hepatitis, it is 250 % of the risk; for depression, it is 460 percent. If a patient has seven or more ACEs, their relative risk of ischemic heart disease, the number one killer in the United States, is 360 %—more than three-and-a-half times the risk of someone who has never undergone adverse childhood experiences" (ibid p. 1).

Poverty also reduces educational attainment even after controlling for other factors such as quality of schools (Krashen 2002). This is hardly rocket science. For example, there is abundant evidence of the powerful impact of poverty on literacy. Poor children are likely to have much less access to reading material due to fewer, if any, books at home and poorer and lower quality public school and classroom libraries (Duke 2000; Neuman and Celano 2001). Poor children thus have fewer opportunities to read and, not surprisingly, due to these and many other factors, are less likely to become proficient readers.

Similarly, in the USA as a result of growing income inequality, the Scholastic Aptitude Test (SAT) score gap between students from bottom 10 % and top 90 % of family incomes grew by 40 % over the last 30 years with a similar pattern for college completion and highly selective college attendance (Reardon 2013). Even for students who finish high school and do well on the SAT, the gap continues. Students with the highest SAT scores from bottom income quintile families are less likely to graduate from college than the lowest SAT score students from the highest income quintile families (Tough 2014; Carnevlae and Strohl 2010).

Moreover, regardless of educational attainment, childhood poverty increases the likelihood of adult poverty and the poverty of one's children, especially in countries with low social mobility like the USA. One recent study of the USA, Denmark, Sweden, Finland, Norway, and the UK found that in the USA 42 % of sons of fathers born in the lowest income quintile remained in the lowest quintile, versus 30 % in the UK, and 25–28 % in Denmark, Sweden, Finland, and Norway (Friedman 2012).

Another broader study of Australia, Canada, Denmark, Finland, France, Germany, Italy, Norway, Sweden, and USA looked at "income mobility elasticity" (the percentage increase in a son's income that can be associated with a 1 % increase in his father's income) and found that the USA again has significantly lower mobility than other wealthy countries. For example, the income of a US adult male is almost twice as dependent on his father's income as that of a Canadian adult male.[24] And in terms of "rags to riches" mobility, the percentage of sons born into the lowest income quintile who ended up in highest income quintile in the USA was 7.9 %, *far lower* than the six other countries above where the rates ranged from 10.9 to 14.4 %.[25]

And income generally correlates with "life satisfaction" both across countries and within countries and is even related to cross country "minimum-wage" level comparisons (Stevenson and Wolfers 2008; Krassa and Radcliff 2014). Similarly, unemployment has been correlated with depression, suicide, and other kinds of mental illness, as well as domestic violence, bankruptcy, and divorce (Rochman 2011; Goldsmith and Diette 2012; Anderberg et al. 2013).

Can there really be any doubt that poverty, inequality, and unemployment are *bad* for humans: individuals, families, and children, that is, that these conditions are *not* conducive to human *well-being* but rather *are* conducive to human *ill-being*. In fact there is little dispute that poverty and unemployment are bad for people, and recent research increasingly confirms the economic ill-effects of extreme inequality.[26]

As Harris (2010) notes, though there are many different ways to lead a "good life" that is conducive to human well-being depending on individuals and cultures, there is a general moral consensus among major moral traditions regarding what constitutes a "bad life." Though many factors can impact well-being, there is no doubt that poverty and economic oppression are conducive to a "bad life." Scientific research clearly shows that poverty, and inequality, particularly if it increases poverty or reduces broad economic opportunity, is bad for human well-being. Undemocratic and

---

[24] Op. cit.
[25] Op. cit.
[26] Op. cit.

arbitrary oppression stemming from economic power is bad for human well-being as it increases stress and disempowers human capacity to support and sustain healthy and meaningful personal, family, and community life. Fear and insecurity of all kinds are obviously also bad for human well-being.

Is It Preposterous to Claim That NC Economics Is Immoral?

Let me conclude again with a personal note.

I have tried to establish that general universal principles of human morality exist and will increasingly be based on evidence and reason. Though I believe that Harris (2010) has made a compelling argument that such a morality should be, at least with regard to basic principles, based on *science*, for the purposes this book it is important only that a universal set of economic moral principles *exists*. Readers who disagree with Harris' or my view with regard to the ultimate basis for such principles may substitute another justification for such a set of universally valid general economic moral principles such as those of John Rawls (1971), Jurgen Habermas (1990), the United Nations Universal Declaration of Human Rights,[27] or the *social doctrine* teachings of the major religions. The justification and precise articulation of these economic moral principles is, for our purposes, unimportant as long as they are supportive of basic principles of economic justice that are widely shared by all major religious and philosophical moral systems.

However, even if one accepts that universal moral principles in economics exist, attempts to moralize economics may appear to be misguided and not useful. Or to put it more bluntly, is it preposterous and an exercise in hubristic self-righteousness for anyone, and especially another economist who should be beyond this, to claim that mainstream or NC economics is immoral?

To counter this view I think it important to make clear that my contention in this book is *not* that I or any other non-NC or radical economist is more personally virtuous than the average NC or mainstream economist. The issue at hand is not one of personal morality, but rather an evaluation of the values upon which a school of thought and its derived policy conclusions are based. As Harris, and many ethical philosophers

---

[27] See: http://www.un.org/en/documents/udhr/

before him, especially Hume, Smith, and other members of the Scottish Enlightenment have noted, the vast majority of us are quite immoral by reasonable objective standards, as our "moral sentiments" are much too acutely influenced by our personal life histories and immediate and proximate sensations and observations, especially with regard to close family or friends, at the expense of more distant and less direct effects of our actions. How many of us would sacrifice our child so that two children whom we do not know might live? Ten children? One hundred? As Smith notes, we would likely be more upset over the loss of our little finger than a natural disaster that befell hundreds of millions of people in China (Smith 1759, p. 192–193). How many of us in the USA would give an arm or an eye so that a million Indians might live? Possibly most of us but it would not be easy. More mundanely, how many of us who live in relative comfort would sacrifice our nights out or our family vacation trips and contribute these funds to the desperately poor in our own or other countries? There are some significantly more moral *persons* in the world like the Princeton philosopher and ethicist Peter Singer (Singer 1999). We all have favorite examples of such people and most of us offer up some charitable donations, but by any objective standard those of us fortunate enough to live in relative comfort are profligately immoral considering the much greater human well-being that could be obtained from, for example, the money that we spend on food for our pets that we choose *not* to donate to charity.

As discussed later in this book, this point can be carried much further. Do we who live in relative comfort work as hard or as long as persons whose products and services we routinely consume and use? Is our economy based on roughly equal exchange of effort relative to our enjoyment of the bounty of human production?[28] The truth is that living in an immorally constructed national and global economy makes it nearly impossible to be truly personally virtuous.[29]

This last statement serves to illustrate an important point. The fact that almost all individual behavior is so colored by personal experience and

---

[28] See (Baiman 2006, 2014) for models showing the workings of "unequal exchange" of labor, and "rentier" extraction of resources with (almost) no exchange for labor, in the world economy.

[29] Readers who have been exposed to the work of one of the most insightful and influential "worldly moral philosophers" of all time, Karl Marx, will recognize these concerns as driving his withering critique of bourgeois "equal exchange ideology."

bonds of family and friendship as to be hopelessly immoral in an objective sense, does not mean that we should not attempt to do better than this when it comes to questions of broad social policy that ultimately have a much greater impact than our individual behavior that does not relate to these critical questions of collective choice. Or to put this differently, following Harris, our almost universally less than perfect personal morality does not mean that we should not attempt to use what we know from behavioral and brain science to better determine the relative morality of different social and economic *policies*. And this is especially important, as the pretense that NC economics is an objective and value neutral science like physics that can be divorced from inherently subjective political consideration, is such a staple of mainstream economic thinking.

BIBLIOGRAPHY

Anderberg, D., Rainer, H., Wadsworth, J., & Wilson, T. (2013). Unemployment and domestic violence: Theory and evidence. *Forschungsinstitut zur Zukunft der Arbeit Institute for the Study of Labor* (IZA). Discussion Paper No. 7515. Retrieved July, from http://ftp.iza.org/dp7515.pdf

Archer, R. (1995). *Economic democracy: The politics of feasible socialism.* Oxford: Oxford University Press.

Arrow, K. (1951/1963). Social choice and individual values (2nd ed.). New Haven: Yale University Press.

Arrow, K., & Bowles, S. (Eds.) (2000). *Meritocracy and economic inequality.* Princeton: Princeton University Press.

Baiman, R. (1997). A proposal for Democratic Constitutional Reform in Cuba. Presented June 17, 1997, at the *VII Enceunetro en Holguin con Filosophos Norteamericanos,* Universidad de Holguin, Cuba, and on June 23, 1997, at the *IV Conferencia Internacional de Ciencias Sociales y Humanisticas,* Universidad de Camaguey, Cuba.

Baiman, R. (2006). Unequal exchange without a labor theory of prices: On the need for a global Marshall plan and a solidarity trading regime. *Review of Radical Political Economics, 38*(1), 71–89.

Baiman, R. (2014). Unequal exchange and the Rentier economy. *Review of Radical Political Economic 46*(4), 536–537.

Baker, Dean. (2014). World's richest man tries to defend wealth inequality: Bill Gates' critique of Thomas Piketty is revealing for what it overlooks. October 16. Al Jazeera: http://america.aljazeera.com/opinions/2014/10/bill-gates-thomaspikettycapitalwealthinequality.html

Bilefsky, Dan. 2008. In Albanian Feuds, Isolation Engulfs Families. July 10. New York Times: http://www.nytimes.com/2008/07/10/world/europe/10feuds. html?_r=0

Carnevlae, A., & Strohl, J. (2010). *Rewarding strivers: Helping low-income students succeed in college.* New York: The Century Foundation Press.

Cudd, Ann. (2013). Contractarianism. The Stanford Encyclopedia of Philosophy (Winter 2013 Edition), Edward N. Zalta, Ed.

Chesbrough, H. (2003). The era of open innovation. *MIT Sloan Manage Review,* 44, 35–42.

Daly, H. (1997). *Beyond growth.* Boston: Beacon Press.

Duke, N. (2000). For the rich it's richer: Print experiences and environments offered to children in very low- and very high-socioeconomic status first-grade classrooms. *American Educational Research Journal, 37*(2), 441–478.

European Commission. (2015). *Open Innovation 2.0 – Yearbook 2015.* Directorate-General for Communications Networks, Content and Technology. Brussels: European Union.

Friedman, H. (2012). The American myth of social mobility. *Huffington Post.* Retrieved July 16, from http://www.huffingtonpost.com/howard-steven-friedman/class-mobility_b_1676931.html

Georgescu-Roegen, N. (1999). *The entropy law and economic processes.* iUniverse Inc.

Gershoff, Elizabeth Thompson. (2002). Corporal Punishment by Parents and Associated Child Behaviors and Experiences: A Meta-Analytic and Theoretical Review. Psychological Bulletin. 128(4), 539 –579

Goldsmith, A., & Diette, T. (2012). Exploring the link between unemployment and mental health outcomes. *American Psychological Association SES Indicator.* Retrieved April, from http://www.apa.org/pi/ses/resources/ indicator/2012/04/unemployment.aspx

Gordon, R. (2012). *Is U.S. economic growth over? Faltering innovation confronts the six headwinds.* NBER Working Paper No. 18315. Retrieved August, from http://www.nber.org/papers/w18315

Habermas, J. (1990). *Moral consciousness and communicative action* (C. Lenhardt & S. W. Nicholsen, Trans.) Cambridge, MA: The MIT Press.

Hahnel, R., & Albert, M. (1990). *Quiet revolution in welfare economics.* Princeton: Princeton University Press.

Harris, S. (2010). *The moral landscape: How science can determine human values.* New York: Free Press.

Harris, N. B. (2014). The chronic stress of poverty: Toxic to children. *The Shriver Report.* Retrieved January 12, from http://shriverreport.org/the-chronic-stress-of-poverty-toxic-to-children-nadine-burke-harris/

Kant, E. (1785). *Groundwork of the metaphysics of morals.* Cambridge, U.K.; New York: Cambridge University Press (1998).

Klein, N. (2014). *This changes everything.* New York: Simon & Schuster.

Krashen, S. (2002). Poverty has a powerful impact on educational attainment, or, don't trust Ed trust. *Substance*. Retrieved February, from http://www.fairtest. org/poverty-has-powerful-impact-educational-attainment-or-dont-trust-ed-trust

Krassa, M., & Radcliff, B. (2014). Does a higher minimum wage make people happier. *Washington Post*. Retrieved May 14, from http://www.washington-post.com/blogs/monkey-cage/wp/2014/05/14/does-a-higher-minimum-wage-make-people-happier/

Marx, K. (1859). *A contribution to the critique of political economy. Preface*. Moscow: Progress Publishers, 1977.

Mortimer M. and Toader A. 2005. Blood Feuds Blight Albanian Lives. September 23. BBC World Service.

Neuman, S., & Celano, D. (2001). Access to print in low-income and middle-income communities. *Reading Research Quarterly*, 36(1), 8–26.

Piketty, T. (2014). *Capital in the twenty-first century*. Cambridge, MA: The Belknap Press of Harvard University Press.

Popper, Karl. (2002). The Logic of Scientific Discovery. NY: Routledge.

Rawls, J. (1971). *A theory of justice*. Cambridge, MA: Harvard University Press.

Reardon, S. F. (2013). No rich child left behind. *New York Times*. Retrieved April 13, from http://opinionator.blogs.nytimes.com/2013/04/27/no-rich-child-left-behind/?_php=true&_type=blogs&_r=0

Rochman, B. (2011). Unemployed men are more likely to divorce. *Time Magazine*. Retrieved July 11, from http://healthland.time.com/2011/07/11/unemployed-men-are-more-likely-to-divorce/

Sen, A. (1987). *On ethics and economics*. Oxford: Blackwell Publishing.

Singer, P. (1999). *Practical ethics*. Cambridge University Press.

Smith, A. (1759). The theory of moral sentiments (6th ed.). London: A. Millar. 1790.

Stevenson, B., & Wolfers, J, (2008). *Economic growth and subjective well-being: Reassessing the Easterlin Paradox*. Institute for the Study of Labor (IZA), Discussion Paper No. 3654. Retrieved August 2008, from http://ftp.iza.org/dp3654.pdf

Taylor, Q. P. (2004, Winter). An original omission? Property in Rawls's political thought. *The Independent Review*, VII(3), 387–400.

Tough, P. (2014). Who gets to graduate. *New York Times*. Retrieved May 15, from http://www.nytimes.com/2014/05/18/magazine/who-gets-to-graduate.html

Tuckness, Alex. 2008. Punishment, Property, and the Limits of Altruism: Locke's International Asymmetry. American Political Science Review, 208, 467–480.

Vohs, K. D. (2013, August 30). The poor's poor mental power. Science, 341, 969–970.

Whyte, W. F., & Whyte, K. K. (1991). *The growth and dynamics of the worker cooperative complex*. Ithaca: Cornell University Press.

CHAPTER 3

Economics as a Moral Science

Though NC economics texts are careful to distinguish between the value-free NC *science* of economics and subjective and *unscientific* thinking about values and morality,[1] economics was traditionally a branch of *moral philosophy* and is a *moral science*. Adam Smith was a professor of moral philosophy (Heilbroner 1992), Keynes believed that "economics is essentially a moral science" (Davis 1991), and economics was part of the "moral sciences tripos" concentration at Cambridge University in the 1930s (Boulding 1969). Recognizing that morality will be increasingly influenced by science or evidence and reason, as discussed in Chap. 2 and that the ultimate purpose of *social science* and economics is to improve human well-being, as discussed in Chap. 1, this chapter attempts to expose the futility of continuing to try to separate *moral science* from *the pursuit of human well-being*, by claiming that both are properly inherent to *economics*.

Though I believe that this link should be obvious and uncontroversial, the unwillingness of NC economists to acknowledge the value basis of economic theory, measurement, data, and interests, and their tendency to denigrate and marginalize colleagues who do acknowledge this, has become a key barrier to progress in economic thinking. This unwillingness to see what is obvious to anyone not trained in the discipline of NC economics

---

[1] See beginning chapters of any introductory NC economics text, for example (Mankiw 2008; Schiller 2013a, 2013b).

© The Editor(s) (if applicable) and The Author(s) 2016
R.P. Baiman, *The Morality of Radical Economics*,
DOI 10.1057/978-1-137-45559-8_3

has led to a narrowness of thinking, inattention to assumptions, and seeming indifference to social and political impact in mainstream economics.

Furthermore, I don't believe that *adjustments* to NC economics, that for example, attempts to incorporate the insights of Rawls (1971) or Sen (1987) to advance a moral economics, are adequate as the most basic methodology of NC economics makes true reform highly unlikely. These reforms include adjusting utility functions to include "malevolence and benevolence" (Boulding 1969), less narrow specialization and more openness including deviations from the "Pareto Criteria" (Shiller and Shiller 2011), and greater incorporation of

> the implications of behavioral economics, consideration of primary goods and capabilities, plurality of criteria, fairness, and the role of individual ethical codes (Atkinson 2011, p. 160).

These are of course welcome suggestions that point in the right direction but they are not likely to fundamentally redirect the core focus and methodology of NC economics away from liberal capitalist political and social legitimation.[2]

Rather, it is essential that economics, as a discipline, acknowledges that an effective *moral economics* must be a *radical economics* that forthrightly addresses the core injustices of capitalism and eschews what Lance Taylor has called "Methodological Individualism and Rational Action" (MIRA) (Taylor 2004, Chap. 2). Rather than MIRA, radical economists privilege issues of class, exploitation, and power in both production and distribution, in their economic thinking, without precluding diversity of thought or inquiry. Radical economics includes, as is the case currently in other more pluralistic social sciences, an abundance of theoretical and empirical disputes, many with divergent policy implications. However, unlike disputes among NC economists, these debates openly acknowledge the moral basis of: assumptions, theoretical constructions, measurement criteria, and focus of analysis, using ideas that draw heavily from the works of past *moral philosophers* like Keynes, Kalecki, Marx, Veblen, and Smith.

---

[2] Ingrid Robeyns (2013) offers a similar, though more philosophical, take on these suggestions: http://crookedtimber.org/2013/10/31/economics-as-a-moral-science/

An excellent synopsis of the fundamental methodological differences between radical, or heterodox, and NC economic approaches is presented by Lavoie (2009), a prominent heterodox economist of the post-Keynesian (PK) and Kaleckian school of thought, that I believe is one of the most important of the radical alternatives to NC economics. Lavoie first outlines common features of heterodox economic thinking in general and then discusses "essential" and "auxiliary" features of PK economics.

Among other things, a quick perusal of these fundamental methodological differences shows why in the years leading up to the 2007 financial crash, NC economists, unlike radical economists who were almost all waiting for the collapse, were either sanguine about the future of the "new economy" or fairly confident or cautious to a fault, as is evident from the papers in the *Journal of Economic Perspectives* issue discussed by Shiller and Shiller (2011). The dominant view was that though there were problems, *markets* would work things out without a major collapse.[3]

Lavoie classifies the fundamental differences between *heterodox* and *NC* approaches into five areas: *epistemology, ontology, rationality, focus of analysis,* and *political core.*

EPISTEMOLOGY: REALISM VS. INSTRUMENTALISM

Heterodox economists generally try to employ the most realistic set of assumptions or *stylized facts* possible, given data, observation, and common sense. These assumptions are justified and debated based on their factual accuracy.

NC economics on the other hand employs unrealistic assumptions such as perfect competition, complete information, agent rationality, and no power in the economy, using an *instrumentalist epistemology* canonically articulated by Friedman in his (1953) paper on "The Methodology of Positive Economics" that is often referenced in NC texts. In Lavoie's words:

> For instrumentalists, a hypothesis is sound for two reasons: it is acceptable, first, provided it allows for accurate predictions, and, second as long as it can help calculate the value of a new equilibrium position. The realism of any particular hypothesis is not of concern. Theories are mere tools or instruments of analysis, largely regardless of their ability to explain the real workings of the economy. (Lavoie 2009, p 7)

---

[3] See related discussion in introduction.

dman made a virtue of using unrealistic assumptions claiming important hypotheses are able to isolate the critical, apparant and "unrealistic," key assumptions that yield accurate ...s (Keen 2011, Chap. 8).

To be fair, many NC practitioners attempt to modify classic orthodox assumptions with more realistic hypotheses regarding information and behavior, see for example Atkinson (2011), but these tend to be *auxiliary* modifications of the underlying model rather than fundamental changes to it. Most importantly, introductory textbooks adhere to and present the underlying classical assumptions as the *core* teachings of the science of economics.

ONTOLOGY: ORGANICISM OR STRUCTURALISM VS. METHODOLOGICAL INDIVIDUALISM

The core NC approach, best exemplified in the Walrasian General Equilibrium model to be discussed in later chapters, mimics the *atomicist* and reductionist approaches of classical mechanics and chemistry in an effort to ground fundamental laws of economics in individual agent behavior (Walras, 1877). This is as true in NC macroeconomics, which is based on *representative agents* who are both consumers and producers, as it is in NC microeconomics, which is based on agents who maximize their *utility* or *profit* subject to constraints.

This core methodological difference is perhaps best exemplified by another prominent PK of the Kaleckian and structuralist school, Thomas Palley, who highlights the futility of Krugman and other NC efforts to retroactively tweak and adjust the NC "neo-Keynesian" mainstream "representative agent" macro model to predict the 2007 Lesser Depression (Palley 2013). To his credit, as most mainstream economists simply ignore heterodox critics, Krugman has attempted (though unsuccessfully in my view) to repute Palley on this point.[4]

Heterodox economists on the other hand emphasize institutional causation that cannot be reduced to individual agents. Heterodox, or Radical, economist favor a *structural* or *organic* approach that assumes a two-way interaction between *agents,* and *institutions, society, culture,* and *class.* Both preferences and motivations evolve and change over time in response to economic, political and social policy decisions, that underpin social and cultural environments

[4] See for example Palley's 4/29/2104 blog post "The Flimflam Defence of Mainstream Economics," at: http://www.thomaspalley.com/?p=425

and affect the behavior of key economic institutions such as corporations, government, unions, and central banks. In this view, institutions are *not* "imperfections" or impediments to a fictional idealized "perfect market" system but, rather often, bring stability and predictability as they mediate and channel power relationships between classes and other powerful institutions such as large corporations and banks.

RATIONALITY: PROCEDURAL VS. SUBSTANTIVE

At its core, NC economics posits *substantive* agent rationality, or behavior based on constrained optimization with *perfect* information. This is the version of NC economics most prominently disseminated in introductory text books. It assumes unique *optimal* equilibrium points based on perfectly known individual *preferences* and *utility* functions and perfectly specified differentiable concave and convex production, profit, and cost functions.

In light of these core methodological differences, even the recent interest in behavioral economics and irrational decision-making (Kahneman 2011), if ever incorporated into introductory textbook economics, would result in *adjustments* rather than an abandonment of basic NC MIRA analysis. Utility functions, that include *empathy* and *jealousy*, would simply be "add-ons" to the basic model that take into account these *imperfections*. As Lavoie notes, NC models based on *imperfect* or *asymmetric information* (Stiglitz 1996), "only serve to reinforce this unreasonable [assumption of an] ability of agents to calculate and optimize information [if they had it]." (Lavoie 2009, p. 9).

Heterodox economists, on the other hand, have always posited *bounded* or *procedural* rationality at the core of their modeling efforts. This is based on *satisficing* habits, conventions, heuristic shortcuts, or *rules of thumb* that characterize realistic consumer and individual behavior (Simon 1976).

For example, PKs distinguish between "needs," akin to Rawls "basic goods", like food, housing, shelter, transportation, and health care, and "wants" that are discretionary and generally *substitutable preferences*. This leads to *lexicographic* utility functions and to class- and culture-based consumption patterns dependent on income, and more limited substitution in consumption (Lavoie 2009, Chap. 2).

The same is true in production where heterodox economists generally assume Leontief production functions with fixed or limited substitution in production rather than Cobb-Douglas or Solow growth models that are based on NC production functions with factor elasticities of substitution of one or greater (Marglin 1984; Taylor 2004).

FOCUS OF ANALYSIS: PRODUCTION VS. EXCHANGE

The conventional and most often used definition of economics repeated in some form in many, if not all NC texts is that of Lionel Robbins (1932):

> Economics is the science which studies human behavior as a relationship between given ends and scarce means which have alternative uses (p. 16).

This reflects the fundamental basis of NC economics in exchange. Thus there are limited goods on offer so that everything consumed or used in production is scarce. This implies that there is an *opportunity cost*, or cost of the choice forgone, for every exchange. This is reinforced in every introductory textbook through the example of the "production possibilities frontier" (PPF) showing the constraints to producing more of either of two goods, often represented as *guns* or *butter*. The PPF demonstrates the *increasing opportunity* cost of specializing in one or the other good along a concave production frontier, see Fig. 3.1 below.[5] In NC economics, as is shown in detail in later chapters, *production* is a species of *exchange* so that the entire economy is, in principle, modeled as *one giant supermarket*.

In contrast, heterodox economists tend to view *production* and the challenge of creating Valuable goods and services, rather than exchanging or consuming them, as the most important focus of economic analysis. Marx focused on production and expanded reproduction, and all heterodox economists are keenly interested in the extent and disposition of *surplus* production, or production over and above current needs, as well as in the causes and effects of growth, unemployment, and technical progress.

Again, to be fair, NC macroeconomists are of course concerned about these issues, but core NC models are rooted in the Walrasian-based ideal of a market-based tendency toward *full-employment* dictating a world of *scarcity* and *opportunity costs* even in the macroeconomy (Weeks 2014). NC economics thus leads to a primary focus on *efficiency* of allocation rather than the elimination of unemployment and sustainable production.

---

[5] See (Schiller 2013a, 2013b, Chap. 1) or any other mainstream introductory economics textbook.

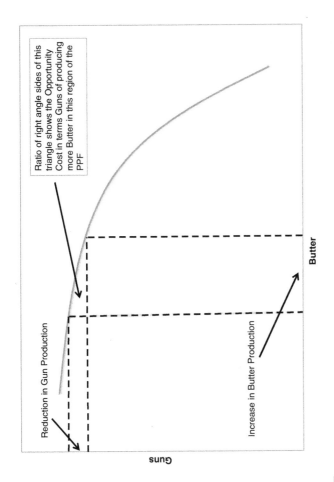

Ratio of right angle sides of this triangle shows the Opportunity Cost in terms Guns of producing more Butter in this region of the PPF

Reduction in Gun Production

Increase in Butter Production

Butter

Guns

Fig. 3.1 PPF

THE POLITICAL SUPPOSITION: MARKETS VS. SOCIAL CHOICE

Underlying these methodology differences is the NC faith in markets as an efficient and optimal mechanism of allocation. In the NC view, this is an *ideal goal*, even if often not feasible for practical reasons in the real economy. In NC economic theory, under ideal conditions of perfect competition, perfect information, and perfect rationality markets and *flexible prices* generate an *optimal* economic equilibrium.[6]

As Lavoie (2009, p. 11) puts it:

> Neoclassical economists often present their argument in the following way: in the short run, because of the presence of imperfections or externalities, state intervention may be needed. In the long run, however, markets are perfectly flexible, being able to guarantee [a beneficial] equilibrium on their own, and hence a minimum level of state equilibrium is optimal since the state is a source of inefficiencies in the long run.

For example, in spite of the current Lesser Depression resulting in a decline in employment-to-population ratio far above anything ever experienced in any prior postwar recession, even after controlling for the long-term general aging of the US labor Force (see Fig. 3.2 below), there has been very little support for a comprehensive federal jobs program even when politically popular funding sources are identified. The implicit elite consensus, driven by the NC economic world view, is that *the economy* will recover *on its own*, or perhaps with heroic *monetary* infusions by the Federal Reserve, but *without any need for direct* public policy measures such as a large scale federal jobs program (Baiman 2015).

In contrast, heterodox economists do *not* place an inherent positive normative value on market outcomes unless markets are explicitly structured and regulated to produce socially beneficial results. In the heterodox view, markets reflect economic power and are *embedded in society* (Polanyi 1944). Markets are creatures of policy and *social choices*. This implies that the allocation and production of large portions of "basic goods" such as health care, housing, education, infrastructure, and social services, need to be

---

[6] As discussed in the Introduction, this is true even for politically progressive NC economists such as Paul Krugman, as Krugman's (2014) comment claiming that a carbon tax is without a doubt the "first best" solution for global warming, shows.

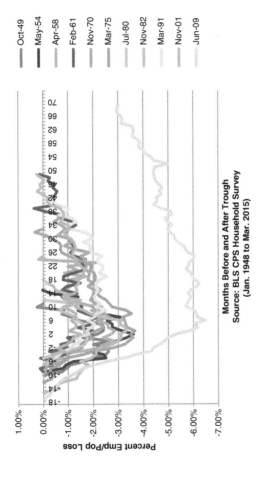

Fig. 3.2 Trends in post-WWII recession in employment-to-population ratios assuming that population age cohorts (16–24, 25–54, 55 and over) are fixed at March 2015 shares

removed from the market. In this view, there is nothing that is necessarily good or efficient about market outcomes, especially in increasingly unequal capitalist economies.

Imbuing market outcomes with unjustifiable *normative content* has led to increased injustice and inequity that becomes harder to address as markets are given ever freer reign over the economy. Unregulated markets are thus more than likely to be a central part of the *problem* as they inevitably lead to more concentrated and unequal economic and political outcomes. Relying on markets as the key driver and *counter factual* ideal for the economy undermines support for even the most pragmatic regulation, or market-constraining or displacing, policies. The ideology of NC economics thus becomes an apologia for greater inequality, and unfairness and immorality in the economy, that fundamentally undermines progressive policy supported by NC *economists* who mistakenly believe that *NC economic science* and *political values* are *separable*.

PK Economics Methodology

PKs are heterodox economists who believe that Keynes' revolutionary insights into, and fundamental transformation of, the basic assumptions and methodology of macroeconomics should be extended and developed further, rather than treated as a special case of institutional rigidity and market inflexibility within an undisturbed "neoclassical synthesis". A synthesis that is based on pre-Keynesian NC Walrasian core theory, in the mainstream NC Keynesian, or neo-Keynesian view (Palley 2013).

Within the PK school of thought, "Keleckians" or "structuralists" build on the work of Polish economist, Michal Kalecki who is widely credited with concurrently and independently developing a macroeconomic theory like that of Keynes, but from a *Marxist* background, rather than the *Marshallian* background of Keynes and most other western economists (Kalecki 1971). Prominent Kaleckian or structuralist PKs, such as Godley, Lavoie, Palley, Taylor, and Nell offer a particularly relevant and important version of *moral economics* as, following Kalecki and Marx, they highlight the importance of class and distribution in the economy and develop realistic economic theory and policy aimed at reducing class power and exploitation, and increasing long-term economic sustainability.

PK economics in general is based on a number of key methodological principles.

The most important of these is the "principle of effective demand" which holds that macroeconomic outcomes are primarily a function of overall or aggregate *demand*. In the PK view, in direct opposition to the dominant NC "Say's Law" view that "supply generates its own demand" and "savings leads to investment," *supply adapts to demand* and *savings is generally determined by investment* (Ridell et al. 2011, Chap. 14).

PKs also emphasize the importance of understanding *dynamic adjustment processes* that occur in real or *historic* time rather than focusing on *equilibrium* states that are arrived at in *theoretical* time that ignores the possibilities of *hysteresis* or *path dependency* of outcomes through time. Keen (2011, Chap. 9) is a particular proponent of the importance of using modern *dynamic* models, rather than the traditional *comparative statics* that still dominates NC economics. Keen (2011), Godley and Lavoie (2007), Cripps and Godley (1976), and Cozzi et al. (2014) have built and used such models for current policy analysis.[7]

Another important aspect of PK economics is an emphasis on the role of *finance and money* in the macroeconomy based on Keynes' insights regarding the importance of finance and investment in modern capitalism. Keynes pointed out that money is not just a *veil* with no impact on the *real* economy other than determining nominal price levels as theorized in NC core doctrine, but that *monetary policy* can have short- *and* long-term impact on the real economy. PKs believe that finance plays a substantive role in the macroeconomy. It can, for example, be the source of increasing instability leading to periodic *financial crashes* that can severely impact the entire economy.

The eminent PK economist, Hyman Minsky, was famously an early proponent of the inherent instability of capitalist financial cycles, and the widespread acceptance of Minsky's views among PKs was one of the reasons for their pervasive agreement on the likelihood of a major economic crash in the pre-2007 years (Keen 2011, Chap. 1; Minsky 1982). The Modern Monetary Theory (MMT) school of PKs, centered around the Economics Department at the University of Missouri at Kansas City, focuses on the importance of monetary policy and the use of government/central bank capacity to create money to support progressive public policy goals (Wray 2012).

---

[7] The econometric model used by Cozzi, McKinley, and Michell is now the Cambridge Alphametrics Model that is based on an earlier model by Godley and Cripps.

Another PK methodological focus is the attention to the negative impact of *falling* prices, rather than the one-sided preoccupation with *inflation* that characterizes much of NC macroeconomics. This again stems from Keynes' critique of the NC assumption of an *automatic* macroeconomic adjustment to equilibrium based on eventual falling of real wages and prices during the Great Depression. Rather, Keynes believed that falling prices would be damaging to the macroeconomy (as they have been in Japan in the last decade and are now in Europe), so that institutional factors that supported *price stability* were important to *sustain* overall macroeconomic prosperity rather than *obstructions* to the price flexibility necessary for free-market stabilization.[8]

PKs, following Keynes, also emphasize the distinction between "fundamental uncertainty" for which probability distributions *cannot* be hypothesized and "risk" for which probability distributions *can* be estimated. Thus PKs believe that the likelihood of a crash from the "irrational exuberance" of investors, for example, cannot be calculated, as was famously being done in financial models prior to the 2007 crash (Taleb 2010).

Finally, PKs believe in a *realistic* microeconomics, that includes *lexicographic* preferences and, as will be discussed in later chapters, non-U-shaped cost curves and a *pluralism* of economics methods rather than a single "scientific" body of theory (Lavoie 2009, p. 15).

General Radical Economics Methodology Points

An introductory discussion of the ways in which *radical* or heterodox economics methodologically deviates from NC economics was developed by Samuel Bowles and Richard Edwards in 1985 in the first edition of their now classic radical economics introductory textbook *Understanding Capitalism: Competition, Command, and Change* (Bowles and Edwards 1985), which is currently in its third edition with an additional author, Frank Roosevelt (Bowles et al. 2005).[9]

---

[8] The second edition of PK economist David Colander's Intro text on Macroeconomics has an excellent review of these Keynesian arguments (Colander 1994).

[9] Interestingly Samuel Bowles, for many years a preeminent radical economist at the University of Massachusetts at Amherst (one of the six PhD-granting heterodox economics departments in the USA) and a founding member of the Union for Radical Political Economics (URPE), the professional association of radical economists in the USA, is now, with equally prominent former radical economist and long-time co-author and colleague Herb Gintis, at the Santa Fe Institute for evolutionary economics in New Mexico. Gintis and Bowles now

Bowles et al. (2005) define an "economic system" which can be anything from "tribal commonwealths, slavery, and feudalism, to self-sufficient households, capitalism, and state socialism" (p. 52) as

> *all ways of organizing the human labor needed in every society to produce the goods and services that support life.* No matter what type of society it is situated in, an economic system will determine *what* work is done, *how* it is done, and by *whom*, and to *whom* the resulting products are distributed. Economic systems are *relationships among people.* (p. 52)

This contrasts with the standard NC Lionel Robbins' definition (see p. 56 above), which is either reproduced in most NC texts or paraphrased. For example, in the popular NC introductory text by Schiller (2013a, 2013b), "scarcity" is emphasized as the "core" problem of the economy, which leads to

> three core choices that confront every nation:
> WHAT to produce with our limited resource.
> HOW to produce the goods and services we select.
> FOR WHOM the goods and services are produced – that is who should get them.(p. 3).

The focus on "goods and services" and what, how, and for whom to produce them is common in standard texts. There is a key difference between this and the focus of Bowles et al. on the economy as determining relationships between *people* with a focus on *production*, rather than between *people and things*, and *on distribution* and "innate" *scarcity*. Readers who are familiar with Marxist thought will recognize the Marxist origins of the Bowles et al., effort to peel away the "commodity fetishism" of what Marx called "vulgar bourgeois political economy" by highlighting the underlying relationships between people rather than focusing on things, in their definition of economics (Marx 1984).[10]

Expanding on this definition of "political economy" Bowles et al. then suggest that every economic system, and in particular capitalism, can be analyzed in terms of three dimensions: a "horizontal" dimension of

prefer to be called "evolutionary economists" rather than "radical economists," though the distinctions between these species of *heterodox* schools of economic thought may be lost on most (NC) economists.

[10](Marx 1984, p. 956) translation corrected to the German edition.

competition, a "vertical" dimension of *command*, and a "time" dimension of *change*.

The *horizontal* dimension of *competition* refers to

 aspects of economic relationships in which voluntary exchange and choice among a large number of possible buyers and sellers play the predominant role. (54).

The *vertical* dimension of *command* refers to

 aspects of economic relationships in which power plays the predominant role. (54).

Where the *direct power* of one person "over another person" is defined as:

 A has power over B if by imposing costs on B (or threatening to do so) A can cause B to act in a way that is to A's advantage. (55).

And finally the *time* dimension of *change* refers to

the historical evolution of people and economic systems. (p. 55)

Bowles et al. explicitly acknowledge the values basis of economics:

Economics is about values (what ought to be) as well as facts (what is). It is useful to make values – and their role in any particular economic analysis - explicit. The values adopted in this book are simple: an economy should provide all members of a society with an opportunity to lead a flourishing life, and this objective is more likely to be achieved if the economy is *efficient, fair,* and *democratic.* (p. 52).

And they define *political economy* (or what we're calling *radical* economics) as a *three dimensional* inquiry into the competition, command, and time dimensions of economic systems based on values of "efficiency, fairness, and democracy." NC economics is described, in their book, as limiting the core of its analysis to the *competition* dimension and, though it claims to be *value neutral,* to a narrow "Pareto Optimality" definition of efficiency.[11]

---

[11] Pareto Optimality is the NC *high theory* definition of efficiency. It is discussed in detail in Part III.

Other recent economics texts, such as Goodwin et al. (2009), make strides in opening up the standard NC approach to the need for more inclusive measurement criteria and impact assessment, especially with regard to critically important issues of environmental sustainability, in the spirit of the Commission on Measurement of Economic Performance and Social Progress headed by Stiglitz, Sen, and Fitoussi (2009). However, like the aforementioned Atkinson (2011) and Shiller and Shiller (2011) reform proposals, these texts do not place economic morality so directly at the center of economic thinking.

Though there is no question that all of these efforts are worthwhile, without changing the basic methodology of NC economics, or *directly challenging* the NC school's claim to be the *only legitimate scientific and objective* form of economics, it is hard to see how a *moral economics* that can serve as the basis for a more just and sustainable economy will ever emerge as a dominant form of economic inquiry.

THE GENERAL ECONOMICS LAY OF THE LAND IN THE USA

Though many mainstream economists are loath to admit this, it has been long known that many of the most important issues of economic policy cannot be meaningfully addressed through a value neutral *positivist* economic *science*, but rather are fundamentally questions of values and morality.

Classical political economists were well aware of this as they tried to base economic policy on a realistic view of moral behavior following the thinking of famous atheist moral philosophers, such as David Hume (1742) and Jeremy Bentham (1818), rather than religious moral precepts.[12] Though not an atheist himself, Adam Smith, for example, was building on the thinking of Hume and the Scottish Enlightenment when he tried to fashion a Theory of Moral Sentiments and promote competition that, through an "invisible hand," would channel inevitable self-interested behavior toward the unintended service of the public good and promote the "welfare of nations" (Smith 1776).[13] As discussed above,

[12] See, for example, Hume (1742). In spite of his status as one of most preeminent philosophers of his time, David Hume was not permitted to teach at a Scottish University or be buried in a public (religious) cemetery due to his atheist views, which he refused to recant. Similarly, Jeremy Bentham, though not as publicly outspoken an atheist as Hume, made his views clear through such works as Bentham (1818).

[13] Though Smith (1776) is his most famous book, Smith scholars, including the late Robert Heilbroner, author of probably the most influential modern book on the history of economic

core modern-day NC economic theory can be viewed as a footnote to this idea of Smith, as through elaborate mathematical formalism attempts are made to model "microeconomic foundations" based on the self-interested profit-and utility-maximizing behavior of "homo-economicus" employing MIRA methodology that supposedly underlies all fundamental aspects of the economy (Taylor 2004).

Heterodox economists, have been well aware of the value basis of economic theory and policy and have railed against the reigning NC *natural science* paradigm insisting that its attempt to turn economics into a kind of *classical mechanics* based on *value-free* methodological individualism is nothing more than an ideological form of *sciencism* that masks a very distinct set of values—*efficiency and the primacy of private markets* and *capitalism*, Radical economists believe that mainstream NC economics serves as a social *legitimation theory* that justifies the dominant economic and political order, much in the same way that Soviet style "Marxism" sought to justify State Communism with a claim that its particular brand of Marxism was a *science* of human history (Mirowski 2001; Habermas 1975).

However, recognizing that some elements of mainstream economics can be useful tools, particularly in analyzing markets and market behavior when these are reasonably competitive, and with a view to exposing students to the kind of ideas that most other economics students are being exclusively taught, heterodox economics departments (like other more open-minded—and not coincidentally of lower status and of less importance for the legitimation of the social order—social sciences such as sociology, anthropology, and even political science) have tended to offer a range of different, and often conflicting, economic theories and policies based on the ideas of key thinkers.

The following are the economic schools of thought or theories most often taught in these departments: (a) *NC* economics, which is, as noted, based on—at least some of—the ideas of Adam Smith.[14] (b) *Keynesian* economics or more properly *true* Keynesian economics, often referred to as *PK* economics based on the work of John Maynard Keynes, *not* US-style neo-Keynesian, or "bastard Keynesian" in Joan Robinson's well-known

Thought (Heilbroner 1999), believe that the *Theory of Moral Sentiments* (Smith, 1759) was at least as important in laying out the basis of his ideas.

[14] Smith was actually a much more subtle and realistic *enlightenment philosopher* than *free-market* and *small government ideologues* and economics departments generally give him credit for. He supported, among other things, progressive taxes, public education, and strong government regulation of business, see for example (Bowles et al. 2005).

characterization.[15] The latter, as noted above, is based on a "NC synthesis" that tries to shoehorn Keynes into an NC *rational individualist* framework by attempting to construct *microfoundations* for *institutional rigidities* that, under special circumstances, make a *free-market* economy at least temporarily respond to Keynesian policy prescriptions. And (c) Marxist economics based on the ideas of Karl Marx who emphasized capitalist class oppression and exploitation and, in line with the most progressive enlightenment ideas of his day, the need to construct a truly democratic, political, *and* economic social order.[16] These three schools of thought are said to have different and distinct foci emphasizing respectively, *efficiency, employment, and democracy* and *fairness* (Bowles et al. 2005). Some heterodox departments also include "institutional economics" following the work of Veblen (1899), "evolutionary economics" (Bowles and Gintis 2008), "feminist economics" (Ferber and Nelsen 1993), and other more specialized heterodox schools in the mix.

In heterodox departments, students are, at least formally, encouraged to *think for themselves* and select the theory and associated policy emphasis that best fits their own values and understanding of political economic issues. Implicitly of course, teaching in heterodox departments tends to be strongly critical of NC theory in most contexts and supportive of PK and Marxist theory as being more relevant and consistent with economic reality in advanced capitalism. However, a problem with this social science education in cognitive *dissonance*, as the theory and policy prescriptions of these disparate schools of thought often directly conflict, is that it leaves open the question of what should be the preferred policy recommendation— as in the "on the one hand, but on the other hand" well-known joke about economists. This book is an attempt to shed some light on a path out of this intellectual thicket.

CONCLUSION

The world and US economy is currently in the midst of a severe crisis—the worst since the Great Depression. People are crying out for answers. I argue in this book that the root causes of our economic illness lies in the *fundamental immorality* of our economic structure that is legitimated by a

---

[15] See Robinson (1962).
[16] For an insightful, comprehensive, highly formalized mathematical comparison of NC, neo-Keynesian, and neo-Marxist schools of thought, see Marglin (1984).

fundamental immorality in our *economic thinking*. A mainstream economics that refuses to acknowledge the value basis of its own theoretical constructions and policy recommendations, and worse, professes ignorance about its own apologetic function as core legitimator, based on any reasonable set of moral standards (to be further documented in later chapters), of a clearly immoral economic system and social order, will remain at best impotent, and at worst a major obstacle, to formulating and implementing the fundamental policy changes necessary for economic and social justice, prosperity, and environmental sustainability in the twenty-first century. Hence the imperative to expose the immoral basis of mainstream economics.

BIBLIOGRAPHY

Atkinson, Anthony B. 2011. The restoration of welfare economics. *American Economic Review. 101*(3):157–161.
Baiman, R. (2015). National Note. *CPEG Notes* (Vol. 1, Issue 2). Retrieved March, from http://www.cpegonline.org/wp-content/uploads/2015/06/Vol-I-No-2-CPEG-Notes-FINAL-May-2015a.pdf
Bentham, J. (1818). Church of Englandism and its catechism examined. Published 2011 Oxford: Clarendon Press.
Boulding, K. (1969). *American Economic Review, 59*(1), 1–12.
Bowles, S., & Gintis, H. (2008). The evolutionary basis of collective action. In D. A. Wittman, & B. R. Weingast (Eds.), *The Oxford handbook of political economy*. Oxford: Oxford University Press.
Bowles, S., Edwards, R., & Roosevelt Jr., F. (2005). *Understanding capitalism: Competition, command, and change*. New York: Oxford University Press.
Bowles, Samuel and Richard Edwards. 1985. *Understanding Capitalism: Competition, Command and Change in the United States Economy*. Australia: Harper Collins.
Colander, D. (1994). *Macroeconomics* (2nd ed.,). New York: Irwin/McGraw-Hill.
Cozzi, G., McKinley, T., & Michell, J. (2014). Can conventional macroeconomic models prevent persistent stagnation in the European Union. Policy Brief No. 5, *Center for Development Policy and Research* (CDPR). Retrieved from http://www.feps-europe.eu/assets/b2ba4b96-ba66-4f87-aeaf-d91bd91e1eed/201411-pb5-cozzi-mckinley-michellpdf.pdf
Cripps, F., & Godley, W. (1976, November). A formal analysis of the Cambridge Economic Policy Group Model. *Economica (New Series), 43*(172), 335–348.
Davis, John B. 1991. "Keynes's View of Economics as a Moral Science," *in Keynes and Philosophy: Essays on the Origins of Keynes' Thought*. Eds. Bradley W. Bateman and John B. Davis. Aldershot, England: Edward Elgar Publishing, 1991: 89–103.

Ferber, M. A., & Nelson, J. A. (Eds.) (1993). *Beyond economic man: Feminist theory and economics.* Chicago: University of Chicago Press.

Friedman, M. (1953). *Essays in positive economics.* Chicago: University of Chicago Press.

Godley, W., & Lavoie, M. (2007). *Monetary economics: An integrated approach to credit, money, income, production and wealth.* New York: Palgrave Macmillan.

Goodwin, N., Nelson, J. A., & Harris, J. (2009). *Macroeconomics in context.* Armonk: M. E. Sharpe.

Habermas, J. (1975). *Legitimation crisis.* Boston: Beacon Press.

Heilbroner. 1999. *The Worldly Philosophers: The Lives, Times And Ideas Of The Great Economic Thinkers.* NY: Touchstone: Seventh Revised Edition.

Heilbroner, R. L. (1992). *The worldly philosophers: The lives, times and ideas of the great economic thinkers* (6th ed.,). New York: Touchstone/Simon & Schuster.

Hume, D. (1742). *Essays, moral, political, and literary* (Republished 1987). Indianapolis: Liberty Fund Inc.

Kahneman, D. (2011). *Thinking fast and slow.* New York: Macmillan.

Kalecki, M. (1971). *Selected essays on the dynamics of the capitalist economy.* Cambridge: Cambridge University Press.

Keen, S. (2011). *Debunking economics* (2nd ed.,). London: Pluto Press.

Krugman, P. (2014, June 22). The big green test. *The New York Times.*

Lavoie, M. (2009). *Introduction to post-Keynesian economics.* New York: Palgrave Macmillan.

Mankiw, N. G. (2008). *Principles of microeconomics* (5th ed.,). New York: Worth Publishers.

Marglin, S. (1984). *Growth, distribution, and prices.* Cambridge: Harvard University Press.

Marx, K. (1984). In F. Engels (Ed.), *Capital* (Vol. III). London: Penguin, First published 1894.

Minsky, H. (1982). *Can it happen again?: Essays on instability and finance.* Armonk: M. E. Sharpe.

Mirowski, P. (2001). *Dream machines: Economics becomes a Cyborg science.* Cambridge University Press.

Palley, T. I. (2013). *Money, fiscal policy, and interest rates: A critique of Modern Monetary Theory.* Author's working paper. Retrieved January, from http://www.thomaspalley.com/docs/articles/macro_theory/mmt.pdf

Polanyi, K. (1944). *The great transformation.* New York: Beacon.

Rawls, J. (1971). *A theory of justice.* Cambridge, MA: Harvard University Press.

Riddell, T., Shackelford, J., Schneider, G., & Stamos, S. (2011). *Economics: A tool for critically understanding society* (9th ed.,). New York: Addison-Wesley.

Robbins, L. (1932). *An essay on the nature and significance of economic science.* London: Macmillan.

Robeyns, I. (2013). Economics is a moral science. Post on blog: *Out of the Crooked Timber of Humanity no Straight Thing Was Ever Made.* Retrieved October 31, from http://crookedtimber.org/2013/10/31/economics-as-a-moral-science/

Robinson, J. (1962, September). Review of H.G. Johnson's money, trade and economic growth. *Economic Journal,* LXXII 287, 690–692.

Schiller, B. R. (2013a). *The macroeconomy today* (13th ed.,). New York: McGraw-Hill Irwin.

Schiller, B. R. (2013b). *The macroeconomy today* (13th ed.,). Burr Ridge: Irwin/McGraw-Hill.

Sen, Amartya. 1987. *On Ethics and Economics.* Oxford: Blackwell Publishing.

Shiller, Robert J., and Virginia M. Shiller. 2011. Economists as Worldly Philosophers. *American Economic Review.* 101 (3):171–75.

Simon, H. (1976). From substantive to procedural rationality. In S. J. Latsis (Ed.), *Method and appraisal in economics.* Cambridge: Cambridge University Press.

Smith, A. (1759). The theory of moral sentiments (6th ed.). London: A. Millar. 1790.

Smith, A. (1776). An inquiry into the nature and causes of the wealth of nations. New York: Modern Library. Republished 1994.

Stiglitz, J. (1996). *Whither socialism.* M.I.T. Press.

Stiglitz, J. E., Sen, A., & Fitoussi, J.-P. (2009). *Report by the Stiglitz commission on the measurement of economic performance and social progress.* CMEPSP, Paris. Retrieved from http://www.stat.si/doc/drzstat/Stiglitz%20report.pdf

Taleb, N. N. (2010). *The black swan: the impact of the highly improbable* (2nd ed.,). London: Penguin.

Taylor, Q. P. (2004, Winter). An original omission? Property in Rawls's political thought. *The Independent Review,* VII(3), 387–400.

Veblen, T. (1899). *Theory of the leisure class: An economic study in the evolution of institutions.* New York: Macmillan.

Walras, L. (1877). *Elements of Pure Economics.* Reprint 1954. New York: Irwin.

Weeks, J. (2014). *Economics of the 1 %: How mainstream economics serves the rich, obscures reality and distorts policy.* London: Anthem Press.

Wray, R. (2012). *Modern monetary theory: A primer on macroeconomics for Sovereign Monetary Systems.* New York: Palgrave Macmillan.

Textbook Fables Support Immoral Policies: Economics Is Not About Supply and Demand or Aggregate Supply and Demand

Part II was conceived and mostly written during the 7 years (2000–2007) that my friend Mel Rothenberg and I were conducting a senior seminar on globalization at the University of Chicago. We had excellent, motivated, committed students from diverse disciplines—mostly noneconomics social science and social policy majors of various kinds. Many had non-US family backgrounds and most were progressive, but even these students were, in their economic thinking, often captives of mainstream NC economic ideology.

I wrote this then and as I rework it now (in 2015), much of the world, and particularly the USA, appears to be in a state of free fall. More and more serious social, environmental, political, and economic problems fester and remain unresolved. Young people are appalled and angry as they should be. But they are also overwhelmed and confused.[1] They want to do something and are trying to, but on many issues of economic policy they, and the vast majority of our political and intellectual elite, are trapped in an ideological prison. The prison is NC economics and it appears to leave an indelible mark, masquerading as "science," on all who are exposed to it. Like other prisons of the mind—worship of idols, worship of more abstract religious dogma, Soviet communist ideology, and fascist mythology—the primary function of neoclassical economics

---

[1] My son, a former student activist leader at Southern Illinois University and now a union organizer with the Ohio Education Association, is a good example of this new generation of angry and searching, politically active young people.

is to legitimate a social order. In order to change this social order, its underlying ideological principles and constructs need to be directly confronted. Part II is an effort to do this that draws liberally on the excellent but little-known work of an earlier generation of radial economists.

CHAPTER 4

The Supply and Demand Story: A Dystopian Counter-Factual

Though neoclassical (NC) economists claim that their doctrine is an objective science, the economic system that they present as an ideal benchmark, or counterfactual, against which all actual economies should be measured, a "perfectly competitive free market" (PCFM), reflects a very specific set of values. As has been discussed in previous chapters, the self-representation of NC economics as a *science* based on a SDM or free competitive market *meme* is *not* an irrefutable outcome of natural observation like physics or chemistry but rather is an *ideology* that elevates particular values above all others. This chapter examines this proposition in greater detail.

The easiest way to show that NC economies is an ideology is to posit a perfect PCFM world. Assume that all wealth is equally distributed and that PCFM's, including perfect information and perfect enforcement of contract and property rights, reign. Further assume that all legitimate *externalities* and other *market failures*, such as pollution and natural monopolies, have been addressed in as market friendly a way as possible—through taxes, subsidies, and direct regulation only where absolutely necessary. Assume also that all technologies are homogeneous of degree one[1]. This implies that the sum of *factors* times *marginal factor products* equals *total output* ensuring that, 'once price are given', an *apolitical* purely *technological* rule based on the incremental

---

[1] A production function $F(L, K)$ is said to be *homogeneous of degree one*, where L is labor, K is capital, and t is any positive real number, if $F(tL, tK) = tF(L, K)$. Where $F(L, K)$ is output, L is labor factor input and K is capital, or means of production, factor input. This means, for example, that doubling ($t = 2$) all factor inputs ($\partial L, \partial K$) will exactly double output $\partial F(L, K)$.

© The Editor(s) (if applicable) and The Author(s) 2016
R.P. Baiman, *The Morality of Radical Economics*,
DOI 10.1057/978-1-137-45559-8_4

products of inputs times their levels can be used to divide up total output among factors.[2] These are the only kinds of technologies for which such a purely *technocratic* allocation can be implemented. Finally, assume that all technologies have *diminishing marginal products* for all inputs so that increments in output decline as factor inputs increase.[3] This fits with the NC presumption that *power* and politics play no role in a PCFM economy.[4]

What happens under these *ideal* conditions?[5]

A pure *productivity* and *capital ownership* principle of *distribution* prevails as profit-maximizing competitive businesses will refuse to pay *factors of production* any more than, the value of what the last unit of the factor purchased adds to the value of output, or this last factor unit's *marginal factor product value* Assuming *perfectly competitive* factor markets, factors of production will then be able to bid up wages and unit costs of capital to this same value by refusing to contract for anything less than this.[6]

---

[2] This identity $F(L,K) = K\dfrac{\partial F}{\partial K} + L\dfrac{\partial F}{\partial L}$, known as *Euler's rule*, is a straightforward application of the *chain rule* to functions that are homogenous of degree one. If $F(tL, tK) = tF(L, K)$ then:

$$F(L,K) = \frac{\partial(tF(L,K))}{\partial t} = \frac{\partial F(tL,tK)}{\partial t} = \frac{\partial F(tL,tK)}{\partial(tL)}\frac{\partial(tL)}{\partial t} + \frac{\partial F(tL,tK)}{\partial(tK)}\frac{\partial(tK)}{\partial t} = K\frac{\partial F}{\partial K} + L\frac{\partial F}{\partial L},$$

so that a purely technical method of *exhaustively* allocating the total product F(L, K) based on the *marginal* contributions $\dfrac{\partial F}{\partial L}, \dfrac{\partial F}{\partial K}$ of labor and capital is possible. This method of allocation will not generally work for any other class of production function.

[3] This "convexity assumption," pervasive in NC economics, ensures that the productivity and capital ownership allocation method described in the paragraph below will work. Profit maximization will induce firms to increase factor inputs only as long as the value that they contribute to production exceeds their cost. Due to the *diminishing returns* assumption, for each factor there will be a finite point at which the value of the output of additional factor input will be *less* than the fixed cost per unit of the factor. For obvious reasons, this will not necessarily be the case for *constant or increasing returns* technologies. The origins and realism of the diminishing returns or *increasing costs* assumption are extensively discussed in later chapters, as is the issue of whether it is *possible*, even under the most abstract simplifying assumptions, to *measure physical capital* and its marginal product *before* resources have been allocated.

[4] See discussion in earlier chapters.

[5] The following exposition draws liberally from (Schweickart 1993) and (Roemer 1988).

[6] In competitive factor markets, no factor will work for less than its marginal product as *just sufficient* factor supply will cause other producers to pay this competitive rate. As discussed in later chapters, formal models of PCFM include many other assumptions. Here for clarity of exposition, and without loss of generality, we focus on a short list of some of the most important PCFM conditions.

Under these conditions, citing noted Chicago School free-market economist Milton Friedman, resources are approximately allocated (Friedman 1962, Chapter 10, p. 162)[7]:

To each according to what he, and his instruments, produces.

IF PCFMS EXISTED, WOULD THEY BE MORAL?

But is this a good principle? Will adherence to this allocation support broadly agreed upon economic moral principles that further human well-being?

The answer is clearly *no* as, regardless of how helpful this principle may or may not be for motivation, efficiency, wealth creation, and growth, as discussed later, this standard for distribution ignores *need*, *effort*, and the distinction between the productivity of *labor* and that of *capital*. In particular, it ignores the needs and denigrates the value of the less able, homemakers, the elderly, the disabled and all those who *due to factors beyond their control*, such as poor education, poor health, lack of employment opportunities in their place of origin, and abusive, poor, or dysfunctional family background, end up with *low productivity* jobs as measured by *the market*.

Similarly, this principle is unfair to people who because of their meager inheritance own no or very little *capital*. In the USA, for example, as of 2009 the median wealth of white households was 20 times that of black households (Kochhar et al. 2011). This principle also ignores the affects of an unforeseen economic crash in the stock market or housing market. It is also unfair to people with a relative deficit of patrons or class connections to get bank loans, which includes the vast majority of the population in all capitalist economies who have no such background and have little chance of acquiring significant income-earning assets outside of their home or pension, as indicated by the low rates of social mobility that prevail in countries like the USA (OECD 2010, Chapter 1; Isaacs 2008).

---

[7] "Approximately" as allocations depend on *marginal* contributions, which, under the NC diminishing returns assumption, are lower than those of all the other already employed workers or units of capital equipment. In this sense even attempts to justify this system of rewards in terms of productivity are futile. However, this technical detail is glossed over in the ideological discussion below. See Schweickart (1993) for further discussion of this point.

On the other hand, some people will be fortuitously rewarded by the market for highly valued talents or skills they happen to have or are able to acquire. For example, basket ball players Michael Jordan in his glory days, or LeBron James currently, may receive millions of dollars for short commercials that require little work or effort on their part. Similarly, many people receive income from income-earning assets that they have not inherited but nonetheless come to own without significant direct expenditure of labor, effort, or even risk.

And these considerations do not just apply to the high or low end of the market or to the genetic or sociopolitical lottery. Hourly workers in manufacturing will generally receive higher wages than workers in services regardless of their respective working conditions simply because manufacturing generally has higher market-valued productivity than services. For example, the revenue added by the incremental oil refinery operator, or the *marginal revenue product* of this person's labor, is generally much larger than that of a sales clerk or bank teller. The *plant and equipment that a worker employs* can be as important in determining his or her market-valued productivity as his or her skill, effort, and responsibility level.

ALLOCATING THE PRODUCT OF A HOE

As has been discussed in chapter 2, the notion that the owner of income generating property deserves a return derives from the classic liberal belief in *property* as the basis for *liberty* as famously codified in the work of John Locke. But Locke's (1690) statement that a laborer was entitled to "the work of his hands" conflates, the *return to property* with work of the labor that employs the property, and disregards the sense in which *property that includes rented human labor* violates the most basic principles of *democratic freedom*.

It is instructive to illustrate the former, property and labor *conflation* problem, by focusing on the ownership of *personal physical capital* such as a hand tool like a *hoe* that does *not* require or include rented labor power to operate. It might make sense for the owner of a hoe to benefit from the work that she/he performs with the hoe. However, this link between productivity, effort, and reward breaks down when revenue generated from the sales of the product produced with the help of the hoe is allocated to the *owner* of the hoe, when the owner is *not* the worker doing the hoeing.

The owner may have worked hard and saved to buy the hoe that is used by the worker. In this case there may be a reason to reward the owner for her/his act of sacrificing past expenditure and redirecting the social resources that would have been used to satisfy that expenditure toward productive investment that increases potential output in the future.[8] But what if this ability to redirect social resources toward investment for the future came from *luck* in one form or another, such as the social, geographic, or genetic lotteries discussed above, or from lucky investment or speculation such as that of George Soros, who made almost a billion dollars in two weeks in October 1993 by betting on the devaluation of the British pound (Harvey 2007, p. 96). Finally, even if the owner *did* have to sacrifice to purchase the hoe, shouldn't the economically efficient reward be just what is necessary to induce the owner to make the sacrifice rather than an Euler's theorem-based *perpetual return to capital*?

Regarding the first possibility of work and sacrifice leading to investment, we might legitimately ask if it makes sense for *social* investment, or investment that impacts the economic development trajectory for communities and nations, to be dependent on and controlled by *individual* sacrifice, risk, and investment choices? As Keynes famously pointed out, regardless of the source of their wealth, individual *savers* are *not* motivated by social *investment* needs, so what sense does it make to condition the funding of individual *investors* on the savings of individual *savers*, even if the actions and rewards to both groups of individuals could be morally justified?

In other words, what sense does it make to tie *lost benefit from the sacrifice of consumption* to the *productivity of the hoe*? The hoe, of course, can produce nothing by itself, and although the market value of the output may have some relationship to the design and sturdiness of hoe, under a reasonable assumption that hoes of the same general type are not that different, it is likely that most of the variation in the market-valued productivity of the hoe will be linked to the effort and abilities of the *worker* who is using the hoe, *not* to the particular *cost* of the hoe, or to whatever sacrifice may or may not have been incurred by the owner of the hoe in order to secure the funds necessary to buy the hoe.

The level of output of labor and capital is likely to have a very strong relationship with what *workers* are able to produce with the hoe and very little, if any, relationship to the level of *sacrifice* that the capitalist owner of the hoe may or may not have made to acquire ownership of the hoe. The reward, if any, to the *owners* should, as noted above, perhaps be just enough to offset the loss of sacrificed consumption, but this generally

---

[8] This is called "roundaboutness" in Austrian economics (von Bohm Bawerk 1884).

has *no* or, at most, a very indirect and tenuous relationship with the productivity, or lack thereof, that the sacrificed consumption may facilitate. What, for example, does the "Euler's Rule" principle have to do with sacrificed consumption? If workers come up with a more efficient way of using the hoe, why should a share of this increase in output be attributed to the owners of the hoe, as it *will* be under this principle?

A PCFM-BASED ECONOMY WOULD CONTRADICT LIBERTY AND DEMOCRACY

The *marginal productivity distribution principle* above becomes even harder to justify when we go beyond simple Lockeian conflation and note that the perfect NC world includes *wage labor* as part of "his or her instruments" as in the Freidman citation above. Even if perfectly competitive markets did reward workers based on their effort, skill, or responsibility, why should markets reward individuals whose funds are used to *employ* these workers, or rent their labor power as an instrument to be used to achieve the employer's goals? Or in less euphemistic terms, why should the owners of funds used to rent *labor power* (with some legally imposed restrictions, as labor power cannot be separated from the *people* who wield it), receive income from the output of the people that are rented, especially if these fund owners are not actively involved in any aspect of this production? (Ellerman 1992; Archer 1995). This may be the most troubling case of the general problem of rewarding *the owner of the hoe*. As PCFMs are based on owners of capital renting labor and claiming ownership of all of the residual (surplus or profits) produced by this labor, they are, in fact, *a method of domination and control of some people by other people* to serve their interests (Ellerman 2007). Thus, an ideal PCFM economic system directly contradicts the democratic principle that every adult person in full command of their capacities should be treated as a *free* subject whose decisions and actions are equally worthy of respect.[9]

As has been discussed in earlier chapters, this widely held democratic principle includes a notion of *liberty* that is much more extensive than the simple focus on *negative liberty* requiring restraints on despotic

[9] For example, as discussed in Chap. 2, PCFM directly contradicts the Kantian "Categorical Imperative" that all persons should be treated as *ends* and not as *means*.

government power and on a *tyranny of the majority* that the liberal political tradition with its emphasis on *civil liberties* and *civil rights* emphasizes. It also includes *positive liberty* requiring extensive *public action* to equalize education, health care, and basic economic security so that individuals have comparable *capacity* to realize their *individual* choices and equal influence on the *social choices* that affect them.

Because of the high level of interdependence between individuals in modern societies where only limited *individual actions* can be realized without participation in organizations involving *social choices and actions*, true *liberty* becomes intertwined with *democracy* as it requires that all participants who are strongly affected by *social choices* have more or less equal say over those social choices.[10]

As discussed in Chap. 1, the standard NC and liberal political response to the question, "Where's the democracy in a property-based economic system?" is that, in PCFMs, no individual has *power* over others as all choices are dictated by *consumer sovereignty* exercised through *individual choice* in the economy in the market (Bowles and Gintis 1987). Of course the extreme inequalities of income and wealth, and thus market "dollar votes" typical of capitalist societies, ensure that if *consumer sovereignty* exists, it is a *class*-based form of social choice based on *one dollar one vote*, not a *democratic* system based on *one person one vote*. However, even disregarding this, few serious analysts would accept the notion that there is no *power* in the economy of capital over labor; of big business over small business; and in the ability of "private" companies to make *social* decisions that have global, national, regional, or community impact, in their own *private* interest.

A PCFM IS NOT BASED ON "VOLUNTARY EQUAL EXCHANGE"

Finally, one might contend that though their *liberty* may be compromised, in PCFM: "Aren't workers at least getting paid for their work?" Isn't this just a case of *free and fair voluntary equal exchange* just like when I trade my apple for your orange such as, for example, paying for a plumber to

---

[10]Archer (1995), op. cit., includes an excellent analysis of *liberty*: both *positive* and *negative*, *individual* and *social* (or *democratic*).

fix your toilet?[11] The answer is, "no," for many reasons that have been explained by generations of socialists and Marxists including Marx himself who coined the term "unequal exchange ideology."

Labor power unlike apples and oranges is *not alienable*, or cannot be *separated*, from the people who do the work so that PCFM is incompatible with democratic (with a small "d") societies. These societies are based on the principles of *individual and social* liberty, that people should be free to make their own individual choices among options that primarily affect them and their families, *and* should have comparable ability to influence *social* choices that affect large groups of people *together*. Social choices are particularly necessary for outcomes involving *public goods* that cannot be easily, efficiently, or at all, divvied up among individuals such as national defense, highway systems, basic research, education, health care, fire prevention, and other forms of insurance or risk sharing. As has been discussed in prior chapters any choices made by individuals in powerful positions in the supposedly "private" economy that have significant impact on more than themselves and their immediate families are *social* (and not *individual* choices) that in democratic societies should be made as accountable as possible to those affected.

In this sense the private renting of individual labor is a manifest violation of liberty. In privately owned corporations, unlike in worker cooperatives or in "codetermined" stakeholder corporations in European countries that mandate fixed shares of worker representatives on large corporate boards (Hill 2010), workers *do not* delegate authority to an elected representative to serve their interests. Rather, they are *subjugated* to the authority of the owners and their agents to serve the interests of the owners. The capitalist–worker labor "exchange" without a union contract or codetermination law is an indentured service contract whereby the worker agrees to submit himself/herself to the direct authority of capital for a specified period of time in return for a wage.

Moreover, as wages for this submission-service are based on the second-best alternative or "reservation wages" of a large pool of unemployed workers who do not submit, they are generally lower than the value of

---

[11] Much of this discussion is based on the work of David Ellerman (1992, 2007), who has eloquently pointed out the legal contradictions of the wage-labor relationship in supposedly democratic societies, including the fact that even partially compromising one's *liberty* for money can be viewed, like the *choice* to sell oneself into slavery, as constitutionally illegal. See for example Ellerman's discussion of the "Seabury" decision (Ellerman, 1992).

this labor power to capital. As capital is almost always on the "short side" of the labor market, it exercises effective social power over labor. The labor contract is thus not a free and voluntary exchange (Bowles and Gintis 1993).

A worker who performs a clearly specified service for a preset fee, like a plumber for example, is freely (depending on the fairness of the market) exchanging his or her work for money. But most work in the economy cannot, or cannot efficiently, be contracted out like this (Coase 1937; Penrose 1959; Best 1990). Much production is inherently *social* production requiring organized and often creative team efforts that cannot be precisely or efficiently *prespecified* or monitored through explicit contracts so that *nonmarket*-based production organizations are required. In a democratic society, these should be democratic.

Because choices made by firms generally have *social* consequences, the accountability of Smith's "invisible hand" generated by competitive markets and consumer and worker *exit* power needs to be supplemented by direct democratic mechanisms offering *voice* to workers, communities, and governments (Hirschman 1970; Albert and Hahnel 1991; Bowles and Gintis 1986).[12]

Regardless of whether the exchange of labor power for wages can be supported on moral grounds, in capitalist societies, the unequal class power of the owners of the always scarce means of production is supported through macroeconomic policy. The existence of a *reserve army of labor* is preserved through Central Bank policies that reduce economic growth whenever wages begin to rise or are forecasted to rise due to tightening labor markets. This ensures a healthy rate of profit, necessary to maintain investment and growth in a capitalist economy. But it also constrains the bargaining power of labor vis-à-vis capital. This means that labor is almost always paid less than it produces allowing for *exploitation, profit,* and *accumulation,* all necessary to sustain a capitalist economic system. This particular *class monopoly* or *oligopoly* is a *market imperfection* not discussed in standard NC Economics or "industrial organization" texts though it is central to the very functioning of capitalism (Roemer 1988).

---

[12] As discussed in earlier chapters, Bowels and Gintis (1985) also point out the arbitrariness of limiting democracy to the "public" sector, when much of the "private" sector involves socialized production with large "public" impacts.

MORALITY REQUIRES TAKING LARGE PARTS
OF THE ECONOMY OUT OF THE MARKET

At an even deeper level, addressing issues of what Roemer (1988) calls "self-ownership" as opposed to "outside ownership," that is, delinking rewards from the unfair *genetic* lottery would appear to require an economic system patterned on a standard such as the following:

> From each according to their need, to each according to their ability.

A maxim that appears in Marx (1875), though it apparently originated with Luis Blanc (1851, p. 92). Following Marx, such an economic system may only be possible under utopian conditions of absolute "freedom from need" or scarcity of any kind. However, before we arrive at these exalted social states, there is something we can do here and now to change our dominant pattern of distribution from one that is, at least rhetorically, based on *market-valued productivity* to one that takes *need* and *effort* seriously.

Simply put, the way to do this is to take a large part of the economy *out of the market*, so that it is no longer subjected to market-driven allocation. This can be done either through direct political public sector allocations or with more limited overriding of market generated prices. Note that these *market overrides* would, in many cases, have to go well beyond the much more limited *tax and spend* subsidy regimes and occasional regulation required even under PCFM to deal with unavoidable "market failures." The Swedish workfare state (see Fig 11.4) is a good example of the benefit of *removing* a large part of the economy from the market.

MARKET DETERMINATION OF BROAD MACROECONOMIC
ALLOCATIONS IS UNJUST AND INEFFICIENT

Short of replacing capitalism with a fundamentally different economic system, there are macroeconomic problems, not directly tied to issues of basic liberty and democracy, and efforts even under capitalism, that go a long way toward producing more just societies.

A key macroeconomic problem in capitalist economies is the need to maintain an adequate level of unutilized resources (savings) and sufficient surplus extraction (profit) to induce productive investment that will sustain employment and growth. As investment is dependent on profit expectations, it is typically cyclical with periods of exuberance and overinvestment followed by excessive pessimism and under investment. This cycle is tied to structural forces leading to *profit squeeze* during periods of exuberance as wages increase or interest rates increase due to Central Bank *fears* of a wage increase, and to *wage squeeze, cost repression*, and increased unemployment when investment slows down (Taylor 2004b; Kiefer and Rada 2014).

Since workers receive little or no benefit from profits, they have no incentive to foster accumulation whose direct benefit goes to private owners, especially as this accumulation is derived, at least in part, from employment, and real wage, restraint or cutbacks. Individual capitalists, on the other hand, must maintain high levels of capital accumulation to stay ahead, or to get ahead, of the competition. Over investment can reduce the scarcity of capital, leading to *overaccumulation*, and declining price and profit levels, inducing a general slowdown and long term systemic crises (Dumenil and Levy 2004; Arrighi 2005).

Capital's historic response to profit squeeze has been to pursue technological product and process change creating new poles of monopolistic or oligopolistic market power and profit extraction as well as institutional transformations. These often involve greater concentration and consolidation of capital that enhance monopolies and obigopolies of power and profit. This is facilitated by *financial innovation* and by the expansion of *finance capital*, the *purist* form of homogeneous, liquid, and unattached *capital*. To the extent that it can, capital will also cooperate to repress wage levels and social expenditure and increase its power and freedom vis-à-vis national governments whether they are democratic or not. As is discussed further in Chap. 8, the neoliberal (NL) transformation of the *social relations of production* of the last few decades has also involved capturing and constructing international institutions (such as the International Monetary Fund, World Bank, and The World Trade Organization) that enhance, enforce, and maintain *free trade* freedoms and powers.

These deep long-term structural problems of capitalism need to be addressed through far-reaching democratic transformation of the economy, advancing human freedom and liberty. For example, the problem of investment could be addressed by taking the *net macroeconomic investment and growth* function out of the *market* where it cannot be rationalized or justified for all of the reasons listed above and democratically deciding as a society how much to save from current consumption and the broad guidelines on how to invest it. This would eliminate both the need for *bribery* of private individuals to induce savings and the linking of firm profits to levels and categories of investment that may, or may not be, in the broad social interest. A key current example is the need for fossil fuel companies to invest roughly $150 billion a year to keep reserve replacement ratios at over 100 % to maintain their capitalization levels, though current estimates indicate that harvesting even one quarter of these reserve assets will doom the planet (Klein 2014; Oil Change International 2015). Schweickart, for example, would simply tax capital assets to set up an investment fund (Schweickart 1993, 2011). Roemer proposes a one generation *indicative* stock market (Roemer 1994).

Overriding Market-Determined Wages and Incomes

The current (2015) value of the US federal minimum wage of $7.25 an hour was (in 2011) only 37.2 % of the average hourly wage, down from almost half (49.4 %) in 1964. The federal minimum wage needs to be substantially increased. But why is a *minimum wage* the only broad-based labor compensation mandate? Why not legislate a *maximum* wage or a maximum spread between lowest and highest wages such as the 9:1 maximum wage gap in the Mondragon cooperative with a 50-year history of growth and innovation in Northern Spain?[13] Or, recognizing that labor is *not* a commodity but the product of human beings and that "free" markets strongly favor the class power of capital in wage negotiations, why not use *wage setting boards* to set reasonable wages as used to be the case in Australia (Hancock 2013), a practice not unlike the "prevailing wage standard" rules for US federal projects?

For a long period of time in the 1970s, Swedish unions covering 60–80 % of the work force were able to enforce a "Solidarity Wage Policy" whereby workers with similar skills and responsibilities would receive equal pay regardless of the profitability of the particular firm that they worked/or (Visser 2006). This meant that relatively highly paid workers would receive lower raises than those at the bottom of the labor market. In addition to shrinking income inequality and increasing pay fairness, this forced less productive firms to close or merge with more productive firms,

---

[13] "The current Mondragon Cooperative Corporation-wide average ratio of top to bottom wage rates is 5:1 with a few exceptional cases as high as 8.9:1. Compared to America's ratio of 231:1, this is, of course, a far narrower range of wage rates than typifies capitalist corporations (Democracy at Work 2013), see Chap. 11.

thereby increasing productivity in the economy (Erixon 2008). During this period, extensive job training and "active employment policies" were used to keep unemployment around 2 % (Ginsburg 1982).

Solidarity Wage Policy was part of the active labor market policy implemented in Sweden under the influence of the Rehm-Meidner model from the 1950s through the beginning of the 1970s (Erixon 2008). In 1976 an effort was made to expand the model to address the windfall profits accumulated by high productivity companies that had only to pay average productivity wages because their unions were restrained from bargaining for higher wages due to the Solidarity Wage Policy. The plan advocated taxing these extra profits and using this income to buy shares that would be held by collectively managed worker funds. However, though this plan would have allowed Sweden's wealthiest families to keep their wealth, as it gradually diluted their *control* of stock and company boards of directors, Sweden's capitalist class reacted vehemently against the proposal, and it was a major factor in bringing down the socialist government that had led Sweden for most of the postwar period, in the 1976 elections. However, a watered-down plan was subsequently enacted in 1983 when the Social Democrats regained power so that, by 1994, when the funds were abolished by a nonsocialist government, 8 % of Sweden's stock market was owned by these collective worker funds (Kornai et al. 2001).

Democratizing Investment, Corporate Decision Making, and Central Bank Policies

Under the German General Co-determination Act of 1976 that has now been extended in various forms to other countries in the EU, publicly traded firms with over 2000 employees must have a 50 % employee representation on their Board of Supervisors. Though one of the worker representatives must be a management employee and the employers have veto power over the nomination of the Chair of the Board who can cast a decisive tiebreaking vote, this dramatically constrains the power of capital in these firms (Howard 2009). Similarly, under the Works Constitution Act of 1972 joint-stock companies with 500–2000 employees must have a 33 % employee representation on their Board of Supervisors.[14]

Though the German and Nordic systems are under strain from the free market NL regime being imposed globally by the USA, UK, and its

[14] Op. Cit.

allies, they are examples of *market overrides* that move away from private ownership and control of capital.[15]

Movement toward economic democracy in single, and particularly in small, countries is hard to sustain in the face of a global capitalist regime that is constantly pushing in the opposite direction toward granting ever greater freedom and power to private capital. Capital in highly regulated political and monetary regimes can often find ways to circumvent these policies and exit the country or threaten to do so in order to take advantage of more beneficial circumstances outside national borders. However, all of these programs are examples of market-overrides that attempt to align resource allocation more closely with *need* and *effort*.[16]

Another macroeconomic mechanism, alluded to above in the *wage-profit squeeze* discussion, that is central to capitalist economies is the increasing use of Central Bank *autonomy* over interest rates and the money supply to buttress profits by slowing accumulation, and to do this by rewarding holders of financial assets with higher interest rates and less inflation. This is the flip side of the problem of generating enough productive investment for growth and future needs. On occasion, the macroeconomy needs to slow down as it is generating inflation, and/or resource or environmental pressures (though these are generally ignored in current Central Bank deliberations) that can be damaging to short- and long-run macroeconomic health and viability. The question in this case is why should the owners of vast financial assets and all creditors be rewarded for the necessary economic slowdown by receiving higher interest rates while the much larger and needier group of debtors and workers are penalized? Some macroeconomic central planning levers are needed, but why is interest rate manipulation, or *monetary* policy, the primary tool used in capitalist economies? While *fiscal* or government taxing and spending policies are theoretically available, these have been used much less.

Similar questions can be raised about the Quantitative Easing (QE) policies of the post-2008 Lesser Depression years. As discussed further in Chap. 7, these policies have kept interest rates low but they have effectively funneled trillions of dollars in cash to large banks and financial interests who have hoarded much of these excess reserves (over $1.8 trillion as

---

[15] Archer (1995) op. cit, claims that the German method of gaining co-determination without an outright transfer of property may be more politically feasible.

[16] See Chap. 11.

of January, 2015) and collected interest on them.[17] In fact, in January of 2015 there were indications that the Fed might even raise the interest it has been paying since 2008 on excess reserves to prevent the banks from lending out this money too quickly as QE tapers off (Appelbaum 2015). In this case the legitimate question is why the Fed chose not to directly bailout homeowners and businesses instead of funneling a windfall of cash to the banks to hoard and collect interest on (Keen 2011, p. 370).

DIRECT PRICE AND PROFIT CONTROLS

Policies such as "wage and price" controls, or direct rationing of credit (see Chap. 7), in some cases, using *excise tax* mechanisms that reduce inflation pressures and benefit the government rather than private asset-holders, would appear to be both more efficient and more just.

Though NC economists repeatedly claim in textbooks, based primarily on Nixon's temporary and inconsistent application of controls on wages but not on prices, that wage and price controls do not work, they worked spectacularly well during World War II when the US economy almost doubled its size in 5 years through massive deficit financing without any inflation. During this period inflation was kept in check throuh wage and price controls and rationing of key items (Mills and Rockoff 1983).[18] Yes, wartime sacrifices made this possible, but this suggests that a much more modest 6 %–10 % sustainable "green" growth rate is possible during peace time without excessive inflation until abject poverty is eliminated on the planet.

A final example of the need to break down the prison walls of SDM and free-market thinking applies to the period (May 2011) when oil companies made $32 billion in profits even as gas prices went over $4 a gallon causing enormous hardship for a public stuck in an auto-centered built-environment. It would seem that taxing a good share of these $32 billion in private profits, instead of bestowing an estimated $70 billion in taxpayer subsidies on big oil, and using the proceeds to offset costs to motorists and support alternative energy supply and use as well as conservation would have been an obvious and very popular policy measure (Hanlon 2011).

---

[17] http://www.federalreserve.gov/monetarypolicy/reqresbalances.htm and http://research. stlouisfed.org/fred2/graph/?s[1][id]=EXCRESNS. See also discussion in Chap. 7.
[18] According to the BEA NIPA the GDP Quantity Index (Table 1.1.3 downloaded 8/27/2015) was 8.07 in 1939 and 15.38 in 1945.

CONCLUSION

Even an *ideal* NC PCFM economy cannot be justified on moral grounds. The notion that the SDM PCFM is a natural and objective outcome of external forces and individual choice that cannot be "interfered" with without abrogating individual liberty is unsupportable. This holds true in both the microeconomic and macroeconomic senses. The supply and demand story that furnishes the overriding *meme* upon which the ideal NC PCFM construct rests is a *morally*, and, as is shown in the next chapter, *empirically* unsupportable *ideology*.

BIBLIOGRAPHY

Albert, Michael, and Robin Hahnel. 1991. *The Political Economy of Participatory Economics*. Princeton University Press.

Appelbaum, B. (2015, January 9). Windfall for taxpayers coming to end. *New York Times*.

Archer, R. (1995). *Economic democracy: The politics of feasible socialism*. Oxford: Oxford University Press.

Arrighi, G. (2005). Hegemony unravelling I and II. *New Left Review*, 32(33), March, April, May and June.

Best, Michael H. 1990. *The New Competition: Institutions of Industrial Restructuring*. Harvard University Press.

Blanc, L. (1851). In C. Joubert (Ed.), *Plus de Girondins*. Paris: Passage Dauphine.

Bowles, Samuel and Herbert Gintis. 1987. *Democracy and Capitalism: Property, Community, and the Contradictions of Modern Social Thought*, NY: Basic Books.

Bowles, S., & Gintis, H. (1993). A political and economic case for the democratic enterprise. *Economics and Philosophy*, 9, 75–100.

Breschi, S., Lissoni, F., & Montobbio, F. (2005). The geography of knowledge spillovers: *Conceptual issues and measurement problems*. In S. Breschi & F. Malerba (Eds.), *Clusters, networks, and innovation*. Oxford: Oxford University Press.

Coase, Ronald H. 1937. The Nature of the Firm. *Economica*, New Series, 4, 386-405.

Democracy at Work. (2013). Website data updated January 10, 2013. Accessed February 12, 2015 from http://www.democracyatwork.info/studies/mondragon/

Distefano, F., Gambillara, G., & Di Minin, A. (2016). Extending the innovation paradigm: A double 'I' environment and some evidence from BRIC countries. *Journal of the Knowledge Economy*, 7(1), 126–154.

Dumenil, G., & Levy, D. (2004). *Capital Resurgent*. Cambridge, MA: Harvard University Press.

Ellerman, D. (1992). *Property and contract in economics: The case for economic democracy*. Cambridge, MA: Basil Blackwell Publishers.

Ellerman, D. (2007). On the role of capital in "capitalist" and in labor-managed firms. *Review of Radical Political Economics, 39*(1), 5–26.

Erixon, L. (2008). *The Rehn-Meidner plan: It's rise, challenges, and survival.* Stockholm: Department of Economics, Stockholm University.

Friedman, M. (1962). *Capitalism and freedom.* Chicago: University of Chicago Press.

Ginsburg, H. (1982). How Sweden combats unemployment among young and older workers. *Monthly Labor Review, 105*(10), 22–27.

Hancock, K. (2013). *Australian wage policy: Infancy and adolescence.* Adelaide: University of Adelaide Press.

Hanlon, S. (2011, May 5). Big oil's misbegotten tax gusher: Why they don't need $70 billion from taxpayers amid record profits. *Think Progress.*

Harvey, D. (2007). *A brief history of neoliberalism.* New York: Oxford University Press.

Hill, S. (2010). *Europe's promise: Why the European way is the best hope in an insecure age.* Berkeley: University of California Press.

Hirschman, A. O. (1970). *Exit, voice, and loyalty: Responses to decline in firms, organizations, and states.* Cambridge, MA: Harvard University Press.

Howard, A. (2009). "Codetermination" from website of American Studies at the University of Virginia. http://xroads.virginia.edu/~ma98/pollklas/thesis/codetermination.html. Last updated 9/01/2009. Accessed 26 Aug 2015.

Isaacs, J. (2008). *International comparisons of economic mobility.* PEW/Brookings report based on 1998–2001 data from the International Social Survey Program. Retrieved from http://www.brookings.edu/~/media/research/files/reports/2008/2/economic%20mobility%20sawhill/02_economic_mobility_sawhill_ch3.pdf

Keen, S. (2011). *Debunking economics* (2nd ed.,). Pluto Press.

Kiefer, D., & Rada, C. (2014). Profit maximizing goes global: The race to the bottom. *Cambridge Journal of Economics,* First published online September 29, 2014.

Klein, N. (2014). *This changes everything.* New York: Simon & Schuster.

Kochhar, R., Fry, R., & Taylor, P. (2011). *Wealth gaps rise to record highs between whites, blacks, hispanics.* Pew Research Social & Demographic Trends. Retrieved fromhttp://www.pewsocialtrends.org/2011/07/26/wealth-gaps-rise-to-record-highs-between-whites-blacks-hispanics/

Kornai, J., Haggard, S., & Kaufman, R. R. (2001). *Reforming the state: Fiscal and welfare reform in post-socialist countries.* Cambridge: Cambridge University Press.

Locke, J. (1690). *Second treatise on government.* New York: Barnes & Noble Publishing.

Marx, K. (1875). *Critique of the Gotha program.* Moscow: Progress Publishers, Republished 1970.

Mills, G. T., & Rockoff, H. (1983). Business attitudes toward wage and price controls in World War II. *Business and Economic History, 12.*

OECD. (2010). *Economic policy reforms going for growth.* Retrieved from http://www.oecd.org/tax/public-finance/chapter%205%20gfg%202010.pdf

Oil Change International. (2015). Front page of website downloaded 8/27/15: http://priceofoil.org/thepriceofoil/global-warming/

Penrose, Edith. 1959. *The Theory of the Growth of the Firm.* Oxford University Press.

Porter, M. (1990, March/April). The Competitive Advantage of Nations. *Harvard Business Review, 68*(2), 73–91.

Roemer, J. E. (1988). *Free to lose: An introduction to Marxist philosophy.* Cambridge: Harvard University Press.

Roemer, J. E. (1994). *A future for socialism.* Cambridge: Harvard University Press.

Schweickart, D. (1993). *Against capitalism: Studies in Marxism and social theory.* Cambridge University Press.

Schweickart, D. (2011). *After capitalism* (2nd ed.,). Lanham: Rowan & Littlefield.

Taylor, L. (2004). *Reconstructing macroeconomics: Structuralist proposals and critiques of the mainstream.* Cambridge, MA: Harvard University Press.

Visser, J. (2006). Union membership statistics in 24 countries. *Monthly Labor Review, 1.* Retrieved from http://www.bls.gov/opub/mlr/2006/01/art3full.pdf

von Bohm Bawek, E. (1884). *Capital and interest. Vol 1: History and critique of interest theories.* Republished 1958 by Libertarian Press.

CHAPTER 5

Ghost Curve Ideology: The Supply Curve Generally Does Not Exist, So Why Is It a Core Concept in Almost Every Economics Textbook?

I frequently start a class discussion on the "Supply and Demand Model" (SDM) with a simple question to anyone in the class. If you were a pizza producer how many pizzas would you produce at a price of $15 a pie? Students give me a blank stare. I then elaborate. Consumers will have some idea of how many pizzas they will buy at any given price, assuming other "shift factors" like income, taste, and expectations do not markedly change, but producers can estimate how much they will produce at any given price *only if they know something about demand conditions.* Demand, however, is *not* a factor in constructing the supply curve (SC). Quite the contrary. The SC of introductory economics textbooks is supposed to be completely *independent* of demand. Demand is supposed to have *no influence* on the position or shape of the SC.

Though ubiquitous in economic texts, an independent SC does *not* exist for most of the economy. In most of the *production* economy, firms set prices and levels of production based on *demand and costs.* Introductory textbooks misleadingly pretend that "perfectly competitive free markets" (PCFMs), are representative of *most* markets in the economy.[1]

The SDM story, which assumes that competitive markets drive SDM toward a socially optimal efficient allocation of resources that balances incremental costs and benefits is a hoax. The major purpose of the story, which, as has been noted earlier, is often the only thing that people

---

[1] See any Intermediate Microeconomics textbook, for example (Mansfield 1994).

© The Editor(s) (if applicable) and The Author(s) 2016
R.P. Baiman, *The Morality of Radical Economics,*
DOI 10.1057/978-1-137-45559-8_5

93

remember from their introductory economics training, is to firmly root the PCFM *meme* in the minds of introductory economics students, who later become lawyers, judges, politicians, business people, academics in other fields, citizen voters, and economics professionals, who base their legal or political views on the SDM and PCFM without thinking too much about what it is based on.[2]

In this chapter, we review the underlying SDM story, and show that simple realism dictates that it should be replaced by a "Demand and Cost Model" (DCM) story whereby output and prices are based on *demand and costs, and competition and firm strategy*. DCM derived output levels and prices will *not* satisfy any of the "incremental cost equals incremental benefit" efficiency outcomes that underlie the supposed social optimally of the PCFM. This theme will be taken up again, with greater technical detail, in Part III where *nonintroductory* economics *fall-back* applied microeconomic Ramsey pricing ideology replaces SDM as a meme that supposedly demonstrates the optimality of market pricing even though in these more advanced treatments most markets are acknowledged not have PCFM characteristics.

THE (MOSTLY FAKE) SUPPLY AND DEMAND STORY

Ask a woman or man "in the street" what they know about economics and, if they have had any formal exposure at all in high school or college, they will probably mention the SDM. This, I believe, reflects the extent of the systemic social indoctrination foisted upon the public by the (mostly unwitting) acolytes of NC economics. In one relatively simple story with just enough analytical and graphical content to give it an aura of objectivity and science, the fundamental principles of our social *religion* can be hammered home. As virtually every standard NC (and most heterodox) introductory economics textbook begins with this partial equilibrium story derived from Alfred Marshall's "scissors diagram," I present just a bare outline of the story below (Marshall 1890, Book V, Chap. 3).[3]

---

[2] For example, Rep. Paul Ryan, the current Republican Chair of the House Budget Committee, was by all accounts a devoted student of ultra PCFM libertarian economics professor Richard Hart at Miami University, Ohio, Ryan's alma mater (Tanfani 2012).

[3] Though heterodox texts often highlight critiques and limitations of the supply and demand story, they do not generally present an alternative (Bowles et al. 2005, Chaps. 8–9; Riddell et al. 2011, Chap. 7).

According to the SDM, Markets may be generally analyzed t.
of a supply curve (SC) and a demand curve (DC). For a given ma.
is a schedule of how much of the good in question consumers w.
at different "own-prices". Assuming "all else is constant," or "cet.
bus," the DC will slope downward. In other words, as the own-price c.
"quantity demanded" of the good will increase as it will then become rela   .y
cheaper than its substitutes, whose prices, by assumption, remain constant.[4]
The curve will be stable, or remain in place, as long as exogenous parameters
or "shift factors" that affect overall demand, such as income, tastes, market
size, and the number and prices of substitutes and complements, remain
constant. In this case, changes in own-price will cause "*movements* along the
DC." Changes in shift factors on the other hand will cause *shifts* in demand
or in the DC. Neither the shape nor placement of the DC will be affected by
supply factors. By definition the DC is independent of supply.

Analogously, an upward-sloping SC is a schedule of how much producers
will *produce* at different own-prices of the good in question if all other "shift
factors of supply," including prices of inputs, productivity, number of suppliers, their supply quantities, and expectations of supply, are constant. The SC
will normally be upward-sloping as the higher the own-price a producer can
get for the product, the more they will produce for the market.

Given a stable DC and SC, or *constant* supply and demand shift-fac-
tors, competitive markets will "clear" at the unique equilibrium price and
quantity where DC and SC intersect and where "quantity supplied" equals
"quantity demanded." This is a self-adjusting stable equilibrium that will
be arrived at through individual consumer and producer reactions to
"price signals" (Fig. 5.1).

This (partial) equilibrium is *stable* as it includes a "dynamic adjustment
mechanism," whereby individual-agent price signal responses will automatically move the system back to its original equilibrium, or to the appropriate new market-clearing equilibrium, if the SC or DC shifts.

For example if the DC shifts to the right due to say increased incomes,
a surplus in quantity demanded will occur at the original equilibrium price
causing producers to raise their prices and move up their SC to satisfy the
increased quantity demanded. This will then cause consumers to lower their
quantity demanded a bit by moving up their rightward shifted DC to a new
market-clearing equilibrium at a *higher* price and quantity point. The opposite
will occur if the DC shifts down (left) instead of up (right) (Figs. 5.2 and 5.3).

---

[4]For expensive goods quantity demanded may also increase as price declines due to an
"income effect". Consumers have more money to spend when the price of the good declines.

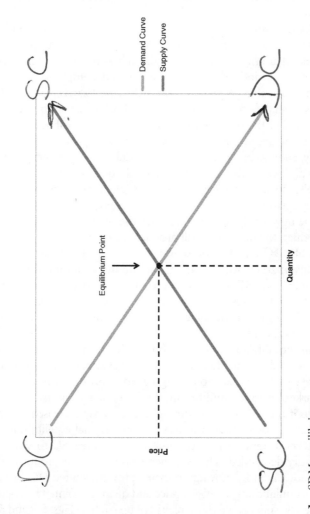

Fig. 5.1 SDM equilibrium

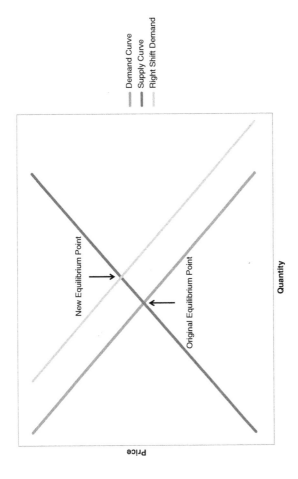

Fig. 5.2 SDM demand increase

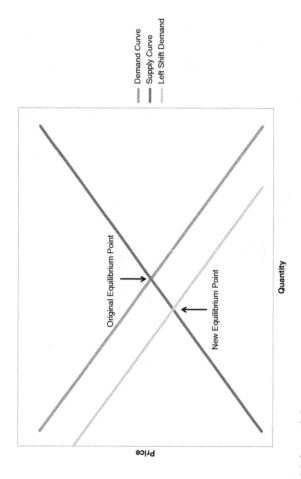

Fig. 5.3   SDM demand decrease

Similarly if the SC shifts right due to say increased productivity, a surplus in quantity supplied will appear at the original equilibrium price, causing producers to lower their prices and move down their SC to reduce unwanted inventory accumulation. This will then cause consumers to move down their DC to a new, *lower* market clearing equilibrium price and *higher* equilibrium quantity, point. The opposite will occur if the SC shifts (left) instead of up (right) (Figs. 5.4 and 5.5).

In introductory and applied economic texts, the concepts of "consumer surplus" (CS) and "producer surplus" (PS) are employed to generate a normative justification for PCFM SDM equilibriums, see Figure 5.6. CS is defined as the area under the DC showing the *sum* of the differences between the prices that consumers would have been willing to pay and what they actually paid at the (always by definition) lower *equilibrium* price level determined by a horizontal line through the intersection of the DC and the SC. PS is defined as the (necessarily positive or zero) profit that equals the area above the SC and below the horizontal equilibrium price line. Standard NC introductory economic texts explain that a PCFM SDM equilibrium maximizes the sum of consumer and producer surplus and that the imposition of any *nonmarket* price or quantity restriction will diminish this measure of overall social welfare.[5]

This is because any "government intervention" into the "free market" that artificially attempts to keep prices low (like rent control) or high (like agricultural price supports) will lead to shortages or surpluses and "deadweight" CS + PS loss relative to the CS+PS that would have resulted from the "Pareto Optimal" welfare-maximizing (unconstrained) market equilibrium price and quantity, or the PCFM SDM equilibrium (Fig. 5.6).

This fundamentally Walrasian[6] SDM story is presented in introductory texts as a description of the workings of Adam Smith's *invisible hand*. The latter is an automatic feedback dynamic story explaining how, in competitive markets, greater demand drives up prices and profits, stimulating increased investment that leads to greater supply. SDM thus supposedly supplies a rigorous foundation for the rhetorical message of objective market

[5] See, for example, the popular (Mankiw 2008, Introductory economics text). For a simple critique of CS and PS methodology see (Hill and Myatt 2010, Chap. 4). For in-depth critiques of CS and PS, see Part III of this text.

[6] For a more advanced discussion of the difference between "Walrasian" and "*Post-Keynesian*" or "Ricardian" theories of growth and value or output and pricing, see (Nell 1967) reprinted in (Nell 1992, Chap. 2).

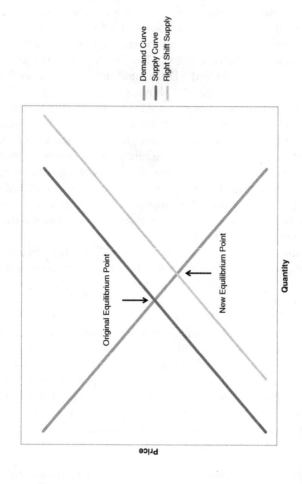

Fig. 5.4 SDM supply increase

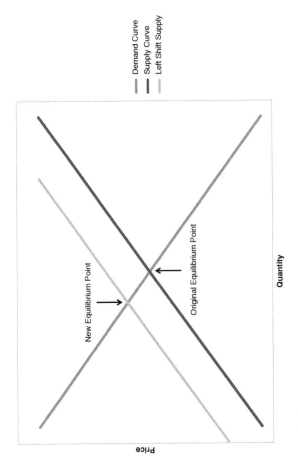

Fig. 5.5 SDM supply decrease

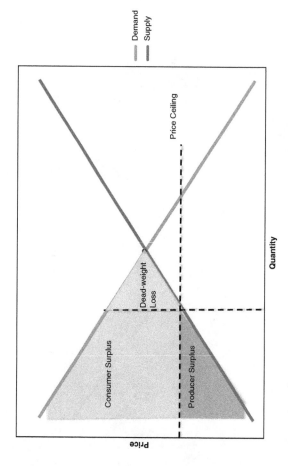

Fig. 5.6 SDM producer and consumer surplus deadweight loss from price ceiling

forces coordinating individual self-interest and providing a beneficial and balanced social equilibrium through freely adjusting price signals.

Given exogenous technological and natural constraints (see Chap. 1), the SDM shows that capitalist *market* economies *gravitate toward a social welfare-maximizing, stable, market-clearing equilibrium that is perfectly determined by natural conditions and individual choice*, as:

(a) "Objective" market forces are produced by aggregations of *agent* choices in such a way that no *individual* buyer or seller can significantly affect overall SCs or DCs. PCFM equilibrium prices and quantities are determined by *nature, technology*, and (almost as sacrosanct in liberal political thinking) "free and voluntary" *individual*-agent *choices* in their own self-interest. These free market equilibrium prices *perfectly and deterministically* balance the objective and inviolate forces of supply and demand so that *quantity supplied* exactly equals *quantity demanded*, resulting in an equilibrium *clearing* of all markets. The SDM thus provides a scientific and objective solution to the central economic problem of "allocating scarce means to competing ends" that is *free and fair* as it properly reflects "consumer sovereignty" and individual choice.

(b) *Shifts* and *movements along* these curves not only generate unique, objective, and fair equilibrium prices and quantities, but the equilibrium so obtained is a "self-correcting" *stable equilibrium*. In the absence of SC or DC shifts, any movement away from equilibrium price or quantity will automatically generate price changes (or "price signals") that will induce individual producers and consumers to make choices based on their own self-interest, that will return the system to (the prior existing) equilibrium. The SDM thus includes a dynamic self-adjustment mechanism that moves the system toward its unique equilibrium position and sustains this equilibrium once it is obtained.

(c) Finally, as the SDM equilibrium generated by individual self-interested agent choice, subject only to (exogenous) constraints of nature and technology, *maximizes social welfare*, the SDM is a modern and rigorous formalization of Adam Smith's "invisible hand" doctrine. The SDM thus provides "objective scientific" support for the cornerstone ideology of NC economics: that competitive markets will cause actions motivated by private self-interest to

serve the public good. The SDM thus shows that PCFMs are optimally socially efficient.

Now any, more or less, formal model ignores some aspects of reality so
that it would serve little purpose to critique SDM for not *precisely* replicat-
ing reality. It is well known for example that SDM cannot determine distribution (*factor* markets play a role but cannot set "initial endowments") and
disregards *exogenously determined* (in the SDM) *tastes, nature, and technology*.[7] As has been noted in earlier chapters, the standard NC response
to these critiques of the SDM is that factors influencing tastes, nature, and
technology are outside the sphere of economic science. NC's claim that
the proper way to address distribution, for example, is through a political
reconfiguration of initial endowments (or wealth) that does not "interfere"
with the efficient workings of the market as depicted by the SDM. The
construct backing up this position is the "Second Fundamental Theorem
of Welfare Economics" that proves that a PCFM can provide any desired
distributional outcome through an appropriate setting of initial endowments.[8] As has been noted, all of these SDM PCFM outcomes are said to be
"Pareto Optimal"—a term that sounds like *optimal* but, in fact, is defined
as a situation under which no agent can become better off through a voluntary market exchange with another agent. In other words, an outcome that
is a tautological consequence of the workings of a PCFM SDM equilibrium
defined as the result of individual agents trying to improve their welfare
through voluntary market exchanges. PCDM outcomes are deemed pareto
optimal as they maximize the sum of CS plus PS in SDM outcomes.

Critiques of both the measure (Why should the welfare derived from
PS or profit be considered equivalent to welfare derived from CS?) and
its units (Why should a dollar of CS for an extremely wealthy individual
like Donald Trump have the same "social welfare" value as a dollar of CS
for an average income person?) have been rigorously developed (Baiman
2001) (Granqvist and Lind 2004) and are discussed in detail in Part III
of this book. Critiques of these supposedly objective scientific "principles

---

[7] For an advanced discussion the role of *tastes, nature, and technology* in the NC model, see
(Marglin 1984, Chap. 2). For theoretical proofs and discussions of how endogenizing these
factors undermines the "Fundamental Theorems of Welfare Economics," see (Hahnel and
Albert 1990).

[8] See any intermediate or advanced standard NC microeconomics textbook, for example
(Mansfield 1994).

of microeconomics" show that even the presumably more realistic, modi-fied version of SDM widely used by NC applied microeconomists (for example to justify the disastrous deregulation of electricity in California) can be shown to rest on *basic assumptions* reflecting particular sets of *values*, namely the primacy of *efficiency* and *individual choice* over *equity* and *social choice*, and a mistaken belief that the former can be strictly and scien-tifically *separated* from the latter, see Part III and (Baiman 2002).

For now, it is important to demonstrate the complete (not just approxi-mate) lack of realism of the *introductory textbook* SDM, which is, as has already been noted, a model that most students who have any formal exposure to economics at all, never get beyond.

SCs GENERALLY DO NOT EXIST

The standard introductory economics SDM is based on *independent* SCs and DCs that in practice rarely exist. For example, in response to our ques-tion of the afore mentioned pizza producer regarding how many pizza's he or she would *produce* at different possible sales prices, if there was a response at all, it would be: "Well that depends on what I thought demand would be." But the answer to this *demand* question, by assumption, plays *no role* in the construction of the SC that the question address. The SC is supposed to give the number of pizzas that a producer would produce based purely on *supply conditions*—that is the *cost* of producing each addi-tional pizza relative to a given price set by the market. This is based on the assumption that producers will be able to sell *every* pizza that they can produce at the *market price*, that costs of production per unit *increase*, and that no individual producer could possibly produce enough pizzas to change the market price. As far as individual producers are concerned, the SC is supposed to reflect *infinite demand* at every price.

If this sounds hokey, it is. How many producers do you think construct (necessarily purely theoretical) SCs to determine the "maximum" output that they can produce profitably at any market-determined "given price" assuming that demand at these prices will be infinite.

Moreover, what if, because of economies of scale, for example, the cost of production per unit *declines* as more is produced? The model obvi-ously breaks down completely in this case, as every producer will produce an infinite supply. The SC hypothetical construction is premised on an assumption that *every* producer will experience increasing costs per unit as output increases and that these incremental, or *marginal*, unit costs will increase fast enough so that no producer will be able to obtain a large enough share of the market to influence prices (thus becoming an *oligopolist* or *monopolist* instead of a "*perfect competitor*") before this happens. But this is a nonsensical assumption in today's advanced economies in which most major sectors are dominated by giant, often multinational, firms whose reach and profitability are based on constant, or declining costs from large-scale, production, sourcing of inputs, and marketing.

Ask the same question of a hypothetical pizza *consumer* and you are likely to get a fairly well defined downward-sloping DC, provided that nearby pizza shops selling the same kind of pizza are available and that the consumer has a limited pizza budget, so that *effective competition* and *income constraint* conditions hold.

The problem here is that though individual, and after adding them up, *aggregate* DCs are a fairly well-defined theoretical construct, the existence of hypothetically *independent of demand* upward-sloping SCs for firms and for markets, generally, are *not*.

In the short run, assuming some level of *normal* excess capacity, *variable average costs* (costs that vary with the amount of output produced) per unit produced are often relatively *constant* so that average *costs* that include *fixed* overhead and setup costs per unit produced should *decline* as these are defrayed over larger production runs (Lavoie 2009, Chap. 2). Thus, total (variable and fixed) short-run average costs, that are, by definition, supposed to be based *exclusively* on cost-side factors, will generally either be *downward* sloping or, at the very least if there are some offsetting increases in average costs for *unusually* high levels of production such as overtime pay, *flat*.[9]

When SDM is applied to the long run, a period of time over which plant and equipment (or "Capital") can be expanded, there is even greater reason to believe that total average costs for most industries will decline as greater market power and economies of scale (larger plants lowering the cost per unit of output) and scope (franchising reducing joint overhead costs such as marketing and financing) reduce the costs of inputs and of

---

[9] Piero Sraffa first raised (a variant of) this critique of the textbook Marshallian microeconomics story in (Sraffa 1926). It has been reiterated by generations of "Sraffians" and "Post-Keynesians" and other non-NC economists ever since with little apparent impact on NC microeconomic theory. For a comprehensive treatment of this NC attachment to "Household production" as opposed to "Industrial Production" see (Nell 1998).

production. NC economic texts (i.e. almost all economics texts) are forced to resort to dubious claims that "administrative inefficiencies" stemming from large size will inevitably add sufficient costs per unit to offset all of the advantages of large-scale production in order to justify an upward sloping long-run average cost curve assumption.[10]

This is a necessary assumption if PCFMs are to naturally evolve toward an optimally efficient production and pricing configuration at the bottom of a U-shaped long-run average total cost curve. But this is contrary to the actual experience of most advanced capitalist economies in which larger and larger firms achieve cost, marketing, and financial advantages, and affective oligopoly power over numerous industries and large market segments. Walmart and Amazon are just the latest example of the efficiencies of scale, including market (and political) power that adhere to the largest and most concentrated units of capital. The "natural" tendency of capitalism in most cases is to evolve toward greater oligopoly à la Marx, rather than PCFM à la Adam Smith, in complete disregard of standard NC textbook microeconomic theory.[11]

In other words, though "diminishing marginal utility of consumption" which generates downward-sloping DCs, since, as consumers derive less and less satisfaction or "utility" as they purchase more of a commodity they will increase their "quantity demanded" only if relative prices of the commodity decline, makes sense as describing consumption behavior, "diminishing marginal productivity," which generates eventually upward-sloping SCs, since, as marginal costs per unit increase, profit-maximizing suppliers will only produce more if sales prices increase, does *not* generally describe *any* characteristic of production.[12]

Rather, the law of *diminishing marginal productivity* (DMP), or increasing marginal cost, is an ahistorical and *ideological artifact* based on "fixed" rather than "produced" means of production (Sraffa 1960; Nell 1996; Lee 1998). Stemming originally from Ricardo's analysis of rent on increasingly

---

[10] See any introductory or intermediate economics or microeconomics text, for example (Mansfield 1994).

[11] The fundamentally ideological NC U-shaped cost curve assumption should not be confused with the Post-Keynesian "Penrose Effect," which assumes that attempts to increase *growth* will eventually result in a decline in *profit rate*, that underlies the Post-Keynesian long-run theory of the firm (Penrose 1959; Lavoie 2009, Chap. 2). The Penrose effect is a *dynamic* effect that does not stipulate rising costs as firm output increases at any given point in time.

[12] For an outline of a more comprehensive and realistic theory of consumer behavior see (Lavoie 2009, Section 2.1).

less fertile land, it became a central principle after Alfred Marshall developed the now standard *increasing costs* SDM formulation, though Marshall himself was careful to specify that this was one possible type of industry cost configuration along with *decreasing cost* and *constant cost* possibilities (Marshall 1890, Book IV, Chap. 13).

Both Ricardo and Marshall were analyzing nineteenth-century agricultural and manufacturing conditions with limited technology and limited excess capacity in manufacturing. Under these conditions production was generally dependent on work teams whose output could not easily be expanded without loss of efficiency (Nell 1998, Chaps. 1–2, and 9). Of course, even in post-industrial twenty-first-century economies, some sectors like agriculture, natural resource extraction, capital goods production, and *exchange* (rather than production) markets, such as financial markets, may have binding short-term supply constraints and consequent upward-sloping costs and SCs, though generally not based on PCFMs. Also "Fictitious commodities" like labor and land that are *not produced for the market* may also exhibit upward-sloping and even backward sloping SCs.

However, most manufacturing and service sectors in advanced economies have excess capacity and *produced* inputs whose supply can be expanded without increasing overhead and fixed costs per unit, or *slack* inputs like labor for which an excess "reserve army" of unemployed generally exists.

Why then is NC economics so wedded to the nineteenth-century DMP principle?

The answer is clear. Without short-run or long-run DMP, there can be no upward-sloping SC, and price setting devolves to a markup on production costs. In this case, none of the aforementioned (a)—(c) SDM outcomes will occur.

THE (MOSTLY REAL) DEMAND AND COST STORY

Though it is ubiquitous in economic texts, an independent SC does not exist for most of the economy. Rather, textbook SCs exist only for firms in so-called perfectly competitive markets where at normal production levels an *upward*-sloping marginal cost curve *exists* and marginal costs *exceeds* total average costs. These are the only cases where a SC, that is equal to the marginal cost curve, can exist. Approximate examples may occur in a few specialized markets, such as some agricultural or natural resource markets, where prices are set globally, individual producers are small relative to the global market and can sell as much as they can produce at the global market price, and incremental costs of production rise as production increase. (Non-text book) SCs also arise in *barter* markets, such as financial trading markets, where equilibrium prices for offers and bids of financial products are reconciled. *With the exception of these special cases, in the rest of the production economy, firms set prices and levels of production based on costs and demand.*

Most markets in the economy are characterized by a "demand and cost model" (DCM).

The DCM assumes that firms have some *market power* in the sense that they face a downward-sloping DC.[13] This implies that the amount of product that they can sell depends on a price that they have some power to set based on competitive conditions in their market and their long-run marketing and production strategy. "Monopolistically competitive" firms (markets where a large number of firms compete, but each firm has some price-setting power, for example in retail trade) may have only *local* market power based on their locational convenience to customers with very limited price and quantity ranges. "Oligopolistic" firms (markets where a small number of firms have dominant market shares and determine price ranges and major product design for the entire industry, for example, automobile or smart phone producers) may face DCs with steeper slopes and more flexible price and quantity ranges that are still limited by competition. "Monopoly" firms (markets with only one producer, for example, regulated utilities or drug companies with patents) have complete (hopefully subject to some regulation) freedom to set prices and quantities (Allen et al. 2013, Chap. 7).

All firms also face average total cost curves that are generally flat or slightly downward sloping in their normal range of production (Lavoie, Chap. 2) (Lee 1998). For a firm to stay in business, these cost curves must be *below* the DC in normal production ranges.

How are prices and quantities set?

Firms will generally apply a "markup" over costs that will depend on how much they want to sell and on their long-term strategy. If they want to sacrifice short-term profits to increase market share over the long run, they will keep prices relatively low. If they want to maximize short-term profit and care less about market share, they will keep prices high. For a useful "heuristic" introductory story, assume a linear downward-sloping demand curve:

[13] In a PCFM that underlies the SDM, firms are "price takers" facing a horizontal demand curve. They can sell all that they produce at a given price set by the Market. They thus have no *Market power* over price.

$$P = a - bQ,$$

where $a > 0$, $b > 0$ are both constant vertical intercept and slope parameters, and P and Q are price and quantity demanded along the DC. Assume also a constant: average total cost = marginal cost = C,[14] that is lower than P in the normal range of production. Under these conditions short-term profit will be maximized when[15]:

$$P = (a + c)/2$$

An unregulated monopoly firm can maximize its short-term profit by setting its price at this level. For all other firms, this will be an *upper bound on price* as any higher price will both reduce demand *and* profit. Firms will therefore set a price Q that is between C and $(a + C)/2$, with a range of production Q between $(a - C)/2b$ and $(a - C)/b$.[16] As noted, the exact price that firms set within this range will depend on competition and firm strategy. *The amount that firms produce, or the "quantity supplied," will adjust to the level of demand at the price selected by the firm along the demand curve* (Fig. 5.7).

All of the SDM stories regarding shifting DCs and SCs can more realistically be presented using DCM analysis.

For example if the DC shifts to the *right* as in Figure 5.8 below due to, say increased incomes (as with SDM exercises, assume a parallel shift) there will be "surplus quantity demanded" at the starting equilibrium price. The rightward shift of the DC will cause the intercept term to increase: $a' > a$. The producers' *upward* bound on *price* will thus *increase*: $(a' + C)/2 > (a + C)/2$ as will its *lower* bound on quantity produced Q as $(a' - C)/2b > (a - C)/2b$. Its *lower* bound on *price* will remain *constant* at C, but the *upper* bound on *quantity produced* corresponding to this price will *increase* as $(a' - C)/b > (a - C)/b$.

Depending on external competition, internal (to the firm) power relations and structure (vis à vis unions, management, shareholders, etc.), and long-term firm strategy, producers will either increase output at the

---

[14] "Average total cost" is average cost per unit of produced output. "Marginal cost" is the incremental cost of producing one more unit of output. When average costs are constant, marginal costs will be constant and equal to the average cost.

[15] Total Revenue (TR) = $aQ - bQ^2$, so that Marginal Revenue (MR) = $a - 2bQ$. As MC = C is below $P = a - bQ$, MR will intersect C from above at the short-term profit-maximizing point where MR = MC. At this point $a - 2bQ = C$, so that $Q = (a - C)/2b$. (Note that $a - C > 0$ by assumption that the demand curve is above the cost curve in usual production range.) This implies that the profit-maximizing price is $P = a - b(a - C)/2b = (a + C)/2$.

[16] Op. cit. When $P = (a + C)/2$ then $Q = (a - C)/2b$. When $P = a - bQ = C$, then $Q = (a - C)/b$.

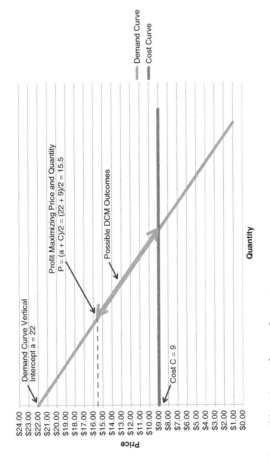

Fig. 5.7 DCM possible price and quantity outcomes

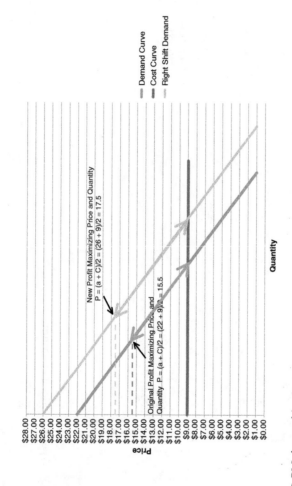

Fig. 5.8 DCM demand increase

same, or moderately higher, price to gain greater long-term market share in response to the increased demand, or raise prices more significantly so as to obtain higher profits and/or wages but cause quantity demanded to decline toward its initial starting level as consumers lower their demand and move up the DC in response to the higher price. The shift in demand will thus, result in a new *higher* equilibrium quantity *and/or* price. The opposite will occur if the DC shifts down (left) instead of up (right) (Figure 5.9 below).

If on the other hand, the *cost* curve shifts *down* as in Figure 5.10 below due to say increased productivity reducing the cost of production to $C' < C$, this will cause the producers' *upward* bound on price $(a + C')/2 < (a + C)/2$ to *decline* and its' corresponding *lower* bound on quantity produced to *increase* $(a - C')/2a > (a - C)/2a$. It will also cause its *lower* bound on price C to *decline* as $C' < C$ and corresponding *upper* bound on quantity supplied to *increase* as $(a - C')/b > (a - C)/b$. As before, depending on external competition and internal power-relations and structure, as well as long-term firm strategy, producers will either *pass through* the lower costs to consumers in the form of lower prices and *higher* quantity supplied, or lower price less, or not at all, without increasing production as much. In general, a shift down in costs will result in a *higher* quantity and/or *lower* price. The opposite will occur if the cost curve shifts up instead of down (Figure 5.11).

As is evident from these examples, the *qualitative* prices and quantities outcomes of the DCM are *similiar* to those of the SDM. But the DCM does *not precisely specify* how much price change will accompany quantity supplied change when the DC shifts, and similarly, how much, price or quantity supplied change will occur when the cost curve shifts. Most importantly, as discussed below, the DCM suggests, and empirical data confirm, that market clearing quantity supplied and demanded is fundamentally determined by *demand* conditions, most often by firms simply increasing or reducing output to match demand with no, or very little, change in price.[17]

---

[17] For example, (Hill and Myatt 2010, p. 57) note that in a survey of a representative sample of 200 nonagricultural firms in the USA (Blinder et al. 1998) found that (a) almost all of the firms in the sample were "price-makers" (as in the DCM) rather than "price takers" (as in the SDM), and (b) though prices were periodically reviewed, they were not determined instantaneously by supply and demand as: "... the median number of price changes for a typical product in a typical year is just 1.4 and almost half of all prices change no more than once annually. Among firms reporting regular price reviews, annual reviews were by far the most

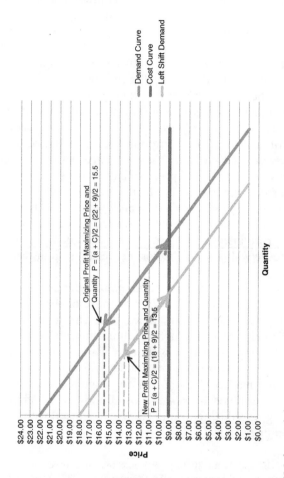

Fig. 5.9 DCM demand decrease

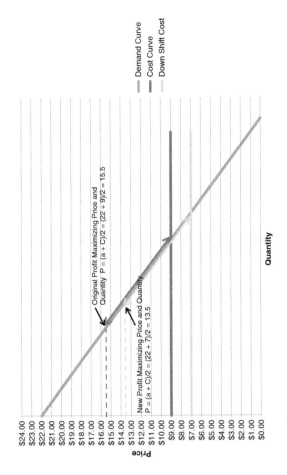

Fig. 5.10 DCM cost decrease

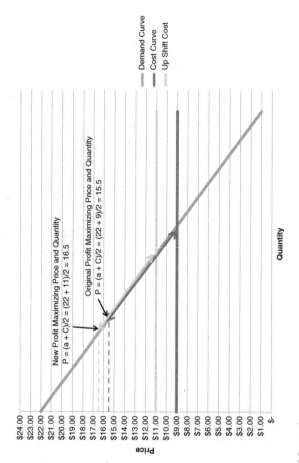

Fig. 5.11 DCM cost increase

For introductory textbook purposes, both models provide an explanation of the workings of demand and cost or "supply," on price. Admittedly the DCM model does not offer as clean and unambiguous an answer, but *qualitatively* both, at least, point to the same possible outcomes in terms of price and quantity changes. Given that the DCM story offers a realistic approximation of reality, whereas the SDM is a fantasy that posits a curve that in most cases cannot be defined, why do introductory economics textbooks almost universally stick with the SDM? Yes, the SDM story is pedagogically simpler to explain, but it is also *patently untrue*, and the DCM model, though a bit more complex, is well within the reach of introductory students. If economics is to maintain its claim to be a "*social science*," should it not be in the business of teaching about *reality* and not purveying *fairy tales*?

It is hard not to conclude that the major reason for the ubiquitous appearance of the SDM in economics textbooks is that it legitimates the PCFM ideology of NC economics as discussed in previous chapters. Most critically, instead of showing that economic outcomes in capitalist market economies gravitate toward a social welfare-maximizing, stable, market-clearing equilibrium that is perfectly determined by natural conditions and individual choice, the DCM shows that price and quantity outcomes in market economies are *subjectively determined, socially embedded choices that reflect institutional and class power, constrained by objective conditions, that result in unstable and generally socially nonoptimal equilibrium price and quantity outcomes* as:

(a) Equilibrium prices are *not precisely* determined as in a mechanical clock by objective (or exogenous to the model) forces of nature, technology, and individual-agent choice, but rather are a product of *external social and market, and internal to the firm, institutional power and strategy* that result in a *selection* of prices and quantities from a *range* determined by demand and cost conditions. Furthermore, empirical studies show that firms mostly *change output levels in response to demand* with little change in price and are unlikely (given that almost all firms in advanced economies have some market power to set prices) to fully "pass through" cost changes to

common. At the other end of the spectrum, only about 10 percent of all prices change as often as once a week, and about 7 percent of all firms schedule price reviews at least weekly." (p. 298).

consumers. As Polanyi (1944) long ago pointed out, markets are *embedded in* and *products of* society rather than a natural or objective force to which society must adapt. Market equilibrium prices and quantities are *not perfectly determined* but rather *are selected from a range* given by demand and cost conditions resulting in active *firm adjustments* of q*uantity supplied* to *quantity demanded* and occasional price changes. These "equilibrium" quantities and prices are thus not objective but *subjective* products of social governance, class power, and firm strategy only partially influenced by cost and individual consumer choices, that are themselves constrained and molded by class, culture, and marketing (Hahnel and Albert 1990).

(b) The equilibrium so obtained is *not* necessarily a "self-correcting" stable equilibrium as it results from *shifting* DCs rather than *shifts along fixed* demand and SCs. If multiple firms adjust output in the same direction, firm output decisions will impact income streams causing shifts in DCs that will lead to a *multiplied* reduction or increase in output, moving the market farther and farther away from its initial equilibrium position. The new equilibrium will clear product markets at the new lower or higher levels of "effective" (backed up by spending) quantity demanded (that, depending especially on income distribution, may have little relationship to actual or optimal levels of *social* output or *needs*), but this new equilibrium, like the old one, will *not* be stable or *clear* labor or capital markets. A free-market equilibrium is thus fully compatible with high levels of unemployment, unutilized capacity, and unmet social and individual needs that could be better satisfied if social resources were more fully employed.[18]

(c) For the reasons discussed above and because the DCM equilibrium does *not* occur, as in the SDM, at the point of intersection of the supply and demand curves, the DCM equilibrium is *not* generally welfare optimal in either the static NC "Pareto Optimal" sense or the more general Keynesian sense of fully employing underutilized resources.[19] Thus the DCM supports a post-Keynesian or Keleckian understanding of the modern capitalist market economy

[18] This was one of (Keynes 1936) central points that is elaborated upon in later chapters.
[19] In the later part of this text, we show that more advanced, and widely used "applied microeconomic" generalizations of the SDM can be similarly shown to be social welfare *reducing* rather than optimizing.

and fundamentally *undermines* Adam Smith's "invisible hand" doctrine and, with it, "objective scientific" support for the Walrasian cornerstone ideology of NC economics.[20]

(d) For a heuristic demonstration of the point above, note that though CS and PS can be defined in a DCM model as in the SDM (see Fig. 5.6 above), in the DCM the *optimal* equilibrium point maximizing CS plus PS would be a zero profit price where PS = 0 and CS is maximized as in Fig. 5.12 below. Thus, the DCM shows that social welfare of from a static allocation is dependent on the *relative power* of the final producer. The less power the final producer has to set prices above costs, the greater the immediate social welfare benefits from allocating current production. Of course, immediate benefits from consumption are not the only goal of economic output, but CS and PS analysis using the DCM accurately shows that the question of what proportion of current resources should be devoted to widespread current benefit (CS) and what proportion should be devoted to producer profit, depreciation, investment and growth (PS), is fundamentally a *social and political* decision.

The DCM and Social Choice

The *social* choice implications of DCM also differ in important ways from the *individual choice*-based SDM. In the DCM individual producer choices are influenced by social and institutional factors, and product quantity and price levels clear product markets but do *not* maximize social welfare in the narrow individual choice-based "Pareto Optimality" sense discussed above.

In the DCM world, social welfare and efficiency depend on *the degree of* competition in demand and cost markets as these will determine how the relative incentives for *static* and *dynamic* efficiency gains are distributed. High demand and robust short-term price competition among producers will result in reduced prices and higher output in the short run, providing *static* efficiency gains or increased quantity supplied and demand at lower prices with no changes in plant and equipment. On the other hand, excessive "cut throat" competition, for example, between small firms with little market power, may prevent production units from obtaining a large

---

[20] See schools of economic thought discussion in Chap. 3.

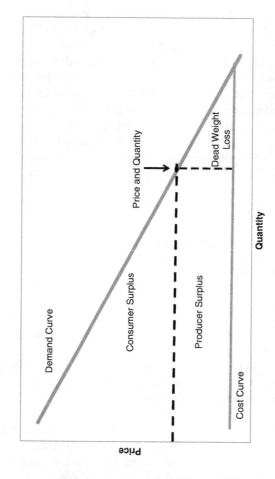

Fig. 5.12 DCM consumer and producer surplus and deadweight loss: the importance of social choice in the economy

enough scale and scope to support significant present and future cost reduction and product innovation, impairing *dynamic* efficiency.[21]

In contrast to the long-run individual choice-based SDM story summarized above and repeated in every NC introductory and intermediate microeconomic text,[22] the DCM model shows that the maintenance of an appropriately competitive but not too competitive industrial structure is *not* an *automatic process* that will result from the purely *individual* choices of firms facing a U-shaped long-run cost curves[23] (that in NC theory include "normal" returns to capital). Rather, like so many important political economic choices, DCM outcomes are *social choices* that will be strongly influenced by institutional history and structure, and by active social policy.

As Marx theorized, the natural tendency of competition is toward ever greater concentration and centralization (Marx 1867). Marx assumed that this would lead to an increasing *socialization* of the economy and eventually to full social ownership and control of production (Marx and Engels 1848). More recent analyses of the role of social choice in political economy likewise have focused on the need to increase "voice" (or workplace, community, and public democratic process) in the economy and not rely exclusively on market competition (or "exit") as the sole mechanism for accountability. This distinction between *exit* and *voice* made by Hirschman (1970) encapsulates the key distinction between *individual choice and markets*, and *social choice and representative democracy*. The SDM story assumes that competitive markets, under conditions of relatively equal income distribution and easily accessible and accurate information for goods (e.g. through repeated sampling) for which there are widely available and affordable substitutes, can provide an efficient form of producer accountability through individual *exit*. In these cases, buyers (the individual agents whose choices aggregate into *DCs*) make their preferences known through their purchasing decisions. They will *exit* away from inferior and costly products and services generating *price signals* that will direct production and investment toward superior and less costly goods and services.

---

[21] Joseph Schumpeter (1942) of the "Austrian School" was a particular advocate of the importance of *dynamic* efficiency or "creative destruction" and the relative unimportance of *static* allocation effi ciency at a given point in time.

[22] This is the case even in the more reasonable applied NC intermediate microeconomic texts such as (Mansfield 1994).

[23] In NC theory average costs initially decline as output increase to optimal plant capacity utilization, but than increase in normal production ranges as discussed earlier in this chapter. Thus total average cost curves are presumed to be "U-shaped" in NC microeconomic theory.

However, *social choices* that have effects on large groups of individuals, communities, nations, or the world economy, generally *cannot* and *should not* be reduced to aggregates of *individual choice*-based votes. This is because individuals, acting as individuals in their own *personal* interest will generally make decisions based on what is best for them (regardless of broader impacts) subject to social, material, or physical (based in the natural world) constraints or influences on their individual choice. But individuals as *social decision makers* and actors are in the business of *setting and changing* these long-run social, material, and sometimes even *natural* constraints, particularly over the long-term.

Only in *particular cases* can individuals disengage themselves from being significantly affected by social choices through an individual choice of *exit* (e.g. by not buying a product) or be party to an automatic transmission mechanism that generates *social choices* that reflect these *aggregated individual choices* (Smith's "invisible hand"—as represented in the SDM allegory).

Consider almost any broad political or economic choice. Suppose I do not like what my country is doing in Iraq. I cannot realistically pick up and move myself and my entire family to another country because of this (though some do). Moreover, even if I did this, my moving would have little to no effect on the social choice made by the government of my country to start a war in Iraq that has disastrously affected people, not just in my country, but throughout the world.

In fact, there is broad agreement that most political choices are social choices for which voting and representative and deliberative democracy are the appropriate or the only realistic decision-making mechanisms, though due to the extraordinary success of *colonization* efforts by NC economists and SDM, many political and social theorists attempt to portray democracy as a *consumer* market that simply reflects aggregate citizen *self-interest*.[24] Most Political Scientists though, I think, agree that such models are wholly inadequate in their representation of political choices in real existing democracies.[25]

---

[24] These are economists and other social scientists of the so-called "Public Choice" school. For a short critical summary of a public choice approach to international trade policy, for example, see (Stretton 1999, p. 684–686).

[25] See, for example, the excellent recent comprehensive paper on US "democracy" which shows that preferences of average citizens matter little, relative to the preferences of economic elites (upper 10 % of income earners) and interest groups (Gilens and Page 2014).

Imagine for example that you are a small business owner with a social conscience. You would like to keep your business in the depressed inner city where it currently is, but do not feel that you can do that if a large share of your network of suppliers and customers leaves for suburban "green fields" that are less costly for *individual* businesses but results in concentrated community poverty that, especially in the long term, is much more costly for *society*. The various tax incentives offered by the city do not come close to offsetting the costs of the loss of these localized *backward* and *forward* linkages that are vital to your business.

Now imagine that these other businesses are in the same position. Unless all of these businesses have a political association through which they can share their desire for a collective *social choice* to stay, they are all likely to follow their *individual choices* to leave. This would be the case even if the preferred *social choice* of a critical number of owners would have been to stay. The problem here is that rather than adding up to a constructive social choice, the individual choices *contradict and undermine* the outcome of the preferred social choice. Moreover, if a critical mass of businesses stays, there is always a danger that eventually individual business owners may abandon and undermine this kind of socially beneficial long-term collective choice outcome and seek short-term individual choice advantage.

Similarly, middle income residents of urban neighborhoods may find themselves having to decide whether to leave their urban neighborhood with all of its unique cultural and educational assets, such as specialized magnet schools, museums, theaters, and diverse neighborhoods and people, and their ties to communities of friends and family, because of overall deterioration in public services and a general perception that all of the other middle income (in the USA, most likely white) families are going to leave. If this perception causes them to leave this would further reduce the tax base and quality of general public services and lead to greater segregation by race and class, rendering the possibility of an economically and racially integrated community unsustainable.

Short of a collective choice option through a government or voluntary organization, even families who might, in principle, prefer to stay *with others* in their situation, will not be able to make this *social choice*. Their only option will be one of maximizing their private individual benefit under the assumption that other families will do the same.

GAME THEORY AND SOCIAL CHOICE HIERARCHY IN THE ECONOMY

The general theory of social choice comes under the rubric of *game theory* and the situations that we have been discussing are examples of *prisoner dilemma games*—one of a set of situations involving contradictions among individual and social choices.

The classic "prisoner's dilemma" is a version of the following simple story. Two thieves rob a bank and are later arrested. The police are quite sure that they have committed a crime but have no hard evidence with which to convict them. The robbers have an inkling that this might be the case. They are thus faced with the following *payoff* matrix (Fig. 5.13). This matrix shows how many years in prison they are likely to serve depending on whether they and their partner confess to the robbery.

The operating assumption for this game is that the *players* (the prisoners) do not trust each other and therefore, in order to avoid a 20-year sentence, will each maximize their *individual* choice under the assumption that the other prisoner will do the same. The *solution* will, therefore, be the upper left-hand corner $[^{10}_{10}]$. This, Nash Equilibrium, defined as a payoff cell that no individual player can unilaterally improve, their payoff by making another choice is, however, clearly an *inferior* outcome for both prisoners as they could achieve an alternative, lower right-hand corner, Nash equilibrium solution of $[^{0}_{0}]$ if they could each make a *social choice* based on mutual trust (or enforced collaboration).

The Prisoner's Dilemma		
	Prisoner #1: Confess	Prisoner #1: Not Confess
Prisoner #2: Confess	10 Years 10 Years	20 Years 10 Years
Prisoner #2: Not Confess	10 Years 20 Years	0 Years 0 Years

Fig. 5.13   The prisoner's dilemma

An understanding of the difference between individual and social choice shows that individual-agent *voluntary equal exchange*, which forms the basis for PCFM ideology is a special case of individual choice that can be applied in, at most, *a limited subset* of economic transactions.

The economy as a whole is probably best viewed as being composed of a hierarchy of actors with varying degrees of power over social and individual choices. A large firm that invests in one location rather than another is effectively making a *social* choice to stimulate the economy and local (especially service sector) businesses where it invests. The firm's decision to downsize or leave for another location will have the opposite effect on the local economy. Similarly, when a large public authority builds a convention center or a transportation hub (such as an airport) it is engaging in a *social* choice with important implications for impacted local economies.

Moreover, as the DCM and various models of monopoly, monopsony, and oligopoly, power show, price markups over costs generally reflect social choice, or *market power*, that allows for the extraction of returns that are not subjected to competitive *individual choice price-taker* constraints. Rather, actors at every level of the economic hierarchy compete as individuals against agents at the *same* level, subject to the conditions and constraints set up by the *social choices* (constrained by objective conditions) of actors at higher levels. Higher level players have greater power to set prices, determine locations, influence tastes, and manufacture and market new products. Regardless of whether these agents are defined as *private* or *public*, *individuals* or *organizations*, the effects of their decisions will extend over local, regional, national, or international, economies.

EVEN WHERE SCs EXIST, THE SDM OFTEN DOES NOT APPLY

As noted above, upward-sloping SCs may exist in markets for "fictitious commodities," such as *labor*, or, credit or *financial capital market allocations* or *natural resources* like land. These are either not produced for profit or the market at all, or produced for the market but subject to seasonal or natural supply constraints. Of these, *pure exchange* transactions, such as those that occur in *financial trading*, may be the only case where an SDM model in the form of "bid" and "offer" curves universally applies.

We have already addressed the contradictory political implications of treating the work of people as an object divorced from the democratic rights of personhood, or treating labor as a *commodity* produced for exchange in the market through the "labor commodity proposition" (Bowles and Gintis 1987, Chap. 3). People are not *produced* in order to make a profit except, in some cases where child labor, or slavery, or bonded servitude is practiced.

Moreover, even if labor power was a commodity, a class monopoly of the owners of the means of production ensures that wage levels are generally not determined through voluntary individual choices between agents of equal power. Rather, in most labor markets, an excess supply of unemployed workers, what Marx called a "reserve army," has been a permanent feature of the capitalist economy.

Various mechanisms ensure that the labor market is generally a buyer's market, including the substitution of machinery (or capital) for labor when real wages rise as was pointed out by Marx, and more directly, especially in recent decades, central bank policies that favor raising interest rates and slowing investment and economic growth in response to real wage increases, even when these are equal or less than labor productivity growth rates (Marx 1867, Chap. 15). The later policies pursued by Central Banks that are "independent" or shielded from direct democratic accountability but dominated by the interests of the financial sector reflects a *social choice* by powerful public authorities favoring the class interests of the owners of capital.[26] Typically, the only periods in which the unemployment rate declines to a *frictional* unemployment level of 2 % or less is during wartime. These periods also generally coincide with the greatest rate of increases in individual real wages, social wages, and improvement in civil rights. The USA during World War II and the Vietnam War are recent examples of this.[27]

The effect of this class monopoly over the means of production is to hold wages close to the *reservation wage* or the next best alternative, lower-paid job or level of social welfare payments (Roemer 1988), or slightly above this in order to facilitate the extraction of quality "labor" from "labor power" as Bowles and Gintis (1993) and later "efficiency wage" theorists have hypothesized. In any case, regardless of the exact level of wages, continuous unemployment in capitalist economies ensures that the supply of labor is almost always greater than demand so that actual wage

---

[26] The seven members of the board of governors of the Federal Reserve are appointed by presidents and confirmed by Congress for 14-year terms, and the Federal Open Market Committee that determines monetary policy also includes five Federal Reserve Bank presidents who are appointed and voted on by the private sector trustees of the regional Federal Reserve Banks.

[27] For example, BLS data indicate that, in 1944, the unemployment rate was 1.2 % and that the late 1960s was the last time (before 2015) that the official unemployment rate was below 4 %, see: http://www.infoplease.com/ipa/A0104719.html

and employment levels are strongly affected by the balance of class power and historical and institutional factors, in addition to the overall level of effective demand. Wages are *not* typically set at SDM market equilibrium levels but rather at levels consistent with a persistent oversupply of labor.

Similarly, as discussed in chapter 1 justification for the class monopoly over *financial capital and the ownership and control of the means of production* that characterizes capitalist economies generally takes the form of what Samuel Bowles and Herb Gintis have called "the asset neutrality proposition" (Bowles and Gintis, Chap. 3). This is the assumption, as Paul Samuelson put it, that anyone, regardless of who they are or where they come from, has equal access to capital and the ability to employ labor rather than serving as employed labor. This view, in effect, extends *equal exchange* SDM ideology to capital markets as well as labor markets by virtue of its claim that all agents have equal power to gain access to the means of authority and control over labor and other means of production.

The asset neutrality proposition assumes that all have equal opportunity to make a profit because the market does not discriminate between the ex-ante *capitalist* or *worker* status of agents and only cares about profitability, itself a function of price signals ultimately determined via SDM and PCFM. However, as has been pointed out, a comprehensive statement of this proposition shows how false it is. Persons with little to no wealth (or large debts) and less education and social–cultural capital in terms of both formal and informal knowledge, such as personal confidence and wealthy social networks, do *not* have equal access to financing relative to other agents who are born into or are able to acquire these "assets." Access to credit is thus class-based and characterized by highly oligopolistic markets and monopolistic (through the Federal Reserve) non-SDM allocation systems, see chap. 7. And Financial trading markets are pure exchange markets with "offer" and "bid" curves that follow a SDM, but not in a PCFM sense. "Money" itself is a fictious commodity that is guaranteed by government. As such it is shrouded in even more obscurity, and violates the basic premises of the PCEM model to an even greater extent that financial capital, Land, and labor, see chapter 7.

Finally, natural resources or "land," the generic label in economics for *extraction* industries including agriculture, are also *not*, in key respects, commodities that are continuously produced for profit, for the market.[28] Rather, crop yields, water, oil, minerals, prime agricultural land, as well as sun, wind,

---

[28] The classic "Holy Trinity" in Marx's words of "Land, Labor, and Capital," have in modern times been reduced to "Capital and Labor," obfuscating the difference between produced physical "Capital" and natural resources.

and hydro-power are given and constrained by nature. In agriculture, for example, based on seasonal production. Aside from the fact that it would appear to make little sense for *private owners* to lay claim to the full returns from these resources for personal benefit,[29] the inherently or seasonally limited supplies of these resources mean that upward-sloping (and often highly inelastic or steeply upward-sloping) SCs often exist in these markets. However, these SCs are not generally equal to the marginal cost curves of PCFMs hypothesized in the textbook SDM. Rather these SCs are typically generated by oligopolists who set prices that are sufficiently *above* marginal costs to ensure healthy static *and* dynamic profits for growth and reinvestment.

The pure SDM and PCFM model does not take any of this into account. The highly inelastic or almost vertical SCs characterizing these markets are generally neither perfect, competitive, or free, typically consisting of a vertical SC that can only be shifted (if at all) over a long period of time relative to more immediate demand fluctuations. The classic case is agriculture.

Because of an almost vertical *highly inelastic* SC that depends on the growing season and cannot be shifted until the next growing season, agricultural free markets often lead to large price fluctuations from season to season, that because of their magnitude can cause suppliers to overshoot (or undershoot) the market in the following growing season. In the case of overshooting, farmers will produce a bumper crop that is likely (because of the vertical SC—see Fig. 5.14 below) to cause a sharp fall in prices possibly below costs inducing bankruptcy and/or major reductions in output. This may result in shortages and scarcity resulting in large increases in prices and windfall profits the following year—and so on. Note that individual farmers have no control over these effects of *social aggregation*.

The tendency for agricultural prices to experience wide fluctuations from season to season is well known and has led to efforts at "price stabilization," or "price support," and to the creation of large *futures markets* for agricultural commodities. In the former *risk socialization* programs the government absorbs losses and gains. In the latter *risk privatization* markets, individual speculators bear the risk. The latter programs do not offer any *long-term* price support as futures markets will most likely reflect past price experience and anticipated future risks rather than long-term costs and fair returns to producers.

In many advanced countries, agricultural price stabilization programs have become agricultural subsidy programs that transfer greater income to

---

[29] As Ricardo famously pointed out in his critique of "rentier" landlords extracting ever greater shares of rent out of profit from agricultural production (Ricardo 1817, Chap. 2).

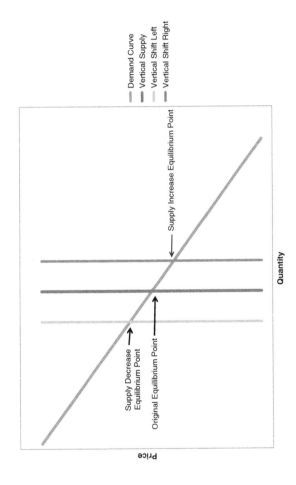

Fig. 5.14   SDM shifting vertical SC

producers than they would likely have earned from stable long-term output and prices. Though these have been roundly criticized by PCFM SDM advocates, their adverse impact on global trade and developing countries is fairly small in aggregate and limited to a select number of products (sugar, cotton, peanuts) and countries (Wright 2003).[30]

In fact, there are often perfectly reasonable and valid social and environmental policy reasons to maintain these programs when they are primarily directed at supporting smaller "family farms." Diverse family farms and rural communities with larger shares of *local* land ownership and control have been linked to significant benefits in terms of environmental stewardship and sustainable rural communities and culture, which more than offset the larger social costs of such programs—especially when the alternative is often large-scale rural depopulation and increased rural and urban poverty from rural immigration. Topsoil depletion, narrowing of genetic diversity in seed stocks, widespread use of genetically modified (sterile and patented) crops that result in an overuse of pesticides, petrochemical derived fertilizers, and water have all been linked to an *unsustainable* nonrenewable fossil fuel-intensive *industrial agricultural extraction* model that cannot continue without increasing the risk of climatic and ecological crises (Klein 2014, Chap. 13).

In terms of natural resources more generally defined, *supply* is clearly determined primarily by nature and the luck or ability to exercise control over land, water, mining, or other "rights" that confer what are essentially monopoly or *monopolistic* pricing power and surplus extraction privileges to the owners of these property rights. Though discovery and/or development may play a large role in accessing and marketing these resources and realizing financial benefits from them, the resource is, by definition, *natural* and, therefore, cannot be *produced*, at least not very easily and quickly, in accordance with market demand via *price signals*.

SCs for natural resources are by nature more rigid, less elastic, and more *vertical* as opposed to just *upward sloping*, and returns to *ownership* of natural resources, as opposed to their extraction, are by definition, unproductive and, therefore, not socially justifiable. Payments of *rent* are essentially extortion payments to those who happen to control these natural resources. Natural resources by their very nature do not satisfy the

---

[30] This is the aggregate net result when the benefits of subsidized cheap food imports are taken into account, though clearly these, often very poor, countries should be able to market their products at unsubsidized higher world prices.

most basic assumptions of individual choice, market signals, and the supply and demand PCFM model.

This means, for example, that oil companies have no "right" to *windfall profits* from oil shortages that are directly related to increasing global demand and fixed, or more slowly growing, supply. The investors and privileged executives who benefit most from this did not produce the unrefined crude lying in the ground. Monopolistic ownership of the scarce resources, just like a class monopoly of the means of production, is not a justifiable reason for claims on profits.

Taxing oil company windfall profits that are above historic average rates of return or implementing quotas and taxes on green house gases emitted by energy production and use would not be cause for serious debate were it not for the ideological grip of PCFM SDM thinking on political elites and on the public. The real debate should be about how the returns on natural resources became *private property* and about the need to eliminate socially destructive monopolistic extortion through private ownership and control of the benefits of "land" and "capital."

The imminent danger of disastrous planetary climate change from global warming highlights the irrational and unjust nature of an economic system that awards massive and unjustifiable returns to ownership of natural resources. The need to wipe out the value of the estimated trillions of dollars of fossil fuel assets through government mandates that they stay in the ground has become an existential imperative (Klein 2014, Chap. 4).

EXTERNALITIES AND PUBLIC GOODS: SDM VIOLATIONS RECOGNIZED BY NC ECONOMISTS

Finally, even mainstream PCFM SDM economic theory recognizes *externalities* and *public goods* as special and exceptional cases of *market failure* where commodity prices either do not correctly allocate the costs and benefits provided or cannot be determined in a way that would efficiently attribute these to individual agents.

Almost all economists recognize that some goods are public goods or goods with large positive or negative *externalities* that will not be taken into account through contracts and prices negotiated exclusively by the parties to the contract. The common definition of an externality is a cost or benefit that is not normally transferred through the market.

A "negative externality" would be for example damaging fumes from a nearby factory whose owners, in the absence of environmental regulation, do not have to reduce or eliminate these toxic emissions. This externality can be *internalized* if the factory owners are required to pay the costs of elimination, or reduction and safe disposal, of these toxic wastes.

Skills and training provided to an employee who then carries them over to another employer is an example of a *positive externality*. While the *employee* may be able to obtain higher pay at the new firm, the company that incurred the costs of the training, and learning by experience, will receive no compensation. Rather, the original employer will incur the explicit costs of finding a replacement and training a new employee and the implicit costs of missing a skilled and experienced employee and possibly additional costs to compete against the firm that hired the original firm's experienced and trained ex-employee.

Because of these and other externality effects, basic general education has long been considered a *public good*, and some countries have devised public or industry-wide union/employer training programs that provide a mechanism for *all* of the beneficiaries to *share* the costs and benefits of training.[31] Alternatively, strong attachment to a single employer and *lifetime* employment norms serve to *internalize* these externalities.[32] More *free and flexible* labor market economies with weak unions have on the other hand often suffered from inadequate investment in long-term training, especially for occupations without professional standards set by regulation or by professional associations.

Some NC economists minimize the number and importance of public goods and externalities based on the Coase Theorem which they claim demonstrates that all externalities can be dealt with through individual contracts between agents. This position ignores the assumptions of the Coase Theorem that stipulate perfect information, zero transactions cost, and equal power (Coase 1960).

---

[31] Germany, for example, has very high quality industry-wide union-employer training programs (Helper et al. 2012).

[32] Japan has had a "lifetime" employment system for the, mostly male, upper tier large company segment of its workforce. However, in recent times this has been breaking down, in part due to slow economic growth and pressure for more market-oriented labor market reform (Koshiro 1984).

Most NC economists, however, acknowledge the existence of externalities, such as training and industrial pollution, but argue that many of these can be most effectively paid for through taxes and subsidies that adjust prices and incomes so that costs are *internalized* or properly accounted and paid for through the market. They claim that goods with very large externalities or *public goods* like *national defense* that are "nonexclusive and nonrival" and, therefore, need to be publicly funded are relatively rare. Goods that are *nonexclusive* are goods whose benefits cannot be realistically or efficiently parceled out to individuals. A *nonrival* good is a good whose benefits to one consumer do not detract from its benefits to other consumers. The number and importance of such public goods is a key policy divide between more liberal (in the US sense) and more conservative economists.

Conclusion: The New Rentier Economy

Mainstream NC economics fails to recognize that PCFM SDM market pricing is an *exception* that only occurs in specialized markets. Under normal conditions, market economies are characterized by pervasive hierarchies of social choices, unequal exchanges, unemployment, and embedded and historically created natural and human-created resources. In these markets *rents* based on control over scarce resources or final productive applications are extracted that bear little relation to the PCFM SDM implied relationship of economic outcomes to reasonable production costs or human effort and to efficient social incentives for their production or utilization.

This is particularly true of *land*, labor, and financial *capital*. The returns to *land* take the form of *rent*, a return to monopoly control that is universally condemned in Classical and Neoclassical political economy, with, however, very different (and clearly ideologically motivated) emphases.[33]

Classical political economists from Smith through Ricardo and Marx focused on the problem of land rent. They beleived that rents were essentially extortion payments by the owners and controllers of scarce productive resources. Rents would also take an ever larger bite out of profits which were more likely to be productively reinvested. For Smith and

---

[33] For a modern critique of mostly financial "Rentierism" see Baiman (2011) and Piketty (2014).

Ricardo, this concern reflected support for the emerging capitalist class and a critique of the parasitic land-owning gentry. The latter, they felt, were wedded to conspicuous consumption, hereditary entitlement, and special monopoly privilege rather than the vigorous competition for ever greater profits that characterized the emerging capitalist class that spurred productive investment and innovation.

Marx extended this "dismal" view of classical political economy, which foresaw ultimate economic stagnation and collapse because of falling profits due to ever higher rent payments, to a "falling rate of profit" (FROP) tied to the characteristics of capitalist "industrial" investment, unrelated to the additional problem of ground rent.[34]

This line of thinking continued with John Maynard Keynes's advocacy of "the euthanasia of the rentier" and socialization of investment to reduce the macroeconomic instability and uncertainty caused by unproductive, speculative, rentier "investment". There is little doubt that Keynes would be appalled at the macroeconomic trends of the last few decades that have led to dramatically higher real interest and dividend payouts, equity bubbles, and ever lower returns to labor.

The new finance-driven, rentier economy has been characterized by greater economic instability, slower growth, higher unemployment, stagnant and declining real wage growth that lags and does not catch up with productivity increases, and large and increasing wealth and income inequality both within and between nations. In particular, the global economic crash of 2008 and ensuing Lesser Depression, widely recognized as caused by the increased power and control of the world economy by *finance capital* has exacerbated the worst features of capitalist market economies. Increased extraction of surplus by unproductive agents with enormous *social choice power* at the top of unequal exchange hierarchies, has, not surprisingly, slowed growth and increased social injustice and inequality (Piketty 2014; Baiman 2014).

---

[34] Though not the iron clad "law of history" proclaimed by some Marxists, there is some evidence that Marx's FROP tendency may be an important factor in recent global macroeconomic trends—see Duminel and Levy (2005). We will discuss this further in the Chapter on Money. Alternatively, recent work by Piketty (2014), Taylor (2014), and Kiefer and Rada (2014), suggests a twenty-first-century tendency toward a "*Rising* Rate of *Rentier* Profit" theory of stagnation. As these two different definitions of profit are not the same, the two perspectives are not necessarily contradictory.

Much of modern NC mainstream economics is, however, directed toward *supporting the rentier economy* by turning the traditional critique of rent against "rent seeking" in the *public sector* and arguing that increasing privatization induces more efficient price formation and macroeconomic performance. The "Public Choice" school of NC economics focuses on the inefficiencies of rent seeking behavior by public officials and social interest groups, advocating more market like mechanisms and competition in the public sector, ignoring the massive macroeconomic failures and microeconomic corruption that such policies have often caused worldwide. Competition and choice can be used to induce greater efficiency when properly guided and regulated, but free market ideologues view markets as a *substitute* for public policy and regulation.

BIBLIOGRAPHY

Allen, B. W., Doherty, N. A., Weigelt, K., & Mansfield, E. (2013). *Managerial economics: Theory, applications, and cases* (8th ed.,). New York: W.W. Norton.

Baiman, R. (2001). Why equity cannot be separated from efficiency: The welfare economics of progressive social pricing. *Review of Radical Political Economics, 33*, 203–221.

Baiman, R. (2002). Why equity cannot be separated from efficiency II: When should social pricing be progressive. *Review of Radical Political Economics, 34*, 311–317.

Baiman, R. (2014). Unequal exchange and the Rentier economy. *Review of Political Economics, 46*, 536–555.

Blinder, A. S., Canetti, E., Lebow, D., & Rudd, J. B. (1998). *Asking about prices: A new approach to understanding price stickiness.* New York: Russel Sage Foundation.

Bowles, S., & Gintis, H. (1993). A political and economic case for the democratic enterprise. *Economics and Philosophy, 9*, 75–100.

Bowles, S., Edwards, R., & Roosevelt Jr., F. (2005). *Understanding capitalism: Competition, command, and change.* New York: Oxford University Press.

Bowles, Samuel and Herbert Gintis. 1987. *Democracy and Capitalism: Property, Community, and the Contradictions of Modern Social Thought.* NY: Basic Books.

Coase, R. H. (1960). The problem of social cost. *Journal of Law and Economics, 3*(1), 1–44.

Friedman, M. (1953). *Essays in positive economics.* Chicago: University of Chicago Press.

Gilens, M., & Page, B. I. (2014, September). Testing theories of American politics: Elites, interest groups, and average citizens. Perspectives on Politics, 12(3), 564–581.

Granqvist, R., & Lind, H. (2004, Fall). Excess burden of an income tax: What do mainstream economists really measure?. *Review of Radical Political Economics*, *37*(4).

Hahnel, R., & Albert, M. (1990). *Quiet revolution in welfare economics*. Princeton: Princeton University Press.

Helper, S., Krueger, T., & Wial, H. (2012). *Why does manufacturing matter? Which manufacturing matters? A policy framework*. February. Brookings Metropolitan Policy Program.

Hill, R., & Myatt, T. (2010). *The economics anti-textbook: A critical thinkers guide to micro-economics*. Halifax and London: Fernwood Publishing and Zed Books.

Hirschman, A. O. (1970). *Exit, voice, and loyalty: Responses to decline in firms, organizations, and states*. Cambridge, MA: Harvard University Press.

Keynes, J. M. (1936). *The general theory of employment, interest, and money*. London: Macmillan/Cambridge University Press.

Kiefer, D., & Rada, C. (2014). Profit maximizing goes global: The race to the bottom. *Cambridge Journal of Economics*, First published online September 29, 2014.

Klein, N. (2014). *This changes everything*. New York: Simon & Schuster.

Koshiro, K. (1984, August). Lifetime employment in Japan: Three models of the concept. *Monthly Labor Review*, *107*, 34–35

Lavoie, M. (2009). *Introduction to post-Keynesian economics*. New York: Palgrave Macmillan.

Lee, F. (1998). *Post Keynesian price theory*. Cambridge: Cambridge University Press.

Mankiw, N. G. (2008). *Principles of microeconomics* (5th ed.,). New York: Worth Publishers.

Mansfield, E. (1994). *Microeconomics: Theory and applications* (8th ed.,). New York: W.W. Norton and Co..

Marglin, S. (1984). *Growth, distribution, and prices*. Cambridge: Harvard University Press.

Marshall, A. (1890). *Principles of economics*. London: Macmillan and Co..

Marx, K. (1867). *Capital* (Vol. I). Moscow: Progress Publishers.

Marx, K., & Engels, F. (1848). *Manifesto of the Communist Party*. Marx/Engles Selected Works Vol. I (1969). Moscow: Progress Publishers.

Nell, E. J. (1967). Theories of growth and theories of value. *Economic Development and Cultural Change*, *16*, 15–16.

Nell, E. J. (1992). *Transformational growth and effective demand*. New York: New York University Press.

Nell, E. J. (1996). *Making sense of a changing economy*. London and New York: Routledge.

Nell, E. J. (1998). *The general theory of transformational growth*. New York: Cambridge University Press.

Penrose, Edith. 1959. *The Theory of the Growth of the Firm*. Oxford University Press.

Piketty, T. (2014). *Capital in the twenty-first century.* Cambridge, MA: The Belknap Press of Harvard University Press.

Polanyi, K. (1944). *The great transformation.* New York: Beacon.

Ricardo, D. (1817). On the principles of political economy and taxation (3rd ed.). London: John Murray (1821).

Riddell, T., Shackelford, J., Schneider, G., & Stamos, S. (2011). *Economics: A tool for critically understanding society* (9th ed.,). New York: Addison-Wesley.

Roemer, J. E. (1988). *Free to lose: An introduction to Marxist philosophy.* Cambridge: Harvard University Press.

Schumpeter, J. (1942). *Capitalism, socialism, and democracy.* New York: Harper & Row.

Sraffa, P. (1926). The law of returns under competitive conditions. *Economic Journal, 36,* 535–550.

Sraffa, P. (1960). *Production of commodities by means of commodities: Prelude to a critique of economic theory.* Cambridge: Cambridge University Press.

Stretton, H. (1999). *Economics: A new introduction.* New York: Pluto Press.

Tanfani, J. (2012). Richard Hart: Paul Ryan's political, economic mentor. *Los Angeles Times.* Retrieved August 15, from http://articles.latimes.com/2012/aug/15/news/la-pn-rich-hart-paul-ryans-political-mentor-20120815

Taylor, L. (2014, May). *The triumph of the Rentier? Thomas Piketty vs. Luigi Pasinetti and John Maynard Keynes.* Center for Economic Policy Analysis, New School for Social Research.

Wright, J. (2003). *The $300 billion question: How much do high-income countries subsidize agriculture?.* Center for Economic and Policy Research. Retrieved December, from http://www.cepr.net/publications/reports/the-300-billion-question-how-much-do-high-income-countries-subsidize-agriculture

Aggregate Supply and Demand in the Macroeconomy: An Ill-Defined and Misapplied Fiction

The use of "aggregate demand" (AD) and "aggregate supply" (AS) modeling (ADASM) in *macroeconomics* is one of the most ideologically driven applications of PCFM and SDM in introductory economics text books.[1] The ADASM eliminates, or pretends to eliminate, the distinction between individual and social choice via an attempt to reduce the most general and most important *social* choices in the economy, the rates of growth of GDP, employment, inflation, investment, and exports and imports, to a "semi-automatic" *individual* choice-driven SDM-like model. The ADASM posits that, in the long run, the best that Central Banks and Legislatures can do is to adopt fiscal and monetary policies, such as adjustments to the money supply and short-term interest rates, taxes and spending, and in extreme cases exchange rates and export and import controls, to steer the economy along its "natural" nonaccelerating inflation rate of unemployment (NAIRU) growth rate. The long-run NAIRU equilibrium itself is determined by the *exogenous and politically neutral* individual choice, technological change, and natural demographic determinants of long-run AD and AS curves. These curves and the ADASM determine *maximal* rates of growth of GDP and employment that can be permanently affected only through *supply side* factors such as technological change, education, labor force growth, personal time preferences (e.g. how much consumption

---

[1] Perhaps surpassed only by "free trade" ideology which applies SDM to the *global* macroeconomy—see Chap. 8.

© The Editor(s) (if applicable) and The Author(s) 2016   139
R.P. Baiman, *The Morality of Radical Economics*,
DOI 10.1057/978-1-137-45559-8_6

now is valued relative to consumption later), and changing institutional impediments to the working of the PCFM such as labor unions, oligopoly power, and government regulations.

Key to the ADASM is the notion that decisions made by executives and boards of directors in response to short-term economic conditions that appear to have social impact are actually reactions to individual choices made in the market and, therefore, not really social choices at all. Similarly, social choices made by public officials in response to short-term economic conditions, should be, or inevitably are, simply ratifications of the AD and AS curves and are, therefore, also not really social choices. As is noted above, the only exceptions to this are *noneconomic political* choices that effect long-term wealth production and distribution. These include infrastructure investment in human and physical capital such as education and research, as well as nonmarket-based and, therefore noneconomic *initial* distributions of wealth and income. In the NC view, public or democratic social choice with regard to short-term AD policies play a minimal role in affecting current or near-term allocation of investment, exports and imports, and income distribution.

The fallacies of this kind of macroeconomics based on individualist reductionism were first pointed out (in the modern period) by John Maynard Keynes and Michal Kalecki in the 1930s.[2] This point was largely accepted by mainstream economists in the postwar period leading to the study of macroeconomics as a separate and distinct discipline from microeconomics. However, this was turned on its head in the 1980s to the point where both introductory and advanced textbooks now present an individualist version of macroeconomics that appears to overturn the Keynesian and Kaleckian revolution in macroeconomics through the use of ADASM and other methodological individualism and rational action-based (MIRA–based) theories that appear to reestablish prewar NC SDM and PCFM principles.[3]

---

[2] Classical, or pre-NC, political economy was unabashedly class-based (Heilbroner 1992).

[3] A detailed technical review and critique of NC macroeconomics that is beyond the scope of this book is provided in Taylor (2004). Taylor takes on some of the most sophisticated versions of NC household and firm, individual utility and profit maximization, macroeconomic models. One of these, the so-called Keynes-Ramsey dynamic optimization model, purports to show that the interest rate or "social rate of discount," modeled as a function of individual *savings preferences* and *time preferences*, is equal to the real profit rate at an *individually optimal* social accumulation rate. Taylor demonstrates that these MIRA "Methodological Individualism and Rational Action" and RBC "Real Business Cycle" models are mathematically unstable, and thus unworkable, and empirically untenable.

This can best be seen by showing how the AD and AS textbook story falls apart as an automatic market-clearing mechanism of aggregating, or optimally transmitting, individual economic choices.

THE "CLASSICAL" ADAS VIEW

The pre-Keynesian pre-1930s PCFM NC view, labeled by Keynes as the "classical" view, of long-run equilibrium in the macroeconomy was one of AD and AS curves coalescing into one vertical line at any given overall nominal price level (Fig. 6.1).[4]

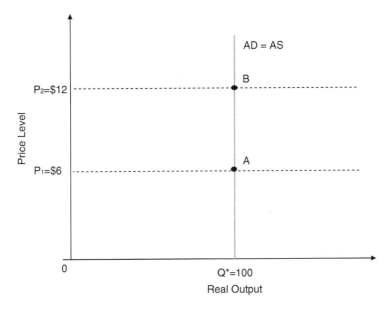

Fig. 6.1 Neoclassical vertical long-run AS = AD

[4]In this section I am largely summarizing David Colander's excellent exposition from Chap. 10 of the second edition of his introductory macroeconomics textbook (Colander 1994). Unfortunately, even Colander, a well-known post-Keynesian, eliminated this clear and unambiguous treatment of Keynesian economics as a radical break from prevailing individual choice-based orthodoxy and replaced these sections with the usual analytically muddled but ideologically coherent (in terms of supporting PCFM and SDM) AD and AS analysis in later editions of his textbook, presumably to make the book more palatable to mainstream trained instructors who are used to this formulation (Colander 1998).

This graph depicts a long-run balancing of AS and AD through free-market forces regardless of the overall nominal price level, reflecting two very important principles of NC economics:

(a) The first principle, "Say's Law," formulated by the classical French political economist Jean-Baptiste Say and also adhered to by British classical political economists David Ricardo and James Mill, stipulated that "supply creates its own demand" and was a central pillar of NC economics.[5] Says Law postulated that since all earnings from production go to workers, managers, owners, or investors who use them for consumption or investment, in the long-run equilibrium, supply of goods and services will equal demand for goods and services.

In fact, as Marx pointed out, in a barter economy without money (such as in the example Jean-Baptist Say must have had in mind) this is self-evident, as in this case, supply and demand are inseparably linked in space and time as part of the same exchange (Marx 1863, Chap. 17). When I exchange my bread for your shoes, my supply is your demand and vice versa. However, with the introduction of money, acts of supplying and demanding become delinked allowing for much more flexible and efficient exchange. And this opens up the possibility of mismatches between savings and investment, leading to "gluts" and to general excesses of supply relative to demand, as described in the well-known Ricardo vs. Malthus debate on this (Malthus 1798; Ricardo 1971, Vol. VI).

In developed market economies with mature financial institutions, Say's law can only be upheld if one assumes that PCFM SDM applies to credit markets so that levels of savings and investment equalize based on freely floating interest rates that will adjust until the credit market clears (Fig. 6.2).

(b) The second principle of long-run NC equilibrium supporting the vertical AD = AS in Figure 6.1, is that of long-run "money neutrality." According to this principle, in the long run, the overall nominal price level will have no effect on the real economy. According to this view, rational individual agents will eventually see through "money illusion" and realize, for example, that if their wages double, and *all* other prices (including interest rates) also double, real purchasing power will not change, so that this will have no effect on *real* economic behavior.

[5] Mill (1808) Chapter VI: Consumption, p. 8, and Ricardo (1971) p. 365.

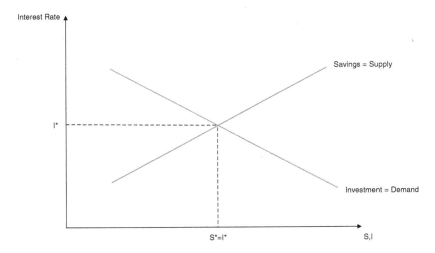

Fig. 6.2 Credit market supply and demand model

Milton Friedman's famous dictum that: "Inflation is always and everywhere a monetary phenomenon" is a corollary of this view (Friedman 1963). Friedman's claim implies that other factors such as distributional conflict or real supply shortages do not cause inflation (though they may result in one-time price increases). Rather, the root cause of all inflations is an excessive and continuous printing of money so that inflation can always be stopped by restricting increases in the money supply with no long-run impact on the real economy.

Based on these principles, pre-1930s NC economists argued that in the long-run, in the absence of *interference* in the natural working of the free market by governments, labor unions, collusions among monopolistic firms, or other forms of collectivist social policy, the macroeconomy will move toward full employment. In this case, there will be no *involuntary unemployment* except for a small amount of *frictional unemployment* due to new labor market entrants and workers who are in between jobs, and stable prices will prevail if the government exercises proper restraint and does not increase the money supply by more than the rate of growth of economic activity. Under these conditions, just as with individual markets in the microeconomy, competitive forces will ensure that price signals reflecting self-interested individual choice will automatically induce optimal adjustments causing AS to equal AD at stable market-clearing prices.

THE SHORT-RUN DISEQUILIBRIUM ADJUSTMENT PROBLEM

As Colander (1994, chap. 10), drawing on Keynes (1936), points out, even if one accepts these principles as valid in a state of long-term equilibrium, they leave open the question of how *disequilibrium adjustment* works in the macroeconomy. In the late 1930s when Keynes was writing, this was not simply a theoretical question but a very practical one. The great depression had left millions unemployed and destitute in the UK and across the globe and caused a colossal breakdown in *macroeconomic coordination*. On the one side, there were millions of workers able and willing to work, and on the other, millions of consumers desperate for the goods and services that this work could provide. But the workers were unable to obtain income generating jobs that would allow them to buy the goods, and businesses would not hire more workers as they could not find customers with money to purchase the resulting increase in supply at profitable prices.

NC economists counseled patience. Markets and the SDM would eventually work through the price system to clear the labor market. If there was a long-term excess supply of labor, it must reflect non-PCFM institutional impediments such as collusion between workers in the form of unions or government intervention in setting too high a wage floor in support of labor. If unions could be weakened or eliminated and if governments would not intervene in the workings of the market, then when a sufficient number of workers finally got the message that wages had declined for the long term and that they had no choice but to offer their labor to employers for lower wages (thus bidding down the wages of the workers who were still employed), the price of labor would fall and labor markets would clear.

Needless to say, after years of Depression, such advice was not popular, but mainstream economists had little else to offer. Even short-term palliatives, such as small increases in job programs, ran up against the complementary money neutrality doctrine of the day that advocated strict limits on government borrowing. Because of the economic collapse, public treasuries were broke so that government borrowing was necessary to fund such programs. But Classial or NC economists of the 1930s believed that government borrowing and spending on job programs would increase the money supply and lead to inflation, undermining attempts to benefit the *real* economy in the *long run* by preventing the fall in prices that was ultimately necessary for sustainable economic recovery. Respectable, academically supported policy advice was thus captured by the vertical AD = AS long-run money-neutral PCFM SDM self-regulating market-equilibrium fiction of Figure 6.1 much as (especially international) economic policy is today.[6]

It was thus not surprising that Keynes' questioning of this doctrine and his focus on the *short-run disequilibrium adjustment mechanism* (what mathematicians and physicists call *dynamics*, or the question of how the system *gets to equilibrium* as opposed to a simple statement of *what the equilibrium is*, or *if there is one*) was viewed with great skepticism. Keynes was accused of political opportunism (Keynes played a prominent role in the Liberal party) and of betrayal of the true bitter medicine (for workers and their dependents) being served up by mainstream theory.[7] In the USA, prominent early "Keynesian" professors, including Samuelson, Galbraith, and Tarshis, became McCarthy era targets and their textbooks were accused of being Marxist or Communist (Backhouse 2006, p. 16; Colander and Landreth 1998). However, as a Cambridge Professor, with hitherto impeccable establishment credentials, Keynes and his followers could not be ignored.[8]

There remained an obvious question: *how* do macroeconomic *free-market* forces lead to the restoration of the hypothesized *long-run equilibrium* where AD = AS at full employment with stable prices, once these supposedly vertical long-run curves have been *displaced* away from each other for a long period of time (Fig. 6.3)? Figure 6.3 below reflects a UK and world economy in which rates of unemployment had soared to 20 % and higher, and unsold inventory had accumulated for years, because of an extreme shortfall of AD that showed no signs of abating (Richardson 1969). When confronted with this rather obvious deconstruction of their, one vertical bar, AS equals AD model (see Fig. 6.1), NC economists were forced to specifically address the *short-run disequilibrium adjustment* story underlying the long-run NC principles described above.

---

[6] See Chap. 8.
[7] This is all very reminiscent of the utterly misguided political support in the USA and in Europe to for unworkable "austerity" policies, see for example Krugman (2015b).
[8] Though, as will be discussed below, Michal Kalecki, a prominent political economist and head of the Central Planning Office in Poland, who also taught at Cambridge and elsewhere and who independently developed a class-based version of what had come to be known as "Keynesian macroeconomics," was pretty much ignored in the Capitalist world.

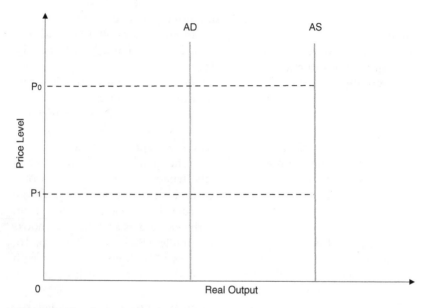

Fig. 6.3   Neoclassical AD shortfall relative to AS

The SDM Short-Run Disequilibrium Adjustment Cannot Be Applied to ADASM

However before discussing the NC response, it is important to underscore another central issue often neglected, obscured, or purposely disregarded in mainstream AS and AD textbooks. Both Keynes and his NC opponents understood that market forces working through competitive individual choice as spelled out in the microeconomics context discussed in Chap. 5, could *not* be applied in a macroeconomics context.

Simply put (even if one assumes for argument's sake that a supply curve (SC) exists), the microeconomic PCFM SDM is entirely dependent on *relative* price comparison and demand *substitution* between commodities. In consumer markets, demand for bananas will decline when the price of bananas goes *up*, creating a downward sloping demand curve (DC), *only* if the all else is constant *partial equilibrium*, ceteris paribus assumption holds. This is because, under this assumption, the nominal price of apples, for example, stays *constant* so that apples become *relatively* less expensive than bananas. Consumers will therefore buy more apples and fewer bananas effectively *substituting* apples for bananas in their preferred *consumption bundles.* This is what causes the *partial-equilibrium microeconomic* DC for bananas (and for every other good for which substitutes exist) to slope *downward.*[9]

Similarly, in *factor markets,* according to NC theory, the demand for "labor" increases as real wages decline because labor then becomes relatively less expensive than capital. Under standard NC substitution assumptions, firms will be able to lower their production costs by substituting *labor* for *capital,* thus increasing demand for labor.[10] In less general models, this may apply to specific types of labor, say the substitution of lower-wage low-skill more replaceable labor (with less bargaining power) for more skilled higher wage labor.

Similarly, the standard NC microeconomic explanation for the upward sloping SC is also dependent on partial equilibrium, *everything else being constant.* The SC, which in the standard SDM story is independent of the DC (see Chap. 5), will rise with increasing product price because, with these greater per-unit sales receipts, producers (given constant costs of labor and higher costs of overtime labor and additional raw materials and other inputs) are able to produce more and still make a *normal* return on unit sales that will add to their profit rate. This individual choice response by competitive price-takers to higher output prices leads to the upward sloping SC.

But neither the downward sloping DC nor the upward sloping SC stories makes any sense in the AD and AS *macroeconomic* context. As the macroeconomy includes *all* prices, there can be *no* relative price decline for any specific good or service in a single market that would induce substitution and a downward sloping DC. Similarly, as the cost of labor and other inputs rises *along with* the output price, suppliers have no incentive to produce more as prices increase.

Moreover, the assumption that supply and demand are hypothetically *independent* is even less sustainable in the macroeconomic context than it

---

[9] As noted in footnote 4 of chapter 5, 'Income effects' may also play a role but are less important than substitution effects for most purchases.

[10] Marglin (1984) has demonstrated that the NC model is dependent on highly elastic factor substitution (with MRTS > 1), whereas more realistic inelastic factor substitution (with MRTS < 1) supports neo-Marxist and post-Keynesian economic models, where MRTS is the "Marginal Rate of Technical Substitution."

is in a microeconomic setting. Movements "along the AS curve" increase employment. But increased employment means that workers have more income and, therefore, spend more. This increased spending (unrelated to the price of the products) should, according to the ADASM, result in a *shift* in the AD curve. In the AD/AS context, one, therefore, *cannot* assume that increased supply will have negligible impact on demand in the particular market being analyzed, even if this were true for *particular specific* markets within the economy.

Similarly, a shift in the AD curve will stimulate production and cause a shift the AS curve and so on. And these interdependent shift effects are the only ways in which the economy can adjust to increasing demand as *overall* price increases or reductions will (at least theoretically) have *no* effect on demand or supply.[11]

The implication of these causal linkages is that the *competitive self-interest individual-choice* assumptions that lie at the core of the SDM PSFM paradigm *cannot* be applied to macroeconomy. This is a key intellectual insight of the Keynesian/Kaleckian "revolution" in economics and the starting point of *macro*, as opposed to *micro*economics, a bifurcation of economic theory that started with Keynes in the postwar period. By using the AD and AS "analogies," mainstream modern macroeconomic texts (at the very least) obscure this critical distinction and, in practice, promote (or at least imply) the contrary, false, and misleading impression that all economics can be modeled with the same SDM paradigm, reflecting a core *individual rational-choice* methodology, descendent from Adam Smith, that *in the NC view* is a defining feature of "rigorous, positive, and scientific" economic analysis.

In fact, within the dominant Marshallian NC thinking at the time of Keynes' writing, the fundamental link between the SDM model, or the "Marshallian cross," and the microeconomic partial equilibrium assumptions that it is based on was well understood.[12] This is why Marshallian trained economists of the time had little to say about downward sloping

---

[11] In fact, as discussed below, there is now considerable evidence that falling overall prices or price *deflation* can lead to prolonged macroeconomic slumps and effective demand shortages, suggesting that the AD curve generally slopes upward rather than downward (Thorpe 2015).

[12] Alfred Marshall's (1890) book *Principles of Economics* included the SDM or "Marshallian cross" as an example of *partial-equilibrium* single market NC analysis under *increasing cost* conditions. Marshall's, more institutionally grounded partial equilibrium NC economics was later overtaken by more formalistic *general-equilibrium* "Walrasian" analysis (see Walras (1877))

AD or upward sloping AS curves. They understood that the Marshallian cross explicitly did *not* apply to the macroeconomy. This is why *vertical* AS and AD curves were hypothesized and little was said about how the vertical curves came to be overlapping. But the Keynesian challenge in the 1930s forced a renewed focus on the question of what the dynamic disequilibrium adjustment mechanism for the *macroeconomy* was.

THE ALTERNATIVE NC ADASM SHORT-RUN DISEQUILIBRIUM ADJUSTMENT STORY

In response to the Keynesian challenge, to sustain the notion of a long-term free-market individual choice-based *macroeconomic* equilibrium, the NC's had to come up with, at least in their own minds, a dynamic price-based adjustment mechanism. This required at least a temporarily *downward sloping* AD curve and, if possible, an *upward sloping* AS curve.

This could have been at best "in their own minds" as even hypothetical temporary downward and upward sloping curves do not address the deeper issues of the possible *interdependence* of these curves in the macroeconomy. In order to produce an AD/AS model that, at least, appears to offer a plausible dynamic adjustment mechanism, the NC mainstream advanced five hypotheses that have wholly or partially been reproduced in introductory macroeconomic texts ever since, particularly since the "monetarist/new classical/rational expectations" resurgence of the 1980s. The then "neoclassicals" that Keynes called the "classical economists" argued that[13]:

(a) Though it is true that *general* price changes will not affect *incomes*, the same cannot be said of wealth with fixed nominal value such as bonds or bank accounts. Clearly, declines in overall nominal price will increase the *real* value of these holdings, and overall price

---

in modern economics texts which treat *increasing marginal costs* as a fundamental economic *principle* rather than a special case—see, for example, Mankiw (2008).

[13] This same debate has been played out over the years at a much more mathematically sophisticated level, with "Ramsey pricing," and "Hamiltonian integration" over *infinite* optimal choice horizons and "saddle path" equilibrium *jumps* worthy of the finest scholasticism or Talmudic scholarship replacing these simple introductory text book stories. As has been already noted, Taylor (2004) shows in rigorous detail that these mathematical contortions are infeasible ideological economic and mathematical fantasies that reflect the hegemonic grip of MIRA on mainstream NC economic theory.

increases will have the opposite effect. This "wealth effect," "real balance effect," or "Pigou effect" (after the economist who first advanced this theory) will cause the AD curve to be downward sloping. A macroeconomic excess of AS over AD will cause an overall price decline that will induce the wealthy to spend more out of their increased *real* balances offsetting the shortfall in demand to bring AD back into equilibrium with AS (Fig. 6.4).

(b) A shortfall of AD or excess of AS causing an overall price decline that is believed to be *temporary* will induce an increase in AD based on an expectation among consumers that future prices will eventually rise back to their "normal" levels.

(c) Similarly, a *national* AD/AS gap that is not shared by trading partners will cause domestic prices to fall below foreign prices, inducing increased exports and reduced imports, leading to a downward sloping AD curve.

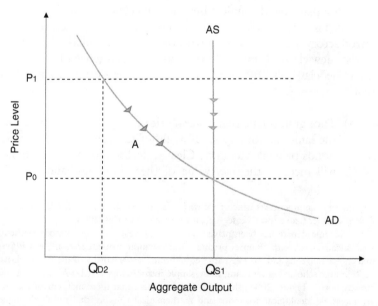

Fig. 6.4 Downward sloping AD and vertical AS

(d) If the money and credit supply are held constant, and one is willing to temporarily suspend the "money neutrality" principle,[14] an overall price decline will reduce the amount of money and credit necessary for *transactions demand* in the economy. This will lead to increased savings and a lowering of interest rates relatively greater than the overall decline in prices. The relatively lower interest rates will induce greater investment and demand for consumer durables causing AD to increase as overall prices decline.

Note that all of these rationales for a downward sloping AD curve rely on some invariant *macroeconomic value* that does not change as all prices fall or rise, either in absolute terms or in their rate of growth, so that particular groups of prices or values in the macroeconomy become *relatively* higher or lower in analogy to the microeconomic adjustment story.[15]

Completing the downward sloping AS hypothesis is an upward sloping AS rationale based on temporarily "sticky" wages.

(e) According to ADASM theory, *supply gluts* or AD shortfall will cause nominal prices to fall more rapidly than wages, as these are "sticky downward" due to longer term contracts and institutional rigidities (like unions and "prevailing wage" legislation). This mismatch between rates of decline (or slower rates of inflation) will cause the AS curve to temporarily bend left as lower prices reduce sales receipts faster than wage costs, thus cutting into profit margins and leading to supply reduction (Fig. 6.5).

Based on these rationales, the ADASM can be characterized by an AS and AD "cross" prominently featured in most mainstream macroeconomic texts that looks just like the microeconomic SDM Marshallian cross, giving unitary ideological SDM/ADASM coherence to the PCFM view of the economy, even though microeconomic and macroeconomic graphs are based on entirely *different* underlying dynamic adjustment mechanisms.

---

[14] This was necessary as this "Keynes' effect" implied that changes in the supply of money (with all prices except interest rates held constant) would, at least temporarily, impact AD, in violation of the "money neutrality" principle.

[15] Though for clarity we have used "price levels" throughout this discussion, since the 1930s, overall price levels have rarely gone down. Instead, they have increased at lower or higher "rates of inflation" leading to the same effects.

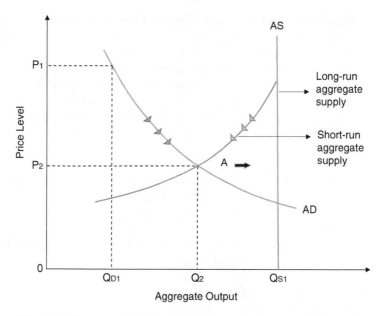

Fig. 6.5   Downward sloping AD and temporarily upward sloping AS

THE KEYNESIAN/POST-KEYNESIAN (PK) CRITIQUE
OF THE NC DYNAMIC ADJUSTMENT STORY

Since they were advanced many decades ago, NC and heterodox (under pressure from publishers) economic texts have almost universally adapted one or more of these arguments and repeated them often and prominently in many different guises (Mankiw 2008; Colander 1994, 1998; Riddell et al. 2011). Just as often, but unfortunately in recent decades, not in mainstream texts and with little institutional power, Keynesians and PKs have been pointing out that though these hypotheses appear to offer possible free-market dynamic adjustment mechanisms leading to long-run AD = AS equilibrium, they fail critical empirical and theoretical tests.

Addressing them in order:

(a) The most popular of these mechanisms, the "wealth effect," or "Pigou effect," is hopelessly one-sided, as it ignores the generally more empirically significant "Fisher Debt effect."[16] Though a tiny

---

[16] See, for example, Palley (2008a).

group of households own significant nominally-fixed financial assets, a much larger group are net debtors, most of whom have fixed mortgage, credit card, and other *payment* obligations. When prices *and wages* decline, these debtor households, that make up a large share of lower and middle income households, are faced with higher fixed nominal payments relative to their incomes as their debt is calibrated to pre-price (or inflation) decline expectations.

Moreover, these lower-income households, unlike the wealth-owning elite, spend almost all, or all and then some, of what they earn so that their increased burden of debt payments is likely to cause an immediate and significant reduction in spending. The reduction in AD caused by such a decline in spending by this large cohort of households is likely to offset and exceed any gain from "wealth effect" spending by wealthy households—a fact that empirical studies appear to confirm. The "Fisher debt effect" thus suggests that if overall price reduction has any effect at all on AD, it is likely to be *negative* rather than positive.[17]

(b) Any temporary increase in AD caused by an anticipated future price increase is likely to dissipate as the prospect of prices returning to their past higher "normal" levels becomes more remote. In particular, such an "intertemporal" effect is not likely to be significant after 10 or more years of depressed conditions. Moreover, any temporary increase in spending brought about by "intertemporal bargain hunting" will simply be a reallocation of spending over time that is likely to result in a reduction in demand in the future that does not bode well for a sustainable downward sloping AD curve that would be necessary to move the economy back to full employment equilibrium.

(c) Similarly, a macroeconomic imbalance may begin in one country and cause a general fall in price levels relative to those of trading partners, but the Great Depression (and 2008 Great Recession or Lesser Depression) eventually spread across the industrialized world, sparing no major trading partner among the advance economies. In such a situation, increases in exports induced by

---

[17] Note that housing price bubble "wealth effect" consumption increases, such as in the U.S from 2000–2006, were not caused by overall AO and AS mismatch but by asset price bubbles in specific markets.

relative price advantage (or by legislation such as the Smoot-Hawley trade bill) could only be temporary.[18]

(d) Finally, Keynesians dismiss the effectiveness of an expansion of credit stimulus through low interest rates in the midst of overall economic decline brought about by lower prices *without* any active Central Bank intervention. They do not believe in an *automatic* monetary stimulus through a *free-market* induced general lowering of prices. Though they believed that lower interest rates *can* increase sustainable economic growth, they do not generally advocate such policies as a remedy for *severe* and long-term economic stagnation from severe AD shortfall.[19]

Rather, in the Keynesian view, *active* efforts by the Central Bank to keep interest rates low are part of comprehensive AD stimulation policies that included *real* increases in public spending and possibly tax cuts. Interest rates, in the Keynesian view, do not *automatically* adjust based on supply and demand for credit but, rather, are a function of bond-holder *liquidity preferences* and Central Bank regulation of short-term money and credit.[20]

Specifically, Keynes argued that in a long-run generalized depression and price decline and efforts by policy makers to reduce interest

[18] And contrary to reigning economics textbook mythology, the Smoot-Haley tariff on 1930 could not have played an important role in *causing or exacerbating* the Great Depression as it was enacted after the depression started, raised (already very high) tariffs on only 1/3 of tradable goods from 44.6 % to 53.2 %, and with the exception of France did not cause a massive "tariff war" retaliation (Fletcher 2009, p. 140–141).

[19] Keynesians (and others) have likened the effect of "interest lowering" monetary policy in this context to "pushing on a string." The claim is that while active credit restraint or "pulling on a string" will certainly reduce AD, the converse is much more uncertain. The recent bout of long-term macroeconomic stagnation in Japan, despite very low and even negative real interest rates, appears to be a good example of an economy stuck in a "liquidity crisis" upon which low interest rates have little to no effect. The tepid growth of the USA and world economies from the 2008 Lesser Depression despite record low, and in some cases negative, interest rates is another good example of the inadequacy of low-interest rate policies in severe recessions.

[20] Though the extent to which the quantity of money can be independently regulated by Central Bank authorities is a debatable issue among Keynesians with some arguing that an *accommodative* credit and money supply that expands and contracts through *endogenous* money creation by banks and other financial institutions according to the needs of investors is more likely, (Lavoie 2009, Chap. 3) see Chapter 7and (Palley 2008b)

rates could run up against a "liquidity trap," which would make it impossible for Central Banks to lower long-term interest rates. In this case, investors would have an insatiable demand for liquidity (or money and short-term credit), which they would hold for speculative purposes with the expectation that bond prices were as high as they could possibly get and would soon fall (leading to a long-term interest rate increase).[21]

Keynesians and PKs argue that an overall price reduction will not cause interest rates to decline automatically even if monetary authorities are able to hold the money supply constant. This is because, in the Keynesian view, interest rates depend primarily on speculative demand for bonds, or decline in liquidity preference as has been noted above, and there is no reason for this demand to increase (causing rates to fall) if bond prices and the prices of alternative investments (such as stocks and real estate) *all* fall in tandem. Moreover, in the Keynesian and PK view, *short term* interest rates are administratively set by central banks and *not* determined through a credit market SDM, see chapter 7.

(e) The temporarily upward sloping SC story is at best transitory as it depends on wage and other factor price stickiness, and to the extent that it is permanent generates a less than full employment equilibrium as it requires a leftward tilt to the long-term full-employment AS curve at odds with the notion of a long-term AD/AS balance at full employment that is the center piece of the AD/AS PCFM model.

In fact, one of the clearest indications of the breakdown in the ADASM is the current post-2008 widespread and well-justified *fear of deflation* among advanced economies noted above. Keynes famously advanced the argument that "real wage downward stickiness" was a positive factor in maintaining AD and that real or nominal reductions in wages and prices would exacerbate recessionary conditions and institutionally destabilize the debt-leveraged financial structures of advanced economics (Colander 1994, Chap. 10; Keynes 1936; Geoghegan 2014, Chap. 6). Clearly, at least in recent decades, the AD curve has been *upward sloping* as low

---

[21] As generic long-term bonds generate fixed nominal returns, when their price rises, the value of the returns relative to the bond price, or effective "interest rate" for buying the bond or lending money to the bond issuer, falls and vice versa when the price of bonds increases.

or negative inflation is linked to slow growth and recession, and not to increased output and employment.

So much for the various attempts to construct a "pseudo Marshallian cross" for macroeconomics. Unfortunately these critiques are generally not raised in macroeconomics texts striving for pedagogic simplicity and coherence based on the microeconomic SDM model.

WHAT IS THE AS CURVE AND DOES THE PHILLIPS CURVE EXIST?

Not only does the ADASM, through neglect or omission, build a false construction, it ignores the deeper theoretical issues relating, as in the microeconomic SDM, to *what exactly is the AS curve*?

The AS curve is clearly not analogous to the SDM PCFM "SC" as again, as in the microeconomic context, the question of what will the entire economy produce at a given overall price level without regard to AD *makes no sense*. What then is the AS curve? Though, mainstream texts are ambiguous on this point, the most reasonable representation appears to be a *cost curve*. That is, the AS curve is the locus of possible output and price levels in the macroeconomy as determined by varying levels of AD, that reflects the impact of overall output increases on costs (Riddell et al. 2011, Chap. 17). This is then related to a "Philips curve" construction showing a "Keynesian range" where the AS is horizontal so that output can be increased without causing overall price increases, an "intermediate range" where the AS curve slopes upward so that increases in output lead to price increases, and a "classical range," where any effort to *move up* the AS curve by shifting AD to the right will simply lead to price increases with no increases in output (equivalent to the AS = AD classical story discussed above) (Colander 1998, Chap. 10). When viewed in this way, the AS curve can be seen (like the mostly nonexistent "SC" in the SDM model) as a stand-in for an *aggregate cost* curve, y*increases* in the overall economy.[22] This may occur in sectors where supplies cannot be easily increased in response to demand such as energy, agriculture, and other commodities, and in labor markets for particular skills, and where a labor movement exists that is able to raise wages (Fig. 6.6).

The Phillips curve, see Figure 6.7 below, that shows an inverse relationship between *inflation* or overall increases in price and *unemployment* directly related

---

[22] More precisely the AS curve is a "final cost", after mark-up, aggregate cost curve, unlike the horizontal pre-mark-up cost curve in the DCM.

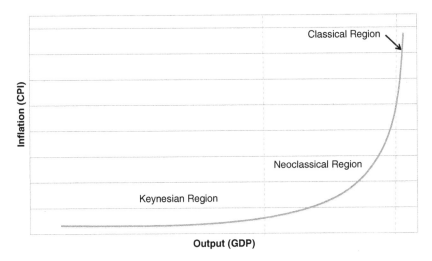

Fig. 6.6 AS with Keynesian, intermediate, and classical regions

to overall output level, can be seen as a *left to right* mirror reflection of the AS curve with the horizontal axis scaled to the unemployment rate (related to the inverse of the output level) and the vertical axis scaled to inflation (directly related to the price level). Mainstream texts and NC economists have largely accepted this view and the corollary focus on what the "Nonaccelerating Inflation Rate of Unemployment" (NAIRU) or lowest "natural" unemployment rate possible in the macroeconomy is. This is the lowest unemployment, or highest output, level possible that does not cause accelerated inflation (Colander 1998, Chap. 14). The NAIRU is an output point in the "Neoclassical Region" where the slope of the AS curve becomes unacceptably steep.

PKs largely reject the notion of a *natural* limit beyond which unemployment cannot be reduced without causing increased inflation and maintain that this is rather a policy-determined outcome that can be changed with suitably designed, and equitable, incomes, and energy and raw-material buffering, policies to maintain full employment and sustainable growth of demand and output. In this view, the key problem of modern macroeconomics is to maintain *adequate demand* and a more *equitable distribution of income and wealth* in an *environmentally sustainable* way (Piketty 2014; Klein 2014). As Geoghegan (2014) forcefully points out, particularly with reference to the US case, this requires greater levels of economic democracy, a stronger labor movement, and more balanced trade policies, and will not emerge, for example, from *class neutral supply-side* improvements in education (Fig. 6.7).[23]

---

[23] Similar points are raised in Baiman (2010, 2011, 2012, 2014).

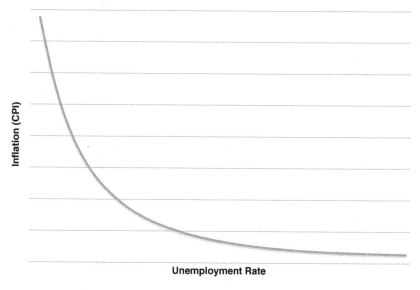

Fig. 6.7   Phillips curve

NC economists continue to belive in the NAIRU in spite of the fact that empirical support for the Phillips curve has largely broken down since the 1970s (Riddell et al. 2011, Chap. 18). In fact, though this is beyond the scope of this book, comprehensive recent work on long-term macro-economic trends in advanced economies supports the PK view that our major concern should be the secular trend of increasing wealth and income flows to rentiers that is causing growing inequality, a secular decline in AD and an increasingly unsustainable economy (Kiefer and Rada 2014; Taylor 2014; Baiman 2015).[24]

[24] Taylor (2014) offers a consistent analytical framework that rejects the unrealistic NC theoretical model used by Piketty (2014), see Varoufakis (2014) and Galbraith (2014). In an interview, Taylor has estimated that a reversal of the doubling since the mid-80s of the income share going to the top 1 % (now about 1/5 of all income) would require a Scandinavian like marginal tax rate on this group of about 60 % (Parramore 2015).

IF IT EXISTED, COULD THE ADASM WORK?

Even if downward sloping AD and upward sloping AS curves existed, the ADASM would not work as *movements along these curves* cannot be separated from *shifts in the curves*. This relates to the fundamental difference between *macro* and *micro* analysis. Any increase in AD or decrease in AS will affect the *entire* economy. Whether initially price-induced or not, increases or shortfalls in AD or AS will change the *non–price-induced behavior* of firms and consumers.

In the macroeconomy, any slowdown or increase in supply or demand will reverberate through *quantity adjustments* linking sales to employment, employment to income, and income to expenditure or sales. In the macroeconomic context in particular, one cannot assume that price-induced substitution will swamp quantity adjustments. To the contrary, in a context of *overall* price decline (disregarding the efforts to relativize "price signals" outlined above), *quantity*, and not *price* adjustments are likely to dominate. And, as Keynes and Kalecki pointed out (and was/is apparently well understood by NC economists then and now, given their intense efforts to find or describe a credible *price*-based dynamic adjustment mechanism), this *eliminates the possibility of an Adam Smith-like, automatic competitive free-market sustainable full-employment equilibrium in the macroeconomy.*

Efforts to superimpose an SDM PCFM on the *macroeconomy* is a misguided attempt to apply an idea with very limited coherence in the sphere of microeconomics to a very different macroeconomic arena *where it cannot even have limited legitimacy.* It is hard not to view the hegemony of ADASM in introductory economics texts as reflecting an effort to show that all of economics can be, in essence, reduced to the simple SDM meme that serves as the underlying foundation of neoliberal Ideology.[25]

Decades of, especially post-World War II business cycle data shows that in the USA and other advanced economies output and employment fluctuate more than prices (Nell 1992, 1998). Moreover, the application of *multiplier* models based on fixed prices to both regional and national economies attests to the widespread practical recognition among applied

---

[25] See, for example, Harvey (2007) on the role of business, foundations, and the state department in fostering neoliberal ideology.

analysts of the power and importance of *quantitative* shifts that are neither induced nor significantly affected by price changes.[26]

KEYNESIAN MACROECONOMIC MODELING

Outside of the intensely ideological realm of macroeconomic theory, planners and other applied macroeconomists have largely embraced the Keynesian/Kaleckian view of *multiplied* shifts in AD along a roughly vertical AS (or aggregate cost) curve that follow each other as a result of reductions (or expansions) in sales leading to employment reduction (or expansion), causing declines (or increases) in income and further reduction (or expansion) of demand. These changes will eventually be reduced to zero or cease due to *leakages* such as savings or profits from one round of income to the next (Colander 1994, Chap. 10) (Fig. 6.8).

This multiplied "tail wagging the dog" view of the short-term adjustment of the macroeconomy implies that, in the absence of outside

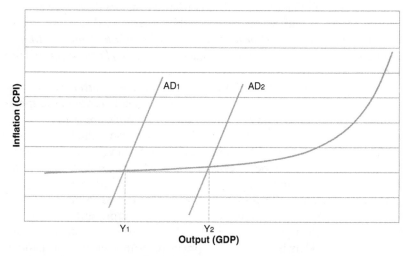

Fig. 6.8 Backward sloping AD shifts along horizontal AS curve

[26] For regional economics, two of the most popular planning software packages, REMI and IMPLAN, are primarily based on input–output fixed-price effects though REMI adds NC price change effects. Social Accounting Matrixes (SAM) and input–output modeling are also used extensively in international development planning (Taylor 2004).

intervention, final automatically obtained equilibria will most likely not be at a full employment level, but rather at a multiplied low, *high unemployment*, or *overheated excessive*, AD level. And as has been noted, a final, not generally full employment, equilibrium *will be obtained* as each round of AD increases or cutbacks will be smaller than the previous round due to leakages like savings, profits, taxes, or net exports from the successive rounds of spending.

This means that though a final equilibrium will generally exist, *it cannot* be found by looking at macroeconomic faux AD/AS macroeconomic Marshallian cross diagrams such as those presented in NC macro texts. Final equilibrium will *not* occur at the intersection of fixed AD and AS curves because AD and AS curves are dependent on each other, and the equilibrium is a result of *shifts* in AD rather than *movements along* AD and AS schedules. A macroeconomic equilibrium point is thus best modeled as a Keynesian cross diagram for which the (ex-post) 'output equal income' point is the only unknown, and the overall price level is assumed to be constant or have a much smaller impact on the equilibrium than quantity changes in aggregate expenditure (AE) or aggregate income (AY) with relatively fixed prices (Fig. 6.9).[27] The macroeconomic adjustment mechanism described in this model will *not*, except by chance drive the economy toward full employment.

KALECKIAN MACROECONOMIC MODELING

The "Kaleckian cross" is an even more useful model of the macroeconomy than the "Keynesian cross."[28] The major difference between the two is that Kalecki assumes that *class distribution* rather than psychological *propensity to consume* is the major factor determining the allocation of income between wages and profits and ultimately between spending and saving, based on the simplified assumption that workers spend all that they earn

---

[27] In macroeconomics, Y often symbolizes "Income" and (ex-post) "Output" as the two flows should be equal to each other in national economic (NIPA) accounts. I is reserved for "Investment."

[28] As has been noted earlier in the text, the Polish Marxist economist Michael Kalecki developed a similar AD-based macro theory independently but simultaneously with Keynes. For alternative Kaleckian cross models, see Nell (2006) and Lavoie (2007, p. 86–96).

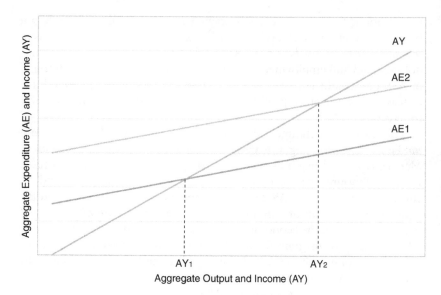

Fig. 6.9   Keynesian cross

and all profits go to capitalists. Kalecki, like Keynes, models investment levels as an independent factor that allows for the realization of profits. As AD from wages cannot exceed the aggregate wage bill, the remainder of AD necessary to support profits must come from investment. Kalecki's model is thus based on his well-known maxim: "workers spend what they earn but capitalists earn what they spend." Wage share or profit share and the level of investment, rather than household propensity to consume become the major determinates of AD in a Keleckian model, reflecting Kalecki's (2009) Marxist understanding of the class nature of capitalism. Keynes' emphasis on consumer psychology and choice reflects his own NC background.

Marc Lavoie proposes a simple version of the Kaleckian model that highlights the way in which the Kalecki approach to macroeconomic modeling expands on Keynesian insights. Lavoie's "Kaleckian Labor Market Model" not only demonstrates the well-known Keynesian "paradox of thrift" showing that *increases* in individual savings out of income rate will cause leakages out of successive rounds of spending leading to *declines* in overall income and savings *levels*, but also includes a "paradox of costs" and a "paradox of productivity."

Lavoie's Kaleckian Labor Market or short-term effective demand model takes the form (see Lavoie, p. 92):

$$RAD = \left(\frac{w}{p}\right)N + a \qquad (6.1)$$

$$q = TN \qquad (6.2)$$

where RAD is Real AD, w is nominal wage, p is overall price level, a is "autonomous" (not dependent on income) investment and capitalist consumption, N is the number of employed workers, and T is output per employed worker, and q is overall economic output. Equation (6.1) is a demand equation stating that RAD equals what workers spend (the total wage bill $(w/p)N$) plus investment and capitalist consumption (a). Equation (6.2) is a supply equation stating that economic output in this simple closed economy (q) will be equal to the number of workers employed (N) times average productivity per worker (T).

At equilibrium AD must equal AS or:

$$RAD = q$$

$$\text{Or: } TN = \left(\frac{w}{p}\right)N + a$$

From which we can derive (Fig. 6.10):

$$\left(\frac{w}{p}\right) = T - \frac{a}{N} \qquad (6.3)$$

The following numerical example highlights the paradoxes of "thrift," "cost," and "productivity" in this simple Kalecki short-term macroeconomic model.

Assume an initial equilibrium where: $T = 50$, $N = 1000$, $a = 20,000$, $w/p = 30$, $RAD = q = 50,000$, $a = 20,000$ So that (6.1) becomes: $50,000 = 30 \times 1000 + 20,000$ and (6.3) becomes: $30 = 50 - (20,000/1000)$.

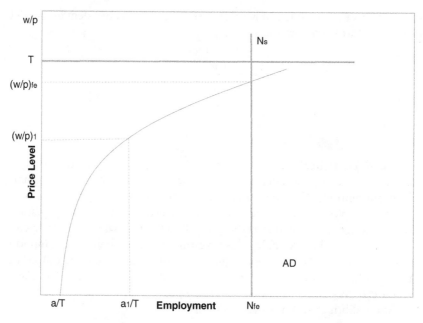

Fig. 6.10   Kaleckian cross

(a) If capitalists decide to increase *saving*, and not spending or investment, by an additional 10,000 out of a, $a = 10,000$, so that if
employment and real wages stay the same *output will decline*:

$$RAD = 30 \times 1000 + 10,000 = 40,000 \text{ instead of } 50,000$$

This is the Kaleckian "paradox of thrift."

(b) If capitalists are able to reduce *costs* by cutting wages so that $w/p = 20$,

$$RAD = 20 \times 1000 + 20,000 = 40,000 \text{ instead of } 50,000$$

In this case, if autonomous spending, productivity, and employment stay the same, output will decline, and *profit will stay the same*
in spite of the decline in real wages. This is the Kaleckian "paradox
of costs."

(c) If due to new investment, labor *productivity* increases from $T = 50$ to $T = 70$ from (6.3) $a/N = T - w/p$:

$$\frac{20,000}{N} = 70 - 30 = 40$$

So that if wages and autonomous spending stay the same, *employment will decline*:

$$N = 500$$

This is the Kaleckian "paradox of productivity."

INFLATION AND ANTIAUSTERITY POLICIES

It should be pointed out that Keynesians do not dispute the fact that if AD increases to the point of driving up costs in natural resources, energy, agriculture, and other production constrained sectors, there will be, in the absence of policy mandated "buffer stocks," *upward* pressure on overall price levels, at least, in the short-term. The extent to which this short-run upward price pressure will increases inflation will, however, depend on input (including labor) capacity constraints in sectors facing high demand.

Long-term evidence suggests that advanced economies have a great deal of *slack* that can be mobilized and expanded without large price increases over the medium and long term under suitable conditions. For example, the USA increased its GDP by over 70 % in four years during World War II, with a large share of the prime-age male labor force in the military and withdrawn from economically productive activity, with almost no inflation.[29] Of course this occurred with wage and price controls, including temporary rationing of some goods and services, in the context of patriotic wartime mobilization efforts that undoubtedly would not have been possible under normal peace-time conditions. But under

[29] Based on US BEA "quantity index" estimates, US real GDP increased by about 73.3 % from 1942 to 1946 while price inflation during this period of stringent price controls was only 3.5 % in spite of a 50 % war time real weekly wage increase in manufacturing (BEA real gross domestic quantity indices 1942–1946) (Tassava 2008; Goodwin 2001).

normal conditions GDP in advanced economies does not increase by over 70 % in four years. This and other examples suggest that when AD growth is sustained over the medium term AS can rapidly expand to meet it and inflation pressures can be kept under control with appropriate policy measures. Keynesians, and especially PKs,[30] have for this reason generally argued that AD is the major constraint in Capitalist economies and that continuous efforts should be made through public policy to expand it to ensure full employment and stable national and global growth.[31]

However, consistent demand stimulation without optional "flexible price control" or "income" policies that can be applied if and when the need arises, such as those in place during the long post-World War II "Keynesian boom," are likely to run into trouble, as they did with the inflation and stagflation of the 1970s.[32] The solution in this case, is not to fall back on fundamentally flawed and misleading AS/AD macroeconomic "Marshallian cross" ideas, but rather to move forward and employ the full arsenal of tools available to public authorities to ensure consistent and sustainable AD growth. In the absence of such policies most advanced capitalist economies, with the exception of periods of war, generally suffer from continuous AD shortfall and unnecessary *involuntary unemployment.*

---

[30] "PKs" generally believe that Keynesian economics is a truly different macroeconomic paradigm than NC microeconomics. They believe that "Keynesianism" applies in the long run as well as in the short run and to finance as well as to the real economy. They are generally very critical of NC economics, especially when applied to the macroeconomy—see, for example, Lavoie (2009), Godley and Lavoie (2007). In contrast, "Keynesians," especially in the USA, often have a much more limited and restricted view of Keynesian ideas as applying to *special case* situations within a general NC long-run paradigm. References to "Keynesians" in this text, in so far as they are contrasted with NC economists, are thus generally most applicable to PKs—the strongest advocates of Keynesian ideas.

[31] Exceptions to this may occur, as, for example, in Nordic countries and much of western Europe in the post-World War II period when worldwide AD was expanding rapidly, so that "supply side" policies of enhanced investment and expanding labor supply (by making it easier for women to work in the Nordic countries and by importing "guest workers" in western European countries other were necessary. These conditions facilitated sucessful "active labor market" (especially in Sweden) full employment policies. See Huber and Stephens' excellent review of this in *Development and Crisis of the Welfare State,* U. Chicago Press, 2001.

[32] For discussion and references on various ways to control prices while allowing for legitimate cost pass-through, see Chase (2000).

One of the major effects of recent laissez faire AD/AS *automatic adjustment* NC macroeconomic ideology supporting neoliberal polices of government spending constraints has been to reduce AD growth causing unnecessary global stagnation and increasing poverty, unemployment, inequality, and environmental degradation on a global scale. Without continuous public sector efforts to stimulate AD, which often requires redistributive measures to increase the income of lower income households who have greater spending needs and reduce that of wealthier households who are likely to spend less and speculate more, AD is likely to be inadequate. Similarly, even in situations where overall AD stimulation may not be necessary, politically crafted *supply side* policies to stimulate productive domestic investment in sectors that produce quality employment, including direct public investment in health, education, and training, as well as long-term paid leave, and child and elder care assistance programs that facilitate productive labor market engagement for both women and men, have been critical factors supporting advanced "workfare" economies.[33]

Even if NC macroeconomists were correct in *theory*, it is highly unlikely that market induced shortfalls in AD would induce large enough price declines to move the macro economy back to a full employment growth path. Such price declines, and especially the real wage cuts prescribed by NC economists to "clear" the labor market, would more likely *harm* the economy than help it, especially if they occurred at a rapid pace. Quantity-based demand-side cuts are likely to predominate over price-based supply-side expansion. Workers with lower, or no income, will buy less, causing businesses to produce less, setting off a *downward multiplier*. Borrowers will find that the real value of their debt has become more onerous and will increasingly default, possibly setting off a chain reaction of bankruptcy that will *multiply* the shrinkage of credit and investment especially in highly leveraged advanced economies.[34] Businesses labor and supply costs at the beginning of the production cycle will be higher than the downward trending real prices (or declining inflation) that they receive when their products are sold.

[33] Op. cit. See. at discussion of "supply side" policies in Nordic social democratic welfare states in Huber and Stephens (2001).

[34] Japan's recent economic recession is a good contemporary case. Note the widespread concern over the role that price *deflation* has had in extending and deepening the stagnation.

For all of these reasons, Keynes and his followers have argued that *sticky wages*, along with *countercyclical* public borrowing and spending, are valuable economic *anchors* for modern macroeconomies as they reduce the risk of downward spirals of price deflation that might occur with more flexible prices and public spending. Large, inflation-indexed, transfer payment programs, like social security, maintain AD during inevitable business cycle recessionary periods. Countercyclical programs like unemployment insurance and welfare, work to automatically *increase* AD during recessions when mandated payments for unemployment and poverty alleviation increase. Thus *public policies and programs* rather than market-induced price declines are critical to maintaining employment and income, especially during recessionary periods.

A final critique of the automatic price-based AD/AS story has to do with timing. As Keynes noted, even if some kind of macroeconomic price adjustment mechanism did exist, it would probably take *too long* to be of any practical use in combating the urgent needs caused by unemployment and poverty in a recession or depression. This argument had particular resonance in the severe downturn of the great depression which lasted roughly a decade in the UK (and USA). How long should society have to wait for "automatic" market forces to make a correction? Certainly 10 years was much too long. The NC's faith in the long run, in fact, prompted Keynes' famous quip that: "In the long run we're all dead" (Keynes 1924, Chap. 3). Similarly, in the post-2008 Lesser Depression world, there is little doubt that both Keynes and Kelecki would argue for massive (environmentally transforming and sustainable) AD stimulation measures, including greater economic democracy leading to radical income and wealth redistribution and stringent financial regulation and repression, to dig the world economy out of its current long-term devastating and unnecessary malaise (Geoghegan 2014, Chap. 6).

BIBLIOGRAPHY

Backhouse, R. E. (2006). *Economics since the Second World War*. University of Birmingham. Retrieved March, from http://www.grammatikhilfe.com/CPNSS/events/Abstracts/HIstoryofPoswarScience/Econsince1945.pdf

Baiman, R. (2010, September). Toward a new political economy for the U.S. *Review of Political Economics, 42*(3), 362.

Baiman, R. (2014). Unequal exchange and the Rentier economy. *Review of Radical Political Economies 46*(4), 536–557.

Baiman, R. (2011). *Eisenhower era income tax rates on the upper 10 % of families would immediately erase the federal deficit.* Chicago Political Economy Group Working Paper 2011-2. Retrieved May, from http://www.cpegonline.org/workingpapers/CPEGWP2011-2.pdf

Baiman, R. (2012). *A 2012 May Day manifesto: 'Left Structuralism' versus 'LiberalCyclicalism',* May. Chicago Political Economy Group (CPEG), see: http://www.cpegonline.org/documents/MayDayManifesto.pdf

Baiman, R. (2015). *The Taylor/Piketty four fundamental laws: A radical/post-Keynesian Macroeconomic Consensus?,* January. Unpublished paper available from the author.

Batelle; R&D Magazine. (2013, December). *2014 Global R&D Funding Forecast.* Retrieved from www.batelle.org: https://www.battelle.org/docs/tpp/2014_global_rd_funding_forecast.pdf

Chase, E. P. (2000). The P-R-I-C-E of full employment, by Elmer P. Chase. In B. Baiman, & D. Saunders (Eds.), *Political economy and contemporary capitalism.* M.E. Sharpe.

Colander, D. (1994). *Macroeconomics* (2nd ed.,). New York: Irwin/McGraw-Hill.

Colander, D. (1998). *Macroeconomics* (3rd ed.,). New York: McGraw-Hill.

Colander, D., & Landreth, H. (1998). Political influence on the textbook Keynesian revolution: God, man and Lorie Tarshis at Yale. In O. F. Hamouda & B. B. Price (Eds.), *Keynesianism and the Keynesian revolution in America: A memorial volume in Honour of Lorie Tarshis* (pp. 59–72). Cheltenham: Edward Elgar. Conn, Matt. 2004.

Deloitte. (2014). *Measuring the return from pharmaceutical innovation.* Retrieved from Deloitte: www2.deloitte.com/content/dam/Deloitte/uk/Documents/life-sciences-health-care/measuring-the-return-from-pharmaceutical-innovation-2014.pdf

European Commission. (2014, May 26). *European Research Area Facts and Figures 2014.* Retrieved from ec.europa.eu: http://ec.europa.eu/research/era/pdf/era.../era_facts&figures_2014.pdf

Eurostat. (2015, September 15). *Eurostat Database.* Retrieved from Eurostat: http://ec.europa.eu/eurostat/data/database

Fletcher, I. (2009). *Free trade doesn't work: Why America needs a tariff.* Washington, DC: U.S. Business & Industry Council.

Friedman, M. (1963). *Inflation causes and consequences.* New York: Asia Publishing House.

Galbraith, J. K. (2014, Spring). Kapital for the twenty first century?. *Dissent.*

Geoghegan, T. (2014). *Only one thing can save us: Why America needs a new kind of labor movement.* New York: The New Press.

Godley, W., & Lavoie, M. (2007). *Monetary economics: An integrated approach to credit, money, income, production and wealth.* New York: Palgrave Macmillan.

Goodwin, D. (2001). The way we won: America's economic breakthrough during World War II. *American Prospect.* Retrieved December 19, from http://prospect.org/article/way-we-won-americas-economic-breakthrough-during-world-war-ii

Harvey, D. (2007). *A brief history of neoliberalism.* New York: Oxford University Press.

Heilbroner, R. L. (1992). *The worldly philosophers: The lives, times and ideas of the great economic thinkers* (6th ed.,). New York: Touchstone/Simon & Schuster.

Huber, E., & Stephens, J. (2001). *Development and crisis of the welfare state: Parties and policies in global markets.* Chicago: University of Chicago Press.

Keynes, J. M. (1924). *A tract on monetary reform.* London: Macmillan and Co. Ltd.

Keynes, J. M. (1936). *The general theory of employment, interest, and money.* London: Macmillan/Cambridge University Press.

Kiefer, D., & Rada, C. (2014). Profit maximizing goes global: The race to the bottom. *Cambridge Journal of Economics,* First published online September 29, 2014.

Klein, N. (2014). *This changes everything.* New York: Simon & Schuster.

Krugman, P. (2015b). The case for cuts was a lie. Why does Britain still believe it? The austerity delusion. April 29. *The Guardian.*

Lavoie, M. (2009). *Introduction to post-Keynesian economics.* New York: Palgrave Macmillan.

Malthus, T. R. (1798). *An essay on the principle of population.* London: J. Johnson is St. Paul's Church Yard.

Mankiw, N. G. (2008). *Principles of microeconomics* (5th ed.,). New York: Worth Publishers.

Marglin, S. (1984). *Growth, distribution, and prices.* Cambridge: Harvard University Press.

Marshall, A. (1890). *Principles of economics.* London: Macmillan and Co.

Marx, K. (1863). *Theories of surplus value.* Moscow: Progress Publishers.

Mill, J. (1808). *Commerce defended. An answer to the arguments by which Mr. Spence, Mr. Cobbett, and Others, have attempted to Prove that Commerce is not a source of National Wealth.* London: C. and R. Baldwin.

Nell, E. J. (1992). *Transformational growth and effective demand.* New York: New York University Press.

Nell, E. J. (1998). *The general theory of transformational growth.* New York: Cambridge University Press.

Nell, E. J. (2006). The simple theory of aggregate demand. *Cambridge Journal of Economics, 30*(4).

Palley, T. I. (2008a). Keynesian models of deflation and depression revisited. *Journal of Economic Behavior & Organization, 68*(1), 167–177.

Palley, T. I. (2008b). *Endogenous money: Implications for the money supply process, interest rates, and macroeconomics.* August. Political Economy Research Institute (PERI), Working Paper 178. Retrieved from http://scholarworks. umass.edu/cgi/viewcontent.cgi?article=1149&context=peri_workingpapers

Parramore, L. (2015). What Thomas Piketty and Larry summers don't tell you about income inequality. Institute for New Economic Thinking and *Huffington Post.* Retrieved February 6, from http://www.huffingtonpost.com/lynn-par-ramore/what-thomas-piketty-and-l_b_6630688.html

Piketty, T. (2014). *Capital in the twenty-first century*. Cambridge, MA: The Belknap Press of Harvard University Press.

Ricardo, D. (1971). *The works and correspondence of David Ricardo, Vol. II. Notes on Malthus's principles of political economy*. Cambridge: Cambridge University Press.

Richardson, H. W. (1969, October). The economic significance of the depression in Britain. *Journal of Contemporary History, 4*(4), 3–19.

Riddell, T., Shackelford, J., Schneider, G., & Stamos, S. (2011). *Economics: A tool for critically understanding society* (9th ed.,). New York: Addison-Wesley.

Tassava, C. (2008). *The American Economy during World War II*. EH. Net Encyclopedia, edited by Robert Whaples. Retrieved February 10, from http://eh.net/encyclopedia/the-american-economy-during-world-war-ii/

Taylor, L. (2004). *Reconstructing macroeconomics: Structuralist proposals and critiques of the mainstream*. Cambridge, MA: Harvard University Press.

Taylor, L. (2014, May). *The triumph of the Rentier? Thomas Piketty vs. Luigi Pasinetti and John Maynard Keynes*. Center for Economic Policy Analysis, New School for Social Research.

Thorpe, J. (2015). The next worry, a deflationary slump like Japan. *Financial Post*. Retrieved July 6, from http://www.financialpost.com/analysis/story.html?id=80453d8f-0110-4999-a295-c6f5469eb155

Varoufakis, Y. (2014). Egalitarianism's latest foe: a critical review of Thomas Piketty's Capital in the Twenty-First Century. *Real-World Economics Review, 69*. Retrieved from http://www.paecon.net/PAEReview/issue69/whole69.pdf

Walras, L. (1877). *Elements of Pure Economics*. Reprint 1954. New York: Irwin.

CHAPTER 7

The Money Supply and Demand Market: The Greatest Myth of Them All

Of the three *fictional commodities*—*land* or natural resources, *labor* power or person-time, and *money* or financial capital—none is more shrouded in obscurity and more *fictional* than *money*.[1] This mystery and obscurity stems from efforts to shoehorn *money* into a supply and demand individual-choice free-market rubric that cannot, even at a superficial level as with *land* and *labor*, be done. The degree to which the pretense of *money as a commodity* is promoted and the extent to which it is surrounded by an esoteric almost mystical aura, masks the way in which the power to create money is *simply transferred* to the private financial sector by supposedly democratic governments under current, historically evolved, monetary systems.

The usual SDM fictions are inadequate for this immense ideological cover up. A vast layer of ritual, special language, multiple layers of opaque institutional shells and reciprocal and overlapping semipublic/semiprivate institutions are necessary to turn the inescapably *social construct* of money into a *pretend commodity* responding to individual choice-based market signals.

---

[1] Much of this account is based on Hugh Stretton's excellent discussion in (Stretton 1999, Chap. 50).

© The Editor(s) (if applicable) and The Author(s) 2016   173
R.P. Baiman, *The Morality of Radical Economics*,
DOI 10.1057/978-1-137-45559-8_7

MONEY AS A PUBLIC GOOD

How has it come to pass that private finance, a.k.a. an elite class of wealthy individuals and their agents, not only own and control the commanding heights of the "private" economy but also are able to produce and benifit from a fictitious commodity, *money*, whose very value depends on government guarantees and continued support?

The answer is tied, as with capitalism itself, to the historical preservation of privileges held by powerful vested interests through institutional gerrymandering and ideological obfuscation in nominally democratic societies. As far as economic historians can tell, goldsmiths and other guardians of precious metals evolved into bankers by issuing *receipts for gold* stored in their vaults that came to be used as a medium of exchange instead of the gold itself that could then be kept safely stored away, see for example (Kim, 2011). Before long, the goldsmiths realized that they could lend out more receipts for gold than they had in their vaults based on the near certainty that all of their customers would not ask to withdraw all of their gold at once.

Thus private money creation based on *fractional reserve banking*, or making money off of other's money by risking its loss but pooling this risk to greatly reduce it without depositors' knowledge or explicit consent, was born. Notice that the banker or goldsmith's ability to *expand* money in this way is wholly dependent on the trust of the depositors who, secure in the knowledge that they can withdraw their gold anytime, do not rush in mass to withdraw it.

Timing is everything in this *confidence scheme*. A goldsmith (or bank) may have more gold owed to him/her (undoubtedly almost all males in those days) than he owes to his depositors, that is, he may be *solvent* in the sense of having positive net worth, but if he cannot immediately come up with the gold demanded for withdrawal by depositors when it is requested, confidence in him (or the bank) will collapse. Moreover, such a *liquidity crisis* for one goldsmith or bank, will cause other depositors with other goldsmiths or banks to immediately demand their gold for fear that it may actually not be in the vault available for withdrawal when they want it. Moreover, this kind of "run on the goldsmith or bank" may cause other smithies to collapse as calculations of how much *liquid* gold they would need to satisfy depositors' requests and the share of their gold that they could lend (one minus the *fractional reserve ratio*) under *normal* circumstances of general depositor confidence will be upended in a period of diminishing confidence.

This example shows that the goldsmith confidence scheme for creating money is critically dependent on *public* confidence and trust in the *entire system*, not just in any one individual goldsmith or bank. In more technical terms, trust in this kind of money is a *public good* whose benefits and costs cannot be neatly parceled out to individual consumers or providers but rather can only be provided to the economy as an *indivisible* whole. Money is therefore a social construct, especially in the case of *paper fiat* or *electronic credit* money. The pieces of paper or numbers on a screen have meaning only because, *we as a society*, have created a *medium of exchange* that must be accepted as *legal tender* for domestic transactions. This construction is based entirely on *social* choice. Without universal or large-scale acceptance of this convention or directive, *money* would be worthless. *Individual choice* of money, or substitution of some other good or symbol for money, is simply not permitted or, with very minor and insignificant exceptions, not socially possible.[2]

EXTERNALITIES AND FRACTIONAL RESERVE MONEY

In a *fractional reserve monetary system* such as exists in the USA and most other countries, "high powered" *fiat* or *paper money* replaces *gold*, and *banks* replace *goldsmiths*. Paper money is printed by the government and injected into the private banking system through Central Bank loans or purchases of securities, usually government bonds, from the banks. The banks are then free to lend this out at higher interest rates and make money from the spread. In normal circumstances in most advanced countries government Central Banks supply necessary new reserves, or *high powered money*, to the private banking system on an *"as needed"* basis, so that the private banking system essentially "creates money" by lending at rates set by the Central Bank (Lavoie, 2005).[3] These loans end up being deposited in other banks who lend out this money to other borrowers. In this way, the banking system *multiplies* the amount of credit in the system just as the goldsmith's did.

A key difference is, however, that modern fractional reserve banking systems are regulated. A common form of regulation is that banks are required to hold, or not lend out, a "required reserve ratio" (RRR) of their

[2] Some small communities and groups have set up their own medium of exchange in *labor time* or *local currency*, or digital currency such as Bitcoin, in an effort to disengage from the broader economy, see, for example: http://www.newciv.org/ncn/moneyteam.html and https://bitcoin.org/en/. But these *alternative money systems* are very small and insignificant in terms of their share of and impact on the overall economy.

[3] Most PKs belive that money is mostly *endogeneous*, meaning that Central Banks by and large *accomodate* private sector landing. The post 2008 *breakdown* of the *money market multiplier* lends further credence to this view, see discussion later in chapter.

deposits as security against higher than usual depositor withdrawals. The new loans are deposited in other banks that keep the RRR and lend out the rest. Like the rounds of successive spending in the traditional Keynesian multiplier, this banking "money multiplier" results in the creation of a *multiplied* amount of money or credit in the economy. Assuming that each bank *fully loans out* its new deposits so that it keeps no extra deposits and that all loans are deposited in the banking system, each new round of money creation will be $(1 - RRR)$ times the previous round.[4] As with the Keynesian multiplier, ignoring other *leakage* complications, the *money multiplier* will be a multiple of the *high powered* (HP) *money* injected into the banking system from the outside, for example, from the Central Bank, times the sum of a geometric series that declines at the rate $(1 - RRR)$ or $1/RRR$.[5] Moreover, as noted above, Central Banks generally *ratify* or *accomodate* private bank lending at short-term interest rates set by the Central Bank by supplying necessary reserve shortfalls to the banking system. Banks are thus able to *multiply* the amount of new money or credit in the economy. This form of *fractional reserve banking*, or money creation has a number of important characteristics:

These are that:

(a) Money is *privately created* by bankers when they *duplicate* depositor's money by lending to other borrowers while the depositors think they have it stored in their banks. The bulk of the money is created through a highly leveraged *multiplication* process as borrowers from one bank deposit their funds in another bank, which then loans these funds to yet another borrower, and so on. Because of this, as we have noted above, fractional reserve money or credit is critically dependent on confidence in the entire banking system and is quite fragile. Lack of trust in the banks will cause a contraction of the money supply that will spread rapidly through the system in a *reverse multiplier* process.

(b) The banks determine who gets the loans. These are disproportionately borrowers who have income or wealth that can be seized if loans are not repaid.

(c) All of the new money is tied to an interest rate to be paid by the borrowers.

---

[4] It turns out that this has not been true in the USA since 2008—see discussion in text below.

[5] New money will be: $HP((1-RRR) + (1-RRR)^2 + (1-RRR)^3 + (1-RRR)^4 \dots = HP/(1-(1-RRR)) = HP/RRR$

Because of (a), a fractional reserve banking system requires extensive government regulation and auditing, or *prudential regulation*, in order to maintain the value of the money supply. Excessive competition can undermine this system by inducing banks to lower their lending rates, raise their deposit rates, and lend to riskier borrowers. This is a classic *public externality* and *market failure* situation as the costs of individual imprudent banking can be rapidly spread through the entire system, whereas the gains are captured by the individual bank.

For this reason, over time, extensive regulations have evolved to stabilize fractional reserve financial systems. These include central bank audits, prohibitions against highly risky lending, and requirements that certain levels and kinds of reserves, such as coins and notes, deposits in Central Banks, and government bonds, be held in reserve by banks. Central Banks have also acted as *lenders of last resort* to bolster public confidence that temporary illiquidity problems, as discussed above, do not cause bank closures and a collapse of the money supply. This is done by offering banks a "discount window" through which they can temporarily borrow at reduced rates directly from the Central Bank, by encouraging banks to borrow reserves overnight from each other "wholesale" reduced "Federal Funds" rate, and through direct emergency *bail-out* measures such as the 1980s savings and loan, and post 2008 financial sector, bailouts in the USA.[6] Finally, banks are required to have deposit insurance, the "Federal Deposit Insurance Corporation" (FDIC) in the USA, that ensures that depositors accounts will be paid in the event of a banking collapse. Though this is supposed to be underwritten by the banks themselves, it is often underfunded requring significant public subsidies during times of banking distress (Evans 2008).

Governments have deployed prudential regulation and economic influence and regulation. The former has included requirements that banks hold a certain share of their loans in specified kinds of reserves that are *not* deposits originating from other commercial banks, usually paper money and coin, central bank deposits, and government bonds, and pass net capital asset requirements depending on the types of assets held. Banks are also prohibited from engaging in highly risky lending and are subject to central bank and other government agency audits and oversight to ensure compliance with these regulations. *Economic* regulation has included efforts by governments to influence and regulate the supply of money and credit and short-term interest rates

---

[6] For example, Felkerson (2011) estimates the total public cost of the 2008 financial bailout at about $29 T.

as a means of affecting investment, employment, inflation, the distribution of wealth and income, and international balance of payments and exchange rates.

Historically, these regulations have included means of influencing the economy and financial conditions through *open market operations*, buying and selling government bonds as a means of setting *short-term rates* for government and interbank overnight borrowing, or by directly regulating interest rates for certain kinds of lending and for certain types of deposits (in competitive financial systems regulating depositor *or* lending rates is usually adequate, as one is keyed to the other). They have also regulated amounts and types of lending and borrowing, the operations of different kinds of financial institutions (savings banks, savings, and loan "building society" banks, credit unions, insurance companies, private pensions, and so on). Finally, governments have often regulated the amount and types of foreign exchange that may be held for different purposes, as well as foreign exchange rates.

It should be clear from this list that there is overlap between *prudential* and *economic* regulations. PCFM reformers who want to do away with *economic* regulations have often revoked regulations with important prudential functions, leading to large scale financial collapse and public bailouts as in the late 1980s and early 1990s Savings and Loan crises in the USA.

In the USA, *economic* regulations have been generally employed exclusively for the macroeconomic purposes of maintaining low interest rates and low unemployment during the postwar Keynesian period until the late 1970s, and since then, in the current neoliberal financial regime, almost exclusively to contain inflation and maintain the value of money and other financial assets. This latter function serves the *prudential* purpose of *socializing* inflationary risks for the financial sector. In addition, the Fed has not hesitated to use the full range of its powers to bailout major banks, hedge funds, savings and loans, and other private financial agents who are "too big to fail" (Felkerson 2011). On a world scale, the IMF and WB have generally employed their considerable power in ways that secure the interests and effectively bail out large money center banks and creditors while forcing the citizens of developing countries to make extreme sacrifices (Stiglitz 2002; Pieper and Taylor 1998). These policy stances reflect the private financial interests that dominate both private domestic and "public" central banks and have exerted dominant influence over IMF and WB policies.

The current international financial regime is discussed in the next chapter. Regarding the policies of the US Federal Reserve System (Fed), critics have long pointed out that the Fed could use its extensive powers in a much more proactive way to combat regional and inner-city poverty and unemployment, rather than focusing purely on financial sector stability and a related constant vigilance against inflation (Dymski et al. 1993).

THE CENTRAL BANK AND GOVERNMENT BORROWING

In the USA, the Central Bank, called the Federal Reserve System or "Fed," is made up of twelve Regional Federal Reserve Banks (New York, Boston, Philadelphia, Richmond, Atlanta, Cleveland, St. Louis, Chicago, Kansas City, Minneapolis, Dallas, and San Francisco) and a national Federal Reserve Bank in Washington. The Federal Open Market Committee (FOMC) is the policy arm of the Fed that sets short-term interest rates and targets for "open market" Treasury bond buying and selling operations. The FOMC is made up of the seven members of the Board of Governors of the Fed including the Chair and Vice Chair, the President of the Federal Reserve Bank of New York, and four presidents of other Regional Federal Reserve Banks who serve on a rotating basis. The seven Fed Governors are appointed by the President and confirmed by Congress for extraordinarily long 14-year terms and rarely retire early except of their own accord, usually to very well paid positions in the private financial sector. The presidents of the regional Federal Reserve Banks are appointed by the private financial sector trustees of these banks. Effectively therefore, though the Fed is widely recognized to have more direct influence on the macroeconomy than any other public authority; especially during periods when the Congress and the executive refrain from large-scale fiscal (tax and spend) policies, the financial sector enjoys disproportionate institutionalized representation on the Fed Board.

As it generally holds a large stock of government bonds from past government borrowing, the Central Bank can decide whether to accommodate an increase in the money supply or *offset* it by selling bonds to the public and, thus, *drain* an equivalent amount of money or credit from the economy, or use its *other monetary tools* to expand or contract the supply of money.[7] Thus, government *deficit spending* may or may *not* cause immediate increases in the money supply depending on Central Bank policies. This is especially the case since, as has been noted "money" in modern economies is primarily a function of *(private sector)* lending.

---

[7] Though as will be described below, this has *not* been the case since 2008 in the U.S.

In modern economies and in the global economy, money or credit has historically been created and maintained by governments through public or quasipublic "independent" Central Banks over which the private financial sector exercises an outsize influence, as in the USA. Under these systems, governments are required to *borrow* funds from domestic or foreign, public or private authorities, including their own Central Banks, when tax revenue falls short of government expenditures. Government borrowing thus incurs debt to either its Central Bank or to other public or private investors when it spends beyond its means.

Historically the buying and selling of Treasury Bills (T-Bills), or "Open Market Operations" has been the Fed's most often used method for setting short-term interest rates. While the Central Bank, or Federal Reserve Bank, in the USA does not directly buy T-Bills from the Treasury, it does hold T-Bills that it acquires in the "Open Market" from dealers in T-Bills or other banks. When the Fed buys T-Bills, it injects new money or "high powered money" from *outside* of the private banking system into that system and into circulation in the economy. Though, in this case, the Fed technically becomes a creditor to the US Government (the issuer of the T-Bill), since most of the interest revenue from these T-Bills is returned to the Treasury, this part of the Federal Government's "debt" is more of an *accounting entry* than an actual *debt* that needs to *repaid*. After all, there is no reason to pay back an *interest-free* "debt."[8]

The Fed decides on its own how much of this public debt to hold and how much to sell to the private sector. Because of this, so-called modern monetary theorists (MMT) have argued for a "functional finance" monetary policy, whereby the government would print (or "borrow" from the Fed) much of its necessary funding and use tax policy as necessary to regulate inflation and unemployment rather than as a means to fund government activities (Wray 2012). Though MMT is not universally accepted, even in heterodox economic circles, it serves to highlight the way in which current institutional arrangements subordinate public spending to "private sector" ownership and creation of credit (Palley 2013).[9]

---

[8] The Fed deducts its cost of operations from the interest and other revenue that it receives. All the rest of the revenue from T-Bill interest payments is forwarded to the US Treasury.

[9] Though Palley's (2013) critique draws on the "real balance effect" that has been questioned in this text, Palley acknowledges that more recent Post Keynesians like Godley and Lavoie (2007) have developed "stock-flow consistent" models that expand upon the real balance effect.

The Fed has wide latitude to use this debt to expand the money supply when and how it deems this necessary, for example, to bail out large hedge funds or banks whose bankruptcy would, it believes, destabilize the financial system. The Fed has thus conceded affective control over money, which exists only because the government guarantees it to the private sector and this is broadly the case in other countries as well (Stretton 2000, Chap. 50). Central Banks that are nominally *public* but are structured so that the *private* financial sector has disproportionate formal and informal influence over their operations, have wide latitude over so-called *monetary policy*. By giving banks special access to cheap discount credit and other bailouts and subsidies and thus lowering the price of money in tough times, governments cover the risks, or *socialize the losses*, while letting banks keep the profits, or *privatize the gains*, from their ability to profit from fractional reserve money creation. In this sense, private fractional reserve banking is a giveaway to private finance. *Private* banks extract profit from *creating money*, a consummate *public good* that is *guaranteed and maintained* at *public* expense.

Ironically, NC economists have traditionally had greater confidence in the *public control* of money than Keynesians or post-Keynesians (PKs), perhaps because this is one of the few areas of *market intervention* that they accept, as they believe that maintaining a *stable* money supply to ensure *the value of money* is one of the key functions of government. This implicit acknowledgement of the inherent social nature of the money construct is related to the doctrine of *long-run money neutrality* described in chapter 6. As readers will recall, according to this doctrine, *real* AD and AS automatically determine long-run macroeconomic equilibrium no matter what the level of *money supply* which will affect only the overall level of prices and have no long-run impact on the *real* (nominal price adjusted) economy. Thus NC's argue that public control of money and credit *cannot* be used as a tool to stimulate sustainable long-run economic *growth*, but only as a means to *temporarily dampen overheated* economic growth and reduce inflation that can spiral out of control if vigilant money supply and credit restrictions are not consistently applied by public authorities.

THE "MONEY MARKET" DOES NOT EXIST

Given the nature of money and how it is created it should not be surprising that *money* or credit falls well outside of the SDM paradigm though one would be hard pressed to find this point explained in a standard economics text. Rather, like *labor* and *land*, *money* and, especially *credit*, are treated like other private commodities as though *market price signals*, in this case interest rates, will *automatically* cause the quantity of credit to adjust to a *market clearing* level so that the supply and demand for credit will equalize. The only difference between money and other commodities, in this view, is that the *money supply* can be publicly controlled. But banking is a system of *administrative* allocation of savings and new money with very large *externality* impacts for the entire society for which *market laws* of competition do not apply and in fact are destructive. Seen in this light, it is clear that "private banking" is an oxymoron that sustains a system of *direct* high level *private* expropriation and control of public wealth through money creation.

How many of us would like to buy a product for which there is always *excess demand* cheaply from the government so that we can sell it at a markup to those in the public whom we deem to be viable customers; and we can have the product and our business guaranteed and maintained by the government at public expense even when we fail to uphold our minimal part of the bargain. The "private" financial sector gets profit, power, and control, and the public gets insurance, regulation, and bailout costs, and a "private" money supply—not a bad deal!

One might think that, at the very least, if we are going to turn over most of our money creation to private financial institutions and create most of it in the form of interest bearing debt backed by fractional reserves, this money should be made to serve *public needs*. Otherwise, fractional reserve money may strike many as an absurd way to supply a growing and changing economic system with the money that it needs, as it is at best a fragile system that tends to reward individual banks for taking more risk and requires constant government maintenance and support to avoid collective systemic breakdowns. The least we could do is to apply *economic* regulation of this process in order to further the general public interest. Such economic regulation would go beyond, and/or would be mixed in with *prudential regulation* that is directed to simply insuring the integrity of the banking system.

Unfortunately, as with most economic policy in a "private" capitalist economy, though economic regulation of fractional reserve money is widely recognized as necessary, it has increasingly, in the neoliberal era, been minimized and pushed aside in favor of "independent" Central Banks who have a primary mission, not of supporting the overall economy, but rather of *maintaining the value of the money* or reducing inflation and maintaining public confidence in the "private" financial system. Thus the appointment of Central Bank administrators and their influence over Central Bank policies have been increasingly distanced from *political* (read *democratic*) influence and placed in the hands of prominent members of the financial sector (by inclination and class usually closely tied to conservative economic interests, ideologies, and political parties) who have, not surprisingly, successfully steered Central Banks toward a focus on low rates of inflation, small government deficits, and loosening regulations on financial speculation while increasing direct or indirect bailouts of major financial institutions in the interests of preserving confidence in the overall financial system.

A key issue with money and credit, as with the other fictional commodities, is that the SDM PCFM model is largely irrelevant to its behavior. The problem, in this case, is not that an upward sloping supply curve (SC) does not exist, but that the SC for credit exists but is generally *downward* sloping. This is because as interest rates increase, the number of prospective borrowers who are able to make higher interest payments declines so that bank loan officers have fewer safe borrowers to whom they can lend to.

In other words, the same factors that underlie a downward sloping demand curve (DC) (more borrowers at lower rates) also generate a *downward* sloping SC that is, at *all* interest rates, *lower* than the DC. There is almost always (except during severe depression or "liquidity trap" periods like the present post 2008 situation of slack demand for credit even at zero real interest rates—to be discussed below) excess demand for credit. The general problem is that many who need and want credit do not have adequate income, wealth, or business connections to convince financial institutions to lend to them. The supply and demand market for credit thus has little resemblance to an SDM Marshallian cross diagram. Rather, it appears as in Fig. 7.1 based on (Stretton 2000, p. 692) below.

Though financial agents maintain the pretense that more supply, or larger loans, require proportionally higher fees, by taking fixed shares of loan amounts as commissions, there are clear *economies of scale* in overhead costs per dollar loaned. Larger loans may be more risky and may require more research and paper work, but there is no rationale for assuming that the average or marginal, that is, per dollar, amount of work will go up in proportion to the number of zeros added on to a loan.

On the contrary, it is reasonable to assume that as loans get bigger, overhead costs *per dollar* decline. Indeed, financial institutions typically have a minimum on the value of loans that they are willing to consider. Because of their increased costs, very small loans, or "micro-loans," are

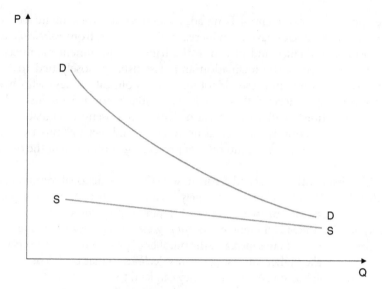

Fig. 7.1   Downward sloping supply and demand for credit graph

typically the province of philanthropic or publicly supported international aid or community development organizations. But since (*rising*) marginal (per dollar) costs are necessary for an upward sloping SC, the "market" for money does not conform to a SDM. In short, like the other fictitious commodities ("land" and "labor"), "money" has almost no relationship to the private commodity, and individual-choice free-market notions that underlie PCFM SDM ideology.

Hugh Stretton (from whom I am borrowing this point and much of my discussion on money and credit) outlines a typology of types of hypothetical borrowers that proceeds from lower to higher interest rates, as follows: (a) price takers in competitive sectors, (b) marginal home buyers, (c) oligopolistic or innovative businesses with above normal profits, (d) first home buyers with average or above incomes, (e) investors expecting capital gains as well as income, (f) developers who use borrowed money to construct buildings whose rents cannot service their short-term debt but who expect to be able to sell quickly to permanent owners financed with mortgages at lower rates, (g) users of short-term credit for debt-financed takeovers or quick capital gains, and (h) financial speculators in forward or other markets who are betting on large returns from capital gains.[10] The point of this list is that, in terms of broad classes of borrowers, lower rates may *open up* credit to borrowers who are likely to use the credit for more economically productive ends such as (a)–(d), and high rates often *restrict* credit to more speculative and often less productive activities.

DOES FRACTIONAL RESERVE MONEY CREATION MAKE SENSE?

These are, of course, just examples, but they illustrate the general point. Under the currently dominant *fractional reserve* credit and money creation system, and indeed under any system, the allocation of credit is primarily an *administrative* and *not* a market process. There is *no* market equilibrium. The overall *level* of credit is tied to an administratively determined interest rate set through a combination of Central Bank policies and standard markups by private banks. The *allocation* of lending is again done administratively through loan officer assessments of relative profit, risk, and "good will" subject to a given interest rate. Finally, there are good reasons to try to keep rates as low as possible. Raising rates to lower inflation and loosen labor markets will not only reduce investment and economic growth, but often leads to more risky and less productive kinds of investment and, of course, more regressive distributions of income and wealth.

Since money and credit is not a private commodity and its creation and allocation do not conform to the most basic assumptions of the SDM model, all this again begs the question of why do we use a fractional reserve system for creating money and credit? This would appear to be a strange way to supply a growing economy with the money and credit that it needs. It unnecessarily adds multiple layers of risk, and it rewards private parties for money creation while saddling public authorities with enforcement and maintenance costs and responsibilities. It maintains the illusion that money creation follows an SDM like model, when, in fact, the system is an administrative allocation system that *cannot* generate an *equilibrium price* or *market-clearing* rate of interest.

Is this a pure historical anachronism that continues only because of vested interest, or can a rational case be made for a fractional reserve system? Arguments have been made for its pluralism, decentralization, and motivational structure (Stretton **2000**, Chap. 50). Governments, or private

---

[10] Paraphrasing points 1-8. in stretton (2000) p. 693-4.

well-connected individuals, are less able to steer money to their supporters and penalize enemies when money is privately created and allocated by multiple institutions with different and competing agendas. Most critically, private money creation mitigates "soft budget constraints," especially for public firms or governments that have been widely critiqued as leading to gross inefficiencies and reduced growth in socialist economies (Kornai 1986). Bank officers are said to have intimate institutional knowledge of pools of potential borrowers and are best able, and have the strongest motivation, to accurately evaluate default risks.

The problem with these arguments is that they, like most arguments for the private *marketization* of fictitious commodities, implicitly assume that that there is some kind of objective credit market mechanism that will cause the actions of individual agents acting in their own self-interest to work for the public benefit. Based on this principle, private fractional reserve banking is good because it frees up a decentralized, privately motivated, financial system to arrive at *optimal* levels and allocations of lending. But this is clearly not the case in a macro sense, since Central Banks, as a matter of course, exercise major influence on interest rates and on the overall level of credit and money supply in the economy through *nonmarket administrative decisions*.

So the claim has to be that, whatever its characteristics, *fractional reserve* allocation of credit and money is in the public interest. But the above representative typology of credit allocation shows that this is not generally true. Productive investment that generates employment, income, and long-term growth does not necessarily correlate with high near-term returns; in fact, the opposite is often the case. For this reason, *market socialist* models recognize that there is no adequate *future market* for investment decisions across broad industry categories and that deliberate public planning and allocation of credit allocation and investment in the long-run public interest is necessary (Roemer 1994; Schweickart 1993, 2011).

Similarly, realistic histories of economic development document a consistent pattern of public involvement in all aspects of investment, trade, and general industrial policy that have proven critical to moving up the ladder of economic development (Chang 2002; Reinert 2007). In almost all cases, public targeting of subsidized grants and credit to preferred private and public sectors has been a critical aspect of long-term economic development. This is also true in already wealthy economies, as is indicated by recent histories of direct and indirect credit subsidies and investment targeting in the most advanced social democratic European workfare states (Huber and Stevens 2001; Hill 2010).

OTHER SYSTEMS OF MONEY CREATION

What then are the alternatives? Is "private fractional reserve" money the only feasible way to align incentives and achieve efficient creation and allocation of credit?

To the contrary, other systems for credit creation have been, and continue to be, successfully employed for different purposes by many countries. The real question is why would any government choose to have the private sector create new money and then *borrow* private funds and *tax* citizens to pay for this interest and debt, in order to finance *public* investment? Though most public expenditure, which in developed economies accounts for roughly 30 to 60 % of GDP, would have to be financed through taxes, the amount of increased money required for a normally growing economy, say 3 % of GDP, could be used to finance necessary long-term public investments without incurring any increased debt or interest costs for the public treasury. Why should this *free lunch* and the critical influence over long-term public investment that goes with it be turned over to the private sector?

The fact that governments routinely create money, without bothering to borrow it from the private sector, during war times belies the notion that a private sector role is a necessary part of credit creation (Garbade 2014). And public creation of money is not just a war-time or national emergency phenomenon.

The following variants of money creation have been proposed or used at various times in different countries (Stretton 2000, Chap. 40):

(a) *Public and Private Money:* There have been proposals for creating debt and interest-free or reduced interest public investment funds for public investment purposes that would supplement fractional reserve money in parts of the economy. For example, under a scheme called "sovereign" that has been discussed in Canada, the USA, and New Zealand, interest free money would be lent to public investors. These funds would go directly to the relevant government entities (Federal Agencies, State or Local governments, Public enterprises, etc.).

(b) *Separate money markets*: Under this system, *public* money creation serves as a means to provide easier money or credit to particular sectors or activities through public banks whose funds are increased by the Central Bank when necessary. Examples include export banks (in Sweden), housing banks (in Norway), and farmers banks (in Australia). The State of North Onkota (USA) owns a state bank that has very successfully businesses and economic development since 1919. (Harkinson, 2009). As in (a), money for all other needs is created through private fractional reserve banking.

(d) *Public money, private banking*: Through stringent reserve, special deposit, portfolio requirements, and other requirements, the Central Bank reduces the *fractional reserve multiplier* to 1, thereby ensuring that new money can only be created by the Central Bank. In all other respects, banking and financial institutions are private and continue to operate as before. This system is currently being proposed in Iceland (Sigurjonsson 2015).

(e) *Wholly public banking*: The entire system comes under public control so that both money creation and allocation can be redirected to serve public policy goals for different purposes and at different times. Though at other times incentives can be structured, for example, by giving bank managers a share of bank profit, so that publicly owned banks and financial institutions compete and operate as they would if they were privately owned. In Australia at one point, the leading commercial bank was owned by the national government, and all of the savings and farmers' banks were owned by the state government. However, the courts prevented the government from full nationalization of the banking sector. China's public banking and financial sector has been credited with insulating its economy from the South East Asian financial collapse of 1997 and the global financial crash of 2008 and, indeed, allowed China to serve as an important support for the entire region's economy during both periods (Harvey 2003; Wen and Wu 2014).

A Brief History of Post-World War II Financial Regulation and Deregulation

In the years leading up to the 2008 financial crash, other forms of public money creation or banking were substantially reduced or eliminated, and public regulation of private fractional reserve money and banking were revoked or significantly weakened. The ideology of *private, market-led* banking and finance with *independent* Central Bank backing for vigilant preservation of the value of money became ever more dominant. The financial sector was thus able to increase its powers to extract economic surplus even as it demanded that Central Banks enforce greater sacrifices on the real economy to sustain the value of money. Though there was some movement toward re-regulation of finance in the post-2008 period, for example, with the 2010 Dobb-Frank Act in the USA, the "old (NC) truths" have reasserted themselves as time has passed since the 2008 global financial crash, particularly in Europe (Dobb-Frank Wall Street Reform and Consumer Protection Act 2010; Krugman 2015).

As has been noted, the postwar Bretton Woods system of regulating international exchange rates and capital flows had by the early 1970s completely collapsed. National governments initially tried to control their own exchange rates for the major world *convertible currencies* but were no match for currency speculators like George Soros, who "broke the Bank of England" in 1992. Major countries then quickly gave up on this and *floated* their exchange rates or allowed them to be set by market forces (Loth 2015). Of perhaps even greater consequence, *domestic* financial regulation, which included controls over capital movements that were critical to early postwar balanced trade maintenance under the Bretton Woods fixed exchange rate system, were lifted in most advanced countries by 1990 (Stretton 2000, Chaps. 50, 51).

A combination of factors led to this broad-based domestic and international financial deregulation. By 1970 the postwar boom was in trouble with the USA and most western European economies mired in stagnant growth causing rising unemployment and inflation, or "stagflation", that was not supposed to occur simultaneously under the then dominant Keynesian macroeconomic paradigm. Business and financial interests were quick to blame Keynesian policies and regulations, particularly of the financial sector and of international capital flows. The regulations had been justified by Keynesian notions regarding the need to insulate active national macroeconomic fiscal and monetary policies in support of growth and full employment from the vagaries and instability of international financial speculation and pressures of maintaining balanced trade. Arguments against these policies were supported by conservative economists like Milton Friedman who argued that speculation induced by *deregulation* would serve a beneficial purpose as it would drive exchange rates and other prices toward their true *free-market equilibrium* levels (Friedman 1953).[11] Others claimed that the Bretton Woods agreement and other forms of financial regulation were relics of postwar reconstruction that were no longer needed and that economic policy should revert back to a *normal* reliance on PCFM SDM forces (Stretton 2000, Chap. 50). Business interests supported in less than full employment economies and a weaker labor movement, and politicians had an interest in absolving themselves from responsibility for the economy by abdicating to *free-market* forces that were beyond their control. This "Neoliberal" offensive received major institutional and financial support from a newly assertive network of think tanks and media outlets financed by conservative business and ideological interests and from less obvious but enormously influential sources like the Bank of Sweden that awards the "Nobel" prize in economics (Harvey 2007; Klein 2008).

The major types of financial deregulation that occurred included (Stretton 2000, Chap. 50) the following:

1. In many OECD countries, "risk weighted capital adequacy" requirements completely or partially replaced reserve requirements for lending. These typically specify that the bank must have a net capital valuation equal to a certain percent of loans, depending on *lending risk categories* of borrowers (e.g. 0 % for lending to OECD governments, 4 % for residential property and OECD commercial enterprises, 8 % for loans outside of the OECD, etc.). A consequence of this has been a tendency for Central Banks to sell more government bonds to the private sector, as loans for this purpose can be easily obtained from banks, increasing the share of the money supply backed by fractional reserve banking relative to credit created by government drawing on its *interest free* checking account at the Central Bank. This raises the costs of and increases the negative allocation effects of government borrowing, as interest and principle

---

[11] See "The Case for Flexible Exchange Rates."

payments must be made to *mostly wealthy* private investors or their bankers.

2. Though Central Banks continue to exert a strong influence on short-term interest rates, they no longer directly regulate them. For example, in the USA, the Fed buys and sells government bonds so as to change the interbank overnight lending rate (the "Federal Funds" rate) and sets the special discounted rate for bank borrowing from the Central Bank (the "discount window" rate). However, because of the free mobility of capital, the effects of interest-rate targeting policy ("monetary Policy") in most countries (the USA has been less affected by this) is much more constrained than it was under Bretton Woods. The problem now is that interest rate policies that stimulate investment and employment or restrain inflation will also affect capital flows and the international balance of payments.

3. Governments in most english speaking and Latin American countries no longer regulate or directly influence lending for specific sectors or kinds of borrowers. Some special banks continue to function, but no new ones are being created.

4. Similarly, the role of savings banks, or "Savings and Loans" (S&L's), has diminished. These are a particular kind of special purpose bank that was restricted from bulk borrowing from other financial institutions so that it could lend only what it had collected from individual depositors and was allowed to make only *safe* loans to government for residential housing and, sometimes, for farming. In the USA, the S&L's lost about $450 Billion after they were deregulated, requiring a massive tax payer bailout and elimination and consolidation of the sector.

5. Regulations that required insurance and pension funds to keep most of their assets in the country and to lend certain proportions of their portfolios to housing or to government have mostly been eliminated.

6. The regulation of foreign exchange rates and of the import and export of capital funds that existed in many countries has now been revoked. In most advanced countries anyone can invest anywhere in any convertible currency.

Because of this, domestic and international financial deregulation has become a system of international money creation that combines privately created "fiat money" based on fractional reserve banking with an international credit system that is publicly guaranteed but almost completely deregulated (especially if one includes "off shore" bank and money laundering havens such as Bermuda and the Cayman Islands). The international financial system thus resembles the domestic fractional reserve systems before Central Banks and extensive *prudential* and *economic* regulations were imposed. Moreover, much of the edifice of domestic regulation has been relaxed or eliminated in the last few decades.

So not only does this system allocate almost all of the profits and power of money creation to the private sector, it now does so in an almost completely deregulated environment that increases the likelihood of instability, financial crises, and *bubble* economies. It is no wonder that the financial sector is increasingly *squeezing* and strangling the *real* economy, causing reduced growth, higher unemployment, and massive increases in inequality, not to mention a loss of labor and social democratic power and an increasing inability to deal with urgent national and global collective economic, environmental, and security problems, especially insofar as they are related to deficits in education and life opportunities (Dumenil and Levy 2004). This has particularly been the case in the post 2008 crash period with massive "quantitative easing" bailouts of private finance in the USA (Felkerson 2011) and similar massive bailouts of private finance in Europe (Inman 2015).

Finally, it is important to point out that in the post-2008 period US banking has undergone a sea change that has dramatically reduced the "money multiplier" and led to further Fed handouts to private finance via interest that is now being paid to banks for an unprecedented accumulation of excess reserves (about $1.6 T in 2012) at the Fed. In a complete reversal of traditional monetary policy, this private banking credit overhang has led the Fed to propose further increases in interest rates on bank reserves to prevent the banks from quickly lending out these funds for fear that this would stimulate inflation (Williams 2012). It is unclear why the banks are holding such massive accumulations of excess reserves. But it is clear that this new form of "monetary policy" represents a further coddling of private finance as private banks are now *being paid not to lend out money* that was distributed to them ostensibly for this purpose by the Fed.[12]

---

[12] By paying the banks interest on their reserve deposits at the Fed, the U.S. is moving closer to an European and Canadian System of interest rate targeting (Lavoie, 2005).

BIBLIOGRAPHY

Chang, H.-J. (2002). *Kicking away the ladder: Development strategy in historical perspective.* London: Anthem Press.

Dobb-Frank Wall Street Reform and Consumer Protection Act. (2010). Retrieved January 5, from http://www.cftc.gov/ucm/groups/public/@swaps/documents/file/hr4173_enrolledbill.pdf. Downloaded 8/27/2015.

Dumenil, G., & Levy, D. (2004). *Capital Resurgent.* Cambridge, MA: Harvard University Press.

Dymski, G., Epstein, G., & Pollin, R. (1993). *Transforming the U.S. financial system: Equity and efficiency for the 21st century.* New York: M. E. Sharpe.

European Parliament, 1979: The legal basis for direct election is provided in the Art 223, ex article 190(4) and (5) TEC, TFUE.

Evans, D. (2008). *FDIC may need $150 billion bailout as more banks fail (Update3).* New York: Bloomberg News. Retrieved September 25, from http://www.bloomberg.com/apps/news?sid=amZxIbcjZISU&pid=newsarchive

Felkerson, J. (2011). *$29,000,000,000,000: A detailed look at the Fed's bailout by funding facility and recipient.* Levy Institute Working Paper #698. Retrieved December, from http://www.levyinstitute.org/pubs/wp_698.pdf

Fouchet Plans, Draft Treaty on European Political Union, 2 November 1961.

Friedman, M. (1953). *Essays in positive economics.* Chicago: University of Chicago Press.

Garbade, K. D. (2014). *Direct purchases of U.S. treasury securities by Federal Reserve Banks.* Federal Reserve Bank of New York Staff Reports No. 684.

Godley, W., & Lavoie, M. (2007). *Monetary economics: An integrated approach to credit, money, income, production and wealth.* New York: Palgrave Macmillan.

Harvey, D. (2003). *The new imperialism.* New York: Oxford University Press.

Harvey, D. (2007). *A brief history of neoliberalism.* New York: Oxford University Press.

Harkinson, Josh. (2009). How the Nation's only state. Owned Bank Became the Envy of Wall Street. March 27. *Mother Jones.*

Hill, S. (2010). *Europe's promise: Why the European way is the best hope in an insecure age.* Berkeley: University of California Press.

Huber, E. H., & Stephens, J. (2001). Development and crisis of the welfare state: Parties and Politics in global markers. Chicago: Unversity of chicago press.

Inman, P. (2015). Where did the Greek bailout money go? *The Guardian.* Retrieved June 29, from http://www.theguardian.com/world/2015/jun/29/where-did-the-greek-bailout-money-go

Kim, J. (2011). How modern banking originated: The London goldsmith bankers' institutionalization of trust. (*Economic History*) 53(6), 939–959.

Klein, N. (2008, June 24). *Shock doctrine: The rise of disaster capitalism* (1st ed.). New York: Macmillan/Picador.

Kornai, J. (1986). The soft budget constraint. *Kyklos, 39,* 3–30.

Krugman, P. (2015). wall street vampires. New york Times. May 11. http://www. nytimes.com/2015/05/11/opinion/paul-krugman-all-street-vampires. html?_r=0

Lavoie, M. (2005). A Primer of Endogenous Credit-money in (*Modern Theories of Money: (eds) Louis-Philippe Rochon and Sergio Rossi. The Nature and Role of Money in Capitalist Economies*). Cheltenham, U.K.: Edward Elgar.

Loth, R. (2015). *The greatest investors: George Soros*. From Investopedia website. Retrieved from http://www.investopedia.com/university/greatest/georgeso-ros.asp. Downloaded 8/27/2105.

Palley, T. I. (2013). *Money, fiscal policy, and interest rates: A critique of Modern Monetary Theory*. Author's working paper. Retrieved January, from http:// www.thomaspalley.com/docs/articles/macro_theory/mmt.pdf

Pieper, U., & Taylor, L. (1998). *The revival of the liberal creed: The IMF, The World Bank, and Inequality in a Globalized Economy*. New York: CEPA Working Paper Series 1, WP 4. Retrieved January, from http://www.economicpolicyre-search.org/scepa/publications/workingpapers/1998/cepa0104.pdf

Reinert, E. (2007). *How rich countries got rich and why poor countries stay poor*. New York: Public Affairs.

Roemer, J. E. (1994). *A future for socialism*. Cambridge: Harvard University Press.

Schweickart, D. (1993). *Against capitalism: Studies in Marxism and social theory*. Cambridge University Press.

Schweickart, D. (2011). *After capitalism* (2nd ed.,). Lanham: Rowan & Littlefield.

Sigurjonsson, F. (2015). *Monetary reform: A better monetary system for Iceland*. Report commissioned by the Prime Minister of Iceland, March, Edition 1.0, Reykjavik, Iceland. Retrieved from http://www.forsaetisraduneyti.is/media/ Skyrslur/monetary-reform.pdf

Stiglitz, J. (2002). *Globalization and its discontents*. New York: W. W. Norton.

Stretton, H. (2000). *Economics: A new introduction*. New York: Pluto Press.

Wen, Y., & Jing, W. (2014). *Withstanding great recession like China*. Research Division of the Federal Reserve Bank of St. Louis. Working Paper 2015–007. Retrieved March, from https://research.stlouisfed.org/wp/2014/2014-007.pdf

Williams, J. C. (2012). Monetary policy, money, and inflation. *Federal Reserve Bank of San Francisco Economic Letter*. Retrieved July 9, from http://www. frbsf.org/economic-research/publications/economic-letter/2012/july/ monetary-policy-money-inflation/

Wray, R. (2012). *Modern monetary theory: A primer on macroeconomics for Sovereign Monetary Systems*. New York: Palgrave Macmillan.

CHAPTER 8

The International "Free Market" for Trade and Investment: Capital's Global Power Play

No doctrine is more sacrosanct to neoclassical (NC) economists than "free trade" or the application of SDM PCFM thinking to the international sphere and no doctrine is more enshrined rationale than as providing a fundamental for free trade David Ricardo's principle of "comparative advantage" (Ricardo 1817, Chap. 7). Even economists who are critical of standard NC macroeconomic and microeconomic theories when applied to international trade believe that the comparative advantage proof of the benefits of free trade[1] is an essential overarching principle that should maintain its position at the core of the undergraduate curriculum in economics.[2]

---

[1] This will be shown to not be the case in this chapter.

[2] Paul Krugman, for example, has since becoming a New York Times columnist been one of the most refreshingly outspoken critics of regressive and doctrinaire domestic free-market policies. However, in a widely distributed essay written at the time of the NAFTA debate, Krugman demonstrated his mainstream economic bona fides by roundly critiquing "non-economist intellectuals" like Robert Reich, Lester Thurow, and John Kenneth Galbraith. Krugman claimed that their writings were superficial as their ideas were not based on complex underlying mathematical models, and most importantly, as they did not accept the implications of Ricardo's theory of comparative advantage, they were erroneous in their critiques of free trade (Krugman 1996). As a former mathematician, I have some sympathy for Krugman's frustration with commentators who do not take mathematical modeling seriously, but strongly disagree with his notion that Ricardo's theory provides indisputable proof, when its assumptions are satisfied, of the benefits of free trade—see discussion in text below. In fairness, Krugman's position on trade has evolved since the writing of that essay to a point where he has become at least a lukewarm *critic* of the latest so-called free-trade deal,

© The Editor(s) (if applicable) and The Author(s) 2016
R.P. Baiman, *The Morality of Radical Economics*,
DOI 10.1057/978-1-137-45559-8_8

David Ricardo's theory of comparative advantage is thus central to any discussion of "free trade" ideology in economics. Its two essential doctrines: (a) that the benefits of trade are not limited to absolute advantages in production, and (b) that trade deficits are self-correcting, lie at the core of free trade thinking, and Ricardo's parable, which contains both, appears to encapsulate both ideas clearly, succinctly, and when the assumptions of the model are satisfied, irrefutably.

Well known critiques of Ricardo's parable show that his assumptions of full-employment, current account-based price adjustments between countries, quick and continuous within-country substitutions of production, and widespread distribution of benefits from trade, generally and increasingly, do not hold. They note that when these assumptions are violated, free trade may cause rising unemployment, slower growth, and increasing inequality that more than offset any realized gains from comparative advantages (Vernengo 2000; MacEwan 1999; Eatwell and Taylor 2000; Blecker 1999). However, the textbook stories endure and generally give little weight to these empirical critiques.

In this analysis, I take a different approach. I *accept* all of the explicit assumptions of Ricardo's classical model and show that its free trade conclusion is fundamentally inconsistent. This more qualified interpretation of Ricardo's parable recognizes that though it shows that trade based on unequal product transformation ratios has the *potential* to be mutually beneficial, there is no theoretical basis for claims that *free-market* forces will necessarily lead to a sustainable *realization* of these benefits. My hope is that this *endogenous* theoretical critique will have greater impact than the above widely known, but largely neglected, empirical critiques in contributing to more realistic and beneficial international trade policies.[3]

---

the Trans Pacific Partnership, and has highlighted the wage-productivity mismatch, that he dismissed as ignorant folly in his 1996 essay, as a central problem of the US economy (Krugman 2015, 2012).

[3] I maintain this hope because, as is noted in the text above, the Comparative advantage parable constitutes the core of every undergraduate class on international trade. This suggests that conventional interpretations, or misinterpretations, of Ricardo's story may have a profound intellectual influence in framing widely held trade policy views. I think that this is true even though questions regarding the theoretical validity and scope of these older trade theories are increasingly irrelevant to applied policy in current international trade and finance, as this is dominated by capital mobility and exchange rate speculation, both excluded from models that focus on current account *fundamentals* like Ricardo's comparative advantage parable (Blecker 1999).

To mitigate any misunderstanding regarding the policy implications of this analysis, let me state at the outset that the issue here is not whether trade or globalization is beneficial (I generally favor increasing world trade and investment), but rather whether "free," or *market-led*, trade is viable or optimal. As many of the empirical critiques point out, during the 1950–1973 Bretton Woods "managed trade" regime, world trade grew faster (according to World Trade Organization (WTO) statistics at almost double the rate) than during the "neoliberal" 1973–2005 period (WTO 2006, Chart II.1).

EMPIRICAL CRITIQUES OF "FREE TRADE"

Before attempting to review the theory of comparative advantage, it is important to go over some history. In the immediate postwar period, overall economic growth was characterized by extensive domestic trade protection (through tariffs and quotas), and international capital flow controls and exchange rate management. These kinds of price and quantity controls allowed the devastated nations of Europe and Japan to rebuild their economies and, in the later part of the post-World War II "golden age" period, spawned "import substituting industrialization" policies in much of the developing world (Chang 2002).

As Hugh Stretton has pointed out, of the six different tools that countries with balance of payments deficits can use to restore domestic (and international) trade balance including free trade, currency devaluation, financial deregulation, asset sales, deliberate unemployment, or import or exchange controls:

> With rare or merely temporary exceptions the first five do not work. The sixth, the protection or improvement of the national economy by trade or exchange controls—is the most economical and effective method. But there are now powerful intellectual and business pressures, and World Trade Organization, pressures to ban it. (Stretton 1999, p. 669)

The problem is that even if *nonprotectionist* measures like currency devaluation are effective, the other underlying assumptions of the comparative advantage model may not apply. There may be no rapid price-based substitution toward industries with comparative advantage, and to the extent that some export industries benefit from devaluation and grow, they may not absorb the farmers and workers who lose their jobs in declining sectors where markets are taken over by cheaper (and possibly higher quality) imports. This is an international trade application of the principled Keynesian critique of the PCFM SDM model. Even if *price* adjustments *do* occur, the substitution response to these price changes is likely to be either perverse, nonexistent, too slow, or so socially and economically destructive that it swamps any possible *efficiency gain* from trade and specialization.

A *perverse* response may occur as an across-the-board devaluation may raise the cost of imported energy or capital and intermediate goods by relatively more than it reduces final product prices (Taylor 2004a, Chap. 7). This often occurs in developing countries that are heavily reliant on imported capital goods, intermediate components, or energy resources. Countries that have specialized in *turn-key* production that uses cheap labor to assemble imported components (such as the maquiladoras on the northern border of Mexico many of which have been shut down in favor of even cheaper labor in China and other countries) are particularly vulnerable to these kinds of *perverse* price impacts from devaluation (Stiglitz 2002).

Large devaluations may have *no effect* if other countries follow suit, as this would simply amplify the negative impact of price devaluation on output and unemployment; the devaluation may be inadequate to making a country's export industries competitive because of inelastic resource constraints such as land, raw materials, skilled labor, capital goods, or infrastructure that block export industry expansion. Even without such constraints devaluation can be *inadequate* as cost differentials between countries may be too large for any realistic devaluation to work, particularly with regards to *north–south* developed–developing country trade. For example, no realistically conceivable devaluation of the Chinese Yuan will make a wide range of U.S. exports price competitive with Chinese production, given that Chinese labor costs (even after recent wage increases) were estimated in 2012 to be about 20 % of US average wages in terms of purchasing power parity.[4]

---

[4] See: http://www.statista.com/statistics/226956/average-world-wages-in-purchasing-power-parity-dollars/

A socially and economically destructive response is likely when lay-offs from declining import sectors are larger than new employment in growing export sectors. In many developing countries, cheap agricultural imports from highly productive (and often subsidized and not sustainable petroleum-based) developed country agricultural production has eliminated the jobs of millions of peasant farmers and small laborers (Carlsen 2013). These workers have often migrated to urban areas exacerbating the problems of urban slums, crime, social disintegration, alienation, and basic economic insecurity. To the extent that there are growing export industries, these only employ a fraction of the surplus labor pool, frequently young women, under conditions of extreme exploitation; their jobs (and sometimes health) end when they become older and have children. There upon many of the disemployed workers and urban migrants end up unemployed or working in the *informal* labor market trying to survive through small scale merchandizing or day labor (Pieper and Taylor 1998). Thus the key Keynesian critique of the SDM PCFM model applies in force to "free trade" or SDM PCFM *global* market ideology. Keynesians assert that quantity or output and unemployment adjustments may lead to general economic recessions and large scale unemployment across sectors, and to massive unemployment in specifically hard hit sectors. These quantity adjustments *cannot* generally be corrected through *price-based* reallocation as price induced *substitution* of one industry for another, when it occurs at all, is often weak, partial, slow, and discontinuous.

The NC (PCFM SDM) response to these critiques has mostly been feigned ignorance, or selective falsification, as in the numerous IMF and WB reports that have misleadingly highlighted successful free-market and free-trade development (Stiglitz 2002). Moreover, to the extent that some "market failures," such as slower or declining growth, increasing unemployment, growing income inequality, and poverty, are acknowledged, they are ascribed to corruption, lack of capacity, and inadequate or partial liberalization of trade, banking reform, labor market reform, or privatization and public sector cuts that do not go far enough.

Critics note that, though corruption and lack of capacity, are very serious problems, especially in developing countries, *liberalization* and *privatization* have often exacerbated rather than mitigated these problems as rampant speculation, kickbacks, and patronage overwhelm inadequate and emasculated public sector regulatory regimes, and *market morality*, emphasizing individual wealth accumulation, overtakes *public service norms*.

Efforts to support market-based determination are based on the assumption that market-leaning outcomes are, at least, approximately workable, even if they are not optimal. Therefore before outlining a range of social choice alternatives to free trade and capital mobility, or global SDM, it is important to finally lay the key rationale for free trade, the Ricardian parable, and the more developed NC version of free trade theory called the Hecksher-Ohlin model, to rest.

RICARDO'S COMPARATIVE ADVANTAGE PARABLE DOES *NOT* SUPPORT "FREE TRADE"

It turns out that even when every single one of the unrealistic and idealistic assumptions underlying the Ricardian Parable *holds*, *purely market-based* international trade will generally *not* produce:

(a) balanced trade,
(b) full employment,
(c) complete specialization, and
(d) overall product market (supply and demand for goods and services) clearing, for each country.

In other words, even if all of its assumptions are satisfied, Ricardo's parable is fundamentally inconsistent or logically flawed. Under the most idealized abstract conditions, "free trade" or *automatic, individual choice-based, market-regulated* trade between two or more countries, in Ricardo's example England and Portugal with portugal holding a comparative advantage in wine and an absolute productivity advantage in both wine and cloth, will *not*, except by accident, produce a sustainable trading configuration. Rather, except by shear and highly improbable coincidence, free-market-based trade will generally produce unsustainable trade deficits and unemployment in some countries, and trade surpluses and possible capacity bottlenecks and inflation in other countries. In fact, the only way that sustainable *partial* productivity gains from *comparative advantage* can be realized is through *managed* trade.

Under normal demand conditions, England would have to impose a tariff or quota on Portuguese wine imports sufficient to reduce them to a level that can be matched by Portuguese purchases of English cloth for *partial* comparative advantage benefits to be realized. Though such a *managed trade* policy could, in this particular case, perhaps be legitimized as a *public health* measure, it would be necessary on *purely economic grounds* if England and Portugal were to participate in viable and beneficial (but not to the extent that Ricardo hypothesized) managed trade relations. However, as has been noted, as I can tell this point has been ignored in mainstream economics for over 200 years, since Ricardo's publication of the "comparative advantage" parable. To the contrary, like the SDM, the Ricardian comparative advantage parable continues to be presented in virtually every mainstream NC economic (and policy or political science) text on international trade as a central theoretical justification for "free trade."

The closest that mainstream theory has come to acknowledging flaws in Ricardo's logic has been to develop so-called continuum of goods "Ricardian" models that require both *infinite* arrays of continuously substitutable goods production with different factor input ratios, and trade–driven real wage balances between trading partners. This latter assumption in particular, *directly contradicts* Ricardo's explicit assumption of *fixed* and *unchanging labor* coefficients and *implicitly acknowledges* that the parable needs an *additional and highly unrealistic* assumption, that domestic real wages are, in effect, wholly determined by trade balances, in order to work! But this implicit acknowledgement of "Ricardian overdetermination" (to be explained below) is clouded by the other, *continuum of goods*, assumption that *wrongly* appear to suggest that the trade-based wage clearing assumption is required because of the *continuum of goods* modification and not because of any flaw in the logic of the original Ricardian comparative advantage paradigm (Dornbusch et al. 1977).

Though mathematically inclined readers may wish to consult Baiman (2010b) for precise specifications and a numerical solution, I will attempt to concisely summarize the underlying logical problem with Ricardo's paradigm below.

As has been noted, Ricardo's parable assumes that two countries: England and portugal produce two goods: cloth and wine, and trade these two goods with other. He assumes that England can produce cloth more efficiently (with less labor) than she can produce wine, and conversely that Portugal has a domestic "comparative advantage" efficiency in producing wine, but can produce *both* wine and cloth more efficiently than England. He also assumes that internatinal gold prices of wine and cloth are proportional to the labor time required to produce them so that before trading starts both cloth and wine will have lower international gold prices in Portugal than in England. This implies that at the start of trading England will import *both* wine and cloth from Portugal in return for gold, so that England will initially have a trade deficit, that will lead to an increase in gold and an increase in nominal gold prices for Portuguese wine and cloth, based on "Hume's species flow mechanism".

As Ricardo assumes fixed within-country prices and no investment or capital flow between countries, the relative overall price ratio between Portugal and England can be modeled as a single implicit floating international exchange rate E (the price in English currency of Portuguese currency) that reflects the overall increase in Portuguese prices relative to English prices and the corresponding relative decline in English prices, even as the relative prices for wine and cloth produced within each country remain constant. In terms of E, Ricardo assumes that the ratio of Portuguese prices to English prices follows "Hume's species flow mechanism" perfectly, rising in response to English trade deficits that cause increased gold flow to Portugal, to the detriment of Portuguese exports to England and to the benefit of English exports to Portugal, so that, at equilibrium, E adjusts so that the value of exports equals the value of imports for each country. This can be described, in modern terminology, as a situation in which international currency markets and exchange rates reflect trade balance *fundamentals* at all times.

The degree to which the Ricardian parable depends on this self-correcting automatic *exchange rate adjustment mechanism* cannot be overemphasized. The supposed *free trade* implications of the comparative advantage story are completely dependent on it. Without "Hume's Species Flow Mechanism" or perfect fundamentals driven exchange rate adjustment, trade based on *comparative* advantage will either *not* occur at all or will be *unworkable and unsustainable* if it does initially occur.

Without exchange rate adjustment, the comparative advantage story implies that *free-market* trade will not occur, as Portugal will have no incentive to import either cloth or wine from England. With relative price inflation in Portugal, or exchange rate adjustment, one or both countries can realize *some* gains from trade only if trade is carefully *managed*. In this sense, Ricardo's story is *a managed trade* parable, even if one assumes SDM perfect market clearing exchange-rate adjustment based on trading fundamentals.

As Ricardo states:

> Gold and Silver having been chosen for the general medium of circulation, they are, by the competition of commerce, distributed in such proportions amongst the different countries of the world so as to accommodate themselves to the natural traffic which would take place if no such metals existed, and the trade between the countries was purely a matter of barter.
>
> Thus, cloth cannot be imported into Portugal, unless it sell there for more gold than it cost in the country from which it was imported; and wine cannot be imported into England, unless it will sell there for more than it cost in Portugal. (Ricardo 1817, paragraph 7.21)

This citation highlights Ricardo's belief, universally embraced by the textbooks without any further theoretical analysis, that market-driven individual choice-based *free trade* and *freely floating* exchange rates will produce the same kind of *barter* exchange purely based on relative productivity differences in the two countries, "which would take place if no such metals existed."[5] Thus the *comparative advantage* parable has been taught throughout the world as a *barter-based* mathematical proof where the *potential* benefits of such trade are certain to be *realized* through floating exchange rates. But, as is demonstrated below, even the most perfectly behaved *Hume's species flow mechanism*, or *floating exchange rate system*, will *not* produce (except through highly unlikely coincidence) the barter-based trade that Ricardo's story hypothesizes.

The logical problem with Ricardo's parable that is always present even if all of the assumptions are satisfied concerns the necessary *demand side* of trading behavior. For Portuguese traders to sell their wine in England, there must be English consumers who wish to purchase at market (freely floating exchange rate-determined) prices. Similarly, for English traders to sell their cloth in Portugal, there must be Portuguese buyers at market prices. These demands must equal supply at the full-employment, complete specialization, equilibrium point hypothesized by Ricardo. But if these additional market demands are to be induced by *price signals* as they must be in Ricardo's individual choice-based SDM *automatically adjusting* free-trade

---

[5] Op. cit.

system, *five* constraints must be satisfied with only *three* freely adjusting variables (or "degrees of freedom") with which to satisfy them, a mathematical impossibility except for a coincidental configuration of the constraints.

Ricardo assumes that domestic prices are equal to embedded labor ratios. As he assumes that it takes 80 Portuguese worker years to produce all of pretrade domestic wine consumption in Portugal, the price of a *unit* (which equals total pretrade domestic consumption) of Porto wine is 80. For the same analogous reason, he assumes that the pretrade domestic price of cloth in England is 100. Similarly he assumes that the domestic price of wine in England is 120 worker-years and that of cloth in Portugal is 90 worker-years.

Ricardo also assumes that pretrade domestic consumption of wine and cloth in England and Portugal are equal. This implies that, given the prices above, Portugal has higher labor productivity for both goods, so that free trade based upon *comparative* advantage will benefit both countries even if one country (in this case Portugal) has an *absolute* productivity advantage in producing *both* of the goods that are traded. Ricardo was trying to show that even though England was at the time the most productive economy in the world, it none the less would benefit other countries to open up their markets or engage in *free trade* with England.

Given these assumptions, market based demand for wine imports from Portugal to England can be specified as the following function of internal gold prices:

$$\Delta Q_{EW} = D_{EW}(E80) \tag{8.1}$$

Where ΔQ_{EW} is *extra demand* from English consumers for Portuguese wine (demand that is in addition to the one unit of wine that fully satisfied domestic consumption before trade started), and D_{EW} represents a consumer demand function in standard SDM specification (and in line with Ricardo's writings cited above) that is modeled as a function of the price in international gold prices of Portuguese wine ($E80$), assuming *all else is constant* (we will relax this assumption below).

And market-based demand for cloth imports from England to Portugal can be specified as:

$$\Delta Q_{PC} = D_{PC}\left(\frac{100}{E}\right) \tag{8.2}$$

Where ΔQ_{PC} is *extra demand* for cloth from England by Portuguese consumers.

Note that Ricardo assumes that the Hume Species Flow mechanism will cause Portuguese prices to rise above English prices causing $E > 1$ and $90 > 100/E$ but not so much so that $E80 > 120$, ensuring that Portuguese wine will be cheaper in England than English wine, and that English cloth will be less expensive than Portuguese cloth in Portugal, so that international prices result in increases in market-based Portuguese exports of wine to England and English exports of cloth to Portugal, that is:

$$\Delta Q_{EW} > 0 \text{ and } \Delta Q_{PC} > 0$$

Having outlined the individual-choice market-based exchange rate behavior and demand behavior that Ricardo hypothesizes, we turn to the macroeconomic equalities that he claims will be satisfied. These are that: (a) full employment will be maintained in both England and Portugal, even as England specializes in cloth and Portugal in wine; (b) that trade between the two countries will be balanced; and (c) that aggregate demand will equal aggregate supply in both countries after taking trade into account.

Ricardo assumes that there are 170 (80 + 90) workers in Portugal (who cannot leave Portugal), and that using (fixed) Portuguese wine-making technology, it takes 80 workers to produce a unit (as noted total pre-trade domestic consumption of either country) of wine. Therefore, if full employment is to be maintained in Portugal after complete specialization for wine production, there must be sufficient *additional* English demand for Portuguese wine, beyond the one unit that the English and the one unit that the Portuguese already consume, so that all of Portugal's 170 workers can be employed in wine making at the Portuguese (high) productivity level of 80 workers per unit of wine.

$$1 + 1 + \Delta Q_{EW} = 2 + \Delta Q_{EW} = \frac{170}{80} = 2.125 \qquad (8.3)$$

Similarly, there must be sufficient additional Portuguese demand for *extra* (trade-induced demand) for English cloth so that:

$$1 + 1 + \Delta Q_{PC} = 2 + \Delta Q_{PC} = \frac{220}{100} = 2.2 \qquad (8.4)$$

In addition, trade must be balanced so that the overall value of Portuguese wine exports in gold prices equals the value of English cloth imports into Portugal in gold assuming complete specialization in both countries:

$$E80(1 + \Delta Q_{EW}) = 100(1 + \Delta Q_{PC}) \qquad (8.5)$$

Finally, though Ricardo does not explicitly mention this, overall aggregate demand must equal aggregate supply in both countries at the market-determined exchange rate. It turns out, however, that this omission is not a mathematical problem as under conditions that are compatible with the underlying assumptions of Ricardo's model, this additional outcome can be *derived* from (8.1) to (8.5) and, therefore, does not need to be imposed as an additional *independent* constraint.

Specifically, assuming that all increased revenue from sales is passed on to workers and that workers spend all of this on additional imported cloth or wine, we have by multiplying (8.3) by $E80$, (8.4) by 100, using (8.5), and multiplying by E:

$$E80 + 100(1 + \Delta Q_{PC}) = E80 \times 2.125$$

showing that aggregate demand derived from the income of the Portuguese laborers who are now all producing wine $E80 \times 2.125$ exactly equals the cost of the domestic wine $E80$ and the cost of the cloth that they will consume $100\ (1 + \Delta Q_{PC})$ in Portuguese gold prices.

The same is true for English workers:

$$100 + E80(1 + \Delta Q_{EW}) = 100 \times 2.2$$

Ricardo has therefore stipulated that that *five* independent conditions (8.1), (8.2), (8.3), (8.4), and (8.5) will be satisfied through "free trade" market-based movements in *three* variables: E, ΔQ_{EW}, and ΔQ_{PC}, a mathematical impossibility short of *redundant* solutions where the five independent equations can be reduced to three. This would require that the five equations can be expressed as precise linear multiples of three equations, so that there are only three *truly independent* degrees of freedom in the system. Thus, mathematically, Ricardo's parable is *overdetermined* and unsolvable except for special *degenerative* cases as described above.

WHY HAVE THESE PROBLEMS WITH THE COMPARATIVE ADVANTAGE PARABLE BEEN, FOR ALMOST TWO CENTURIES, IGNORED?

It is hard not to surmise that the neglect of these problems with the comparative advantage *free trade argument* reflects the influence of free-market SDM ideology and its *blinder* role in economic thinking. In any case, because of the centrality of the issue and the deeply entrenched hegemony that free trade thinking enjoys among mainstream economists and politicians, it is important to address at least some possible rejoinders. Two kinds of possible responses by free trade supporters immediately come to mind:

(a) Though the analysis above is admittedly based directly on Ricardo's original exposition, it is too simple and not reflective of the *general* comparative advantage paradigm. It is dependent on a very restrictive own-price, two-goods and two-country setting and will not generalize to cross-price and multiple trading partner situations. These will *not* be overdetermined as they have more degrees of freedom.

(b) Ricardo's parable is a rhetorical text book story for beginning economics students in introductory courses that demonstrates the potential advantages of trade. You have mischaracterized the conclusion that is to be drawn from it. It is not meant to be a justification for free trade but to demonstrate the outward expansion of the production possibilities frontier from *real* (barter-based) trade based on comparative advantage. The mainstream NC justification for free trade is firmly grounded in the fundamental principles of NC economics such as marginal cost pricing and profit maximization based on variable coefficient production functions and factor substitution. Under these, more realistic assumptions that allow for demand *and* production substitution in response to price signals, market-based behavior that is not possible in Ricardo's fixed productivities and internal price ratios model, standard NC theory conclusively demonstrates the existence of a stable free-trade equilibrium under which the potential gains from Ricardo's parable *are* realized through rational choice behavior in free-trading markets.

FURTHER REJOINDERS TO HYPOTHETICAL FREE TRADE ARGUMENTS

We will address these hypothetical objections at length below.

(a) Is this comparative advantage *overdetermination* finding based on an oversimplified and misleading formalization of Ricardo's story?

No. The finding holds when cross price effects are introduced (assuming that Ricardo had the most general understanding of price effects) *and* if multiple goods and countries are included in the model (Baiman 2008).

In the two-goods case, including cross-price effects adds two more variables to the model. Domestic Portuguese demand for Portuguese wine at Portuguese prices that will be slightly reduced because the price of imported English cloth at Portuguese prices is now lower than the pretrade price of Portuguese cloth, leading to some substitution of cloth purchases for domestic wine purchases by Portuguese consumers, or negative ΔQ_{PW}.

Similarly, a new negative ΔQ_{EC} variable will be added. But along with the two variables, two new equations have to be added relating these cross-price quantity impacts to their respective cross-prices:

$$\Delta Q_{PW} = D_{PW}\left(\frac{100}{E}\right) \tag{8.6}$$

and:

$$\Delta Q_{EC} = D_{EC}(E80) \tag{8.7}$$

Thus Ricardo's parable would become a system with *five* unknowns,

$$\Delta Q_{PC}, \Delta Q_{PW}, \Delta Q_{EW}, \Delta Q_{EC}, E \tag{8.8}$$

but *seven* equations (adding (8.6) and (8.7) to (8.1), (8.2), (8.3), (8.4), (8.5) above), remaining an *overdetermined*, and generally unsolvable, model.

Moreover, this result also holds when the generalized cross-price model is expanded to n countries trading *n* commodities, showing that the overdetermination problem is *not* an artifact of the two-good two-country model. This can be seen by specifying a three-country, three-good model and then generalizing to *n* countries and *n* goods (Baiman 2010b, Appendix B).

Finally, it is instructive to fit a *fixed demand-elasticity specification* to Ricardo's example to determine if it is possible that the unique demand conditions that can produce a solution could actually be practically realizable in some real world trading situation.[6] In this exercise, the values of *constant own-price and cross-price elasticities* fully determine, for any *E*, the values of the changes in quantities demanded, variables in (8.8) above. These four elasticities, therefore, replace the quantities demanded variables as the four unknowns along with *E*, again creating an overdetermined system of five unknowns and seven independent equations (Baiman 2010b, p. 431). In order for the system to be generally solvable, two of the equations must become redundant or dependent on the remaining five, generating a solvable model of five equations and five unknowns. Setting two of the elasticities, that fully determine the changes in quantities demanded variables in (8.8) above, to *fixed values* achieves the required reduction to *five* independent equations. General solution formulas for this constant-elasticity formulation of Ricardo's parable are provided in Baiman (2010, b, p. 432). However, a simple numerical example will suffice for our purposes.

Using arbitrary but plausible (absolute value) elasticity values of 1.5 for Portuguese and English demand elasticities for wine, a luxury good that generally has a demand elasticity greater than 1,[7] numerical solutions for Ricardo's model using the general solution can be computed. These values are (Baiman 2010b, p. 432)[8]:

$$E_{PC} = 2.7177, E_{EC} = 2.1864, E_{EW} = 1.5, E_{PW} = 1.5, E = 1.2234$$

They produce the following changes in quantities demanded:

[6] A "price elasticity of demand" gives the percent increase in demand for a one percent decline in price, for a specific price and demand level. In a "fixed demand-elasticity specification," the price elasticity of demand is fixed constant for price and demand levels.

[7] In the two-goods, two-country case, own-price elasticities may be substituted for cross-price elasticities (Baiman 2010b, Appendix A).

[8] See Baiman (2010b, Appendix D) which also shows that these values solve (8.1), (8.2), (8.3), (8.4), and (8.5) in the text above.

$$\Delta Q_{PW} = -0.1516, \ \Delta QEW = 0.2766, \ \Delta Q_{PC} = 0.2494, \ \Delta Q_{EC} = -0.0494$$

Where E_{PC}, E_{EC}, E_{EW}, and E_{PW} are demand elasticity solutions for the: Portuguese consumption of imported English cloth, English consumption of domestic English cloth, English consumption of imported Porto wine, and Porto consumption of domestic Porto wine, respectively, ΔQ variables are as noted above, and E is the rate of overall price inflation in Portugal in international gold prices. This result indicates that Ricardo's model is *not* tenable, as a Portuguese price elasticity of demand for cloth of 2.7177 (which is the only elasticity solution possible for moderately elastic values of 1.5 for Portuguese and English demand for wine) is far outside of observed realistic own-price elasticities for cloth, a *necessity* that would be generally have an *inelastic* (<1) price elasticity of demand.

In other words, for a sustainable solution to Ricardo's parable, the derived Portuguese elasticity for cloth must be unrealistically large in order to generate sufficient cloth imports to offset English *additional demand* for (reduced price) Portuguese wine (ΔQ_{EW}). This *unrealistically large* Portuguese import elasticity for English cloth is necessary if full employment and balanced trade is to obtain in both countries because of the elastic nature of wine consumption (an observed empirical fact), captured in our $E_{EW} = 1.5$ and $E_{PW} = 1.5$ own-price elasticities for wine.

This numerical solution of Ricardo's model shows that the only way to sustainably capture *some* benefits from trade based on comparative advantage and specialization in Ricardo's example is to use public policy to *restrict* English imports of Portuguese wine, perhaps as a public health measure!

The example shows that (8.1), (8.2), (8.3), (8.4), and (8.5) can be satisfied under realistic demand assumptions only through *managed trade*. Only with some form of nonmarket policy intervention (e.g. a tariff or quota on Portuguese wine, a price-reducing subsidy for British cloth, or a manipulation of the exchange rate E) can *some* benefits of comparative advantage-based *partial* specialization and trade be realized. English consumers may be able to benefit by purchasing less-expensive Portuguese wine, but this import level will be dependent on Portuguese demand for English cloth. *Active trade management* will be necessary in order to keep English wine imports within the bounds of what England can pay for with its own exports.

Ironically, when carefully studied, even under a generous and expansive interpretation (that includes own-prices and cross-prices, Hume's species flow, perfect elasticity responses, and many countries and commodities), the Ricardian parable demonstrates the need for *managed trade* and the inability of a self-adjusting free trading system to produce mutually advantageous, *sustainable* trade that satisfies Ricardo's assumptions (8.1), (8.2), (8.3), (8.4), and (8.5), based on specialization and comparative advantage.

(b) As was noted, a second rejoinder might be that, in spite of its ubiquitous text book presence *as an argument for free trade*, Ricardo's parable should *not* be taken as *literal* proof of a sustainable free trade equilibrium. In this view, the main purpose of Ricardo's parable is simply to demonstrate the *potential* benefits of comparative advantage-based specialization and trade. Based on this reading, the free-market conclusion is a *rhetorical add-on* that is *not* the key implication of Ricardo's example. Though it is true that Ricardo claimed that these benefits would be an automatic result of *free trade*, the Ricardian parable is not a serious and, as the analysis above shows, *not* a valid argument in favor of *free* trade at all.

Rather, in this view a rigorous proof of the theoretical validity of free trade requires trade models with flexible NC production functions that allow for technological substitution between factors of production (labor and capital) in response to their relative prices. This *theoretically sound* proof of a free-trade equilibrium based on standard *neoclassical* (as opposed to the *classical* economic assumptions used by Ricardo) was demonstrated by James Meade (1952), and it is *this* proof that underlies basic NC international trade theorems such as the Hecksher-Ohlin, Stopler-Samuelson, and Rybczynski, theorems.

Proponents of this view might further acknowledge that the inflexibility and overdetermination of the classic Ricardian parable *is*, at least implicitly, acknowledged by the so-called *continuum of goods* "Ricardian" literature that postulates an infinite *set* of goods in countries with varying wages and production coefficients, a literature that is sometimes covered in advanced international trade courses (Dornbusch et al. 1977). In these models, partial specialization and trade based on comparative advantage becomes sustainable and not overdetermined because of real wage adjustments achieved through shifting production mixes that generate balanced trade and full employment. Thus *high* NC theory transforms the *classical Ricardian* model into an essentially NC *variable coefficient* and *flexible wage-level* model, and through this modified Ricardian model shows the viability of (a modified version of) comparative advantage-based *free trade*.

Needless to say, I found this argument, like the prior one, unconvincing. It seems to me that the continuum of goods "Ricardian" exercise is another demonstration of how far mainstream economists are willing to go to "prove" that the invisible hand of free trade *will* work when basic mathematical reasoning applied to the classical Ricardian model demonstrates that it *cannot* work. Unfortunately, these convoluted pro-market ideological exercises of NC *high theory* (adding variables, postulating magical leaps onto saddle paths, etc.) are a *pervasive part* of advanced mainstream theory, see for example chapter 6 and Taylor 2004. In fact, the Dornbusch et al. (1977) *continuum of goods* "Ricardian" exercise may be one of the less egregious examples, as the authors in this case make clear the utterly artificial and unrealistic assumption necessary to make this version of the "Ricardian" parable work—*that real wages among trading partners adjust to balanced trade.*

Such an approach would prescribe, for example, that in order to capture the benefits of comparative advantage and specialization in trade between the USA and China, real wages in the USA need to fall precipitously, and real wages in China need to rise until the labor cost differential between the two countries disappears. In the meantime (for how many decades? ever?), trade will be unbalanced with growing unemployment and inequality between labor and capital in the USA.

DID MEADE RESOLVE RICARDO'S INCONSISTENCY?

However (as proponents of view (b) above might acknowledge), the continuum of goods "Ricardian" model is a side show to the main approach to constructing a viable *NC free-trade* theory. The central proofs demonstrating a NC free-trade equilibrium based on variable coefficients, diminishing returns or increasing costs in production, and diminishing marginal utility in consumption, were developed by James Meade in 1952 and followed by the foundational NC trade theory, Hecksher-Ohlin, Stolper-Samuelson, and Rybczynski theorems. The latter all depend on Meade's proof of the existence of a stable and unique NC free-trade equilibrium and theorize about the characteristics of such an equilibrium. Though, the fact that these latter NC international trade theorems depend on Meade's existence proof is generally neglected in modern trade theory texts, where discussion is immediately directed toward the question of the characteristics of the equilibrium, reinforcing the implied assumption that the existence and uniqueness of a "free-trade" equilibrium is so obvious that it is not worthy of review.[9]

---

[9] See, for example, Findlay (1995).

In fact, Meade's elaborate proof that a NC free-trade equilibrium exists is far from trivial and, as it turns out, depends not only on the standard neoclassical diminishing returns and maximization of utility assumptions, or *mythology* as these are routinely violated in the long-run as has been repeatedly pointed out in earlier chapters, but also upon additional assumptions (not explicitly articulated in Meade's work or anywhere else, as far as I know) that require that gaps in factor cost ratios between trading partners are *limited* to *technologically comparable* levels.

Though Meade, who reportedly shared ideas with and was a close associate of Keynes, did not directly address this latter point, he did devote considerable effort in his work to investigating *nonincreasing cost* conditions, which shows that he, like Marshall, recognized that production characterized by increasing cost or diminishing marginal returns (that as discussed in this book has become a standard *axiom* in NC models ensuring convexity and unique and stable free-market equilibrium solutions) is only *one* of *many* technological possibilities. None the less, Meade's work, for which he received an Economics "Nobel" Prize in 1977, has entered the NC cannon in a *stripped-down* form as the core demonstration of the existence of a unique and stable free-trade equilibrium under standard NC *increasing cost* conditions. Moreover, as we have pointed out above, once this was established, both Meade's increasing cost demonstration and the fact that this represented only one part of a multipart monograph with equal space devoted to other non-NC production possibilities that were unlikely to converge to optimal free-trade equilibrium, was quickly buried, as focus shifted to the Hecksher-Ohlin, Stoper-Samuelson, and Rybczynski theorems characterizing the features of the unique equilibrium that was *assumed* to exist.

In any case, returning to our tactic of giving neoclassical trade theory as much theoretical weight as possible by accepting all of the standard assumptions and determining whether standard conclusions follow when all of the assumptions are satisfied, we will for the sake of argument accept this selective misreading of Meade and ask: "Does Meade resolve Ricardo's inconsistency?"

The answer is "yes," based on NC assumptions for trade between countries *with comparable production factor costs and capacity utilization*, and "no," otherwise. In less technical terms, Meade's theorem works under strict NC assumptions (requiring high and unrealistic rates of factor substitution[10]) *for trade between countries with comparable social and technological standards and comparable economic capacity* and does not work otherwise.

Though Meade's assumptions generate market-induced changes that reduce the problems of trade disequilibrium to productivity and capacity constraints, even in this highly abstract and unrealistic theoretical model, nonmarket *public policy driven measures* are necessary to foster economic development and raise overall social standards, as only these kinds of measures reduce disequilibrium trading or *unequal exchange* caused by *highly unequal* factor costs.[11] Ironically, the Canonical NC trade theorems alluded to above that are based on Meade's proof, focus attention on precisely the kind of trading to which the theorem *does not generally apply*, providing yet another demonstration that the ideological role of *free trade theory* trumps careful consideration of the actual scientific merit and truth value of the theory that is used to legitimate the ideology.

Though Meade's proof of the existence of a unique Neoclassical free-trade equilibrium is fairly involved, we will attempt a concise summary of it below so that the limits of its conclusions and, by extension, the narrow scope of its application via the other core NC trade theorems can be fully appreciated. For a complete treatment of this see Baiman (2017a).

Meade lists seven assumptions for his basic model (Meade 1952, p. 9):

1. Two countries.
2. Two exportable products
3. "Perfect competition with no external economies or diseconomies"
4. "Price flexibility of one kind or another [that] leads to full employment of resources" [brackets mine]
5. "That each country is made up of a set of citizens with identical tastes and factor endowments, so that the indifference map, while it may differ as between a citizen of A and a citizen of B, is the same for all the citizens in either of the two countries. In these conditions we can derive community-indifference curves directly from individual indifference curves;"

---

[10] See Marglin (1984) for an extensive discussion of this point that lower includes the development of variable coefficient Post-Keynesian models with more realistic lower factor substitution rates (MRTS < 1) that, as expected, generally respond to *quantity- signals* much more than the NC assumption of extensive free-market and free-trade *price-signal* response.

[11] For more on trade and *unequal exchange* see Baiman (2006, 2014).

6. Marginal utilities and productivities for both countries are diminishing

7. Both tastes and factor supplies [in each country] are fixed

These seven assumptions allow Meade to postulate convex *trade indifference curves* that trace out a set of export and import bundles which provide the same level of social-welfare (along the curves), based on convex *social indifference curves* and concave *production possibilities frontiers*, in each country.

With these assumptions, Meade attempts to overcome the problems with Ricardo's fixed production coefficient and consumer demand comparable advantage parable. Meade's construction, like all NC models, assumes highly sensitive price responses for both production factors (or relative usage of capital and labor that is strongly affected by relative cost), and for consumption (so that relative demand for each good in each country will be highly dependent on relative prices), which will, in turn, affect *the terms of trade* or relative price for each good in international trade. Using this model Meade shows, that subject to the restrictions noted above, supply and demand for imports and exports will interact with price sensitive supply and demand in both factor markets and product markets to generate an automatic, unique, and stable or self-correcting, free-trade equilibrium (Baiman 2017a).

This unique free-trade equilibrium satisfies all of the Adam Smith invisible hand outcomes that other SDM PCFM models, using similarly stringent highly elastic individual response rates and convexity assumptions, produce.[12] This free-trade equilibrium is unique and stable in the sense that any deviation from it will induce behavior by self-interested producing and consuming agents that will work to move the system back toward equilibrium. It also ensures, if the assumptions (above) hold, that each country (and each citizen) will be at its highest possible *social indifference curve* level.

In summary, Meade resolves the inconsistencies of Ricardo's *Classical* trade theory for a limited range of interenational trade situations, but only at the cost of introducing *another* set of equally unrealistic *Neoclassical* assumptions into trade theory.

---

[12] See Marglin (1984) op. cit.

INTERNATIONAL FREE TRADE *IS* A *GENERALLY* MATHEMATICALLY INFEASIBLE DOCTRINE

Interestingly, regardless of one's views on the arcane theoretical disputes above, it turns out that *any* possible *price-based* international trade model (Ricardian, NC, Marxist, etc.) will be *mathematically unstable* and, thus, *infeasible as an economic model* and *invalid as an international trade doctrine* (Baiman 2017).

Specifically, it turns out that even if "Marshall-Lerner conditions"[13] hold so that, in theory, trade is price responsive in trade-balancing directions, meaning that bilateral trade universally responds effectively and efficiently to exchange-rate fluctuations[14] and freely floating or (individual country) administered exchange rates react quickly and in a *normal* direction to trade imbalances, exchange-rate price signals *cannot* be expected to produce *globally* balanced international trade. Since trade that is not balanced, or moving into balance, is not sustainable, this finding shows that a global free-trade regime is *not* feasible and that the free-trade doctrine *is fundamentally invalid*.

Though beyond the scope of this book, the proof of this point in summary is based on two fairly simple steps.

First, standard equation and variable counting analysis (for *any* possible price-based international trade model) shows that, if there *is* a globally balanced exchange-rate solution to an international trading system, this solution must be *unique*.

Second, it can be shown, using examples of three or more countries, that any unique balanced trade solution to an *exchange-rate based* trading system will be (barring extraordinary coincidence) mathematically *unstable*. Again, this is well-known in practice but, as far as I know, has never been explicitly pointed out in a general formalized model. If the USA and EU, for example, have trade deficits with China, and the EU a trade surplus with the USA, appreciating the Euro(€) vis a vis the dollar($) will reduce Europe's surplus with the U.S. and appreciating the Yuan(¥) vis a vis the dollar will reduce China's surplus with the U.S.

---

[13] Lerner (1944).

[14] Taylor (2004, Chap. 7) shows that (contrary to the standard NC story) satisfaction of the Marshall-Lerner conditions will *not* in itself ensure "normal" trade flow response in the presence of large trade-induced output changes, as the derivation of these conditions assumes (like most of standard NC high theory) that "Say's Law" or full employment holds at all times.

However, if the €/$ exchange rate goes down faster than the ¥/$ exchange rate the €/¥ exchange rate will go down *increasing* China's surplus with Europe. Formally, it can be shown that there are no forces that ensure that bilateral trade-induced exchange-rate changes among three or more countries trading with each other, by any country will consistently move trade in all *three* countries toward greater balance; so the system as a whole is *unstable*. Since the solution (if it exists) is unstable, there is no mechanism driving the system toward the solution. It therefore, has no economic validity and is an economically infeasible solution. The principled theoretical issue addressed in this finding is whether "normal" exchange-rate response to trade deficits and surpluses can, under the most ideal assumptions, produce sustainable *globally* balanced trade. Since this is not possible, the notion of globally balanced and sustainable world trade based on *free trade*, or even individual country *managed exchange rates*, has no theoretical legitimacy Baiman (2017b).

BIBLIOGRAPHY

Baiman, R. (2006, Winter). Unequal exchange without a labor theory of prices: On the need for a global Marshall plan and a solidarity trading regime. *Review of Radical Political Economics, 38*(1), 71–89.

Baiman, R. (2010a, September). Toward a new political economy for the U.S. *Review of Political Economics, 42*(3), 362.

Baiman, R. (2010b). The infeasibility of free trade in classical theory: Ricardo's comparative advantage parable has no solution. *Review of Political Economy, 22*(3), 419–437.

Baiman, R. (2011b). *Eisenhower era income tax rates on the upper 10 % of families would immediately erase the federal deficit.* Chicago Political Economy Group Working Paper 2011–2. Retrieved May, from http://www.cpegonline.org/workingpapers/CPEGWP2011-2.pdf

Baiman, R. (2014). Unequal exchange and the Rentier economy. *Review of Radical Political Economy, 46*(4), 536–557.

Baiman, R. (2017a). The limits of free trade in neoclassical theory: From Hecksher-Ohlin to unequal exchange. Chapter in forthcoming *The Global Free Trade Error: The Infeasibility of Ricardo's Comparative Advantage Theory*, by R. Baiman. New York: Routledge.

Baiman, R. (2017b). Globally sustainable and balanced International TradeBased on Exchange-Rate adjustment is mathematically unstable and therefore economically infeasible. Chapter in forthcoming *The global free trade error. The infeasibility of Ricardo's comparative advantage theory*, by R. Baiman. New York: Routledge.

Blecker, R. (1999). *Taming global finance.* Washington, DC: Economic Policy Institute.

Carlsen, L. (2013, November 24). Under NAFTA Mexico suffered and the U.S. felt it's pain. *New York Times.*

Chang, H.-J. (2002). *Kicking away the ladder: Development strategy in historical perspective.* London: Anthem Press.

Dornbusch, R., Fischer, S., & Samuelson, P. (1977). Comparative advantage, trade, and payments in a Ricardian model with a continuum of goods. *American Economic Review, 67*(5), 823–839.

Eatwell, J., & Taylor, L. (2000). *Global finance at risk.* New York: New Press.

Findlay, R. (1995). *Factor proportions, trade, and growth.* Cambridge, MA: MIT Press.

Krugman, P. (1996). Ricardo's difficult idea. Published on MIT website: http://web.mit.edu/krugman/www/ricardo.htm. Downloaded 8/272015.

Krugman, P. (2012). Where the productivity went. *The New York Times.* Retrieved April 28, from http://krugman.blogs.nytimes.com/2012/04/28/where-the-productivity-went/

Krugman, P. (2015). TPP at the NABE. *The New York Times.* Retrieved March 11, from http://krugman.blogs.nytimes.com/2015/03/11/tpp-at-the-nabe/

Lerner, A. P. (1944). *The economics of control.* New York: Macmillan.

MacEwan, A. (1999). *Neo-Liberalism or democracy?* New York: Zed Books.

Marglin, S. (1984). *Growth, distribution, and prices.* Cambridge: Harvard University Press.

Pieper, U., & Taylor, L. (1998). *The revival of the liberal creed: The IMF, The World Bank, and Inequality in a Globalized Economy.* New York: CEPA Working Paper Series 1, WP 4. Retrieved January, from http://www.economicpolicyresearch.org/scepa/publications/workingpapers/1998/cepa0104.pdf

Ricardo, D. (1817). On the principles of political economy and taxation (3rd ed.). London: John Murray (1821).

Stiglitz, J. (2002). *Globalization and its discontents.* New York: W. W. Norton.

Stretton, H. (1999). *Economics: A new introduction.* New York: Pluto Press.

Taylor, L. (2004). *Reconstructing macroeconomics: Structuralist proposals and critiques of the mainstream.* Cambridge, MA: Harvard University Press.

Vernengo, M. (2000). What do undergrads really need to know about trade and finance. In R. Baiman, H. Boushey, & D. Saunders (Eds.), *Political economy and contemporary capitalism.* M.E. Sharpe: Armonk.

WTO. (2006). International trade statistics 2006. Washington, D.C, Retrieved 5/31/2016 from: https: //www.wto.org/english/res_e/statis_e/its2006_e/its2006_e.pdf.

PART III

The Morality of Radical Economics: Investigating the Value Neutral Aspect of Neoclassical Economics

As related in Chap. 1, my awareness of the destructive effects of NC economic thinking on public policy took a very practical turn early in my professional career. As a graduate student I had the good fortune to land a job as an economic forecaster for AT&T, a job that allowed me to earn a good living and have time at work, once I found a telecommunication-based topic, to complete my dissertation. I thus began my economics career as a telecommunications economist, an expertise that morphed into "utility regulation economist" shortly thereafter when I left AT&T and took a telecommunications policy job with the New York State Department of Economic Development. At the time (1993) leading NC microeconomists, including the dean of deregulation economists, Alfred Kahn, President Carter's former Civil Aeronautics Board Chair who had just presided over the deregulation of the airlines industry and completed his canonical text on regulation economics (Kahn 1993), were infusing the utility regulation and telecommunications policy community with appeals to *economic science* precepts of *efficient marginal-cost-based* utility pricing. Kahn, a self-described "good liberal Democrat,"[1] who taught at Cornell university, in fact sat, along with an assortment of NYC investment bankers, union reps, and consumer advocates, on the "Telecommunications Exchange" for New York State that I staffed. I was thus immediately thrust into the debate over telecom deregulation that Kahn and company were pushing for. Ironically, the New York State

---

[1] Thierer (2010).

Public Service Commission (PSC) had a reputation of being one of the toughest and most effective utility regulators in the country. I personally witnessed PSC staff's detailed interrogations of New York Telephone (NY Tel) executives using their own separate *shadow accounting* system, forcing the company to reallocate investment to underserved and unprofitable areas in the Bronx. PSC staff were in my experience committed progressives—lawyers and engineers who wanted to serve the public. Nonetheless, at the behest of their boss (a Gov. Mario Cuomo appointee and also, like the governor and most of the PSC staff, a political liberal) PSC staff pushed through *price cap telecommunications deregulation* that was, by any previous standard, inequitable and unfair to lower income consumers. They believed that somehow the market would, as Kahn's book emphasized, enhance overall *consumer welfare.*

In short, market led-pricing was in vogue and the PSC largely gave up its extensive utility monitoring operations. I remember trying to explain that Kahn's utility regulation *marginal cost equal price* rule was, like all of NC economic theory, based on *ignoring* equity. I was told to "go talk to economists" and that is what I did, by getting an academic job in Chicago and writing the papers that underlie much of Part III. Unfortunately, as I write (in 2015), the 2008 financial crash, our apparent collective inability to deal with catastrophic global warming, and the continued sway of neoliberal policy over much of the world, show that the destructive reach of NC economic ideology has not weakened much.

Is there any basis at all to NC *value neutrality* claims? Are *welfare* and *efficiency* separable as NC theory claims? Part III investigates this *value neutral aspect* of NC economics, reviews its actual policy impact, and contrasts it with the *values-based* foundations of radical and heterodox economics.

CHAPTER 9

Equity Cannot Be Separated from Efficiency

In its most sophisticated mathematical formulation that we are now going to address, NC values-opacity is rooted in the refined mathematical formalisms of General Equilibrium Theory considered to be at the core of the theoretical foundations of the neoclassical vision. The three "General Theorems of Welfare Economics" supposedly provide irrefutable proof of Adam Smith's vision that individual agent utility and profit maximization will optimize social welfare in a competitive market economy under assumptions that are thought to be an ideal approximation of how such an economy would work.

THE FUNDAMENTAL THEOREMS OF WELFARE ECONOMICS (FTWE)

Some of the key assumptions of the FTWE are that all individuals behave as rational individual maximizers of their own self-interest in a perfectly competitive market with: *constant returns to scale production, no market externalities* in production and consumption, *diminishing marginal utility*, and *diminishing returns* to capital and labor and numerous other highly idealized simplifying assumptions that are too technical for this presentation.[1]

---

[1] I make no attempt in the following discussion to provide a precisely accurate or comprehensive overview of advanced NC microeconomic theory. Rather, this is simply an effort to

© The Editor(s) (if applicable) and The Author(s) 2016
R.P. Baiman, *The Morality of Radical Economics*,
DOI 10.1057/978-1-137-45559-8_9

One of the key assumptions of this model, and a core assumption of NC economics, is that a technically neutral and value-free definition of *efficiency* and *welfare optimality* can be *strictly separated* from concerns about *equity* or fairness with regard to the distribution of goods and services.[2] It is upon this pillar that NC economics largely rests its claim of value neutrality. But this pillar, upon close inspection, turns out to be a mirage.

The basic premises of the FTWE are: First, *welfare* is defined as a purely ordinal measure of individual agent *utility* or *satisfaction* from either consumption of goods or services (for a human person), or profit (when the *agent* is a business)[3]. Second, this ordinal measure of individual welfare can be assigned to an individual agent but not compared across agents (when agents are persons). Third, welfare optimality is defined as a condition of "Pareto Optimality" whereby no agent can be made better off (get to a higher individual utility ranking, *indifference curve* or *isoqunat curve*[4]) without some other agent being made worse off (being forced to a lower curve). Fourth, in a perfectly competitive economy (where no agent has market power over any other agent) that is free of all *externalities* (extra-market affects like pollution or aesthetic improvement) and where all agents are trying to maximize their respective utility or output levels, all exchanges in both *product* (for goods and services used for consumption) and *factor* markets (where labor and capital to be used for production are bought and sold) will tend toward

$$price = marginal\,cost \qquad\qquad (9.1)$$

highlight some of its most essential elements. For a current canonical overview see the Mas-Colell et al. (1995) text which has got to be one of the most comprehensive modern exercises in institutional scholastics ever produced. See Dorman (2001) for a more detailed technical review of some of the recent problems that have arisen even in this highly idealized and purely theoretical neoclassical economic model.

[2] A discussion of the narrowness of this definition of fairness—as having to do exclusively with *distribution*—would lead us too far astray at this point. This issue is addressed below.

[3] The impact of these NC economic conceptualizations, defining businesses on a par with households as *agents* on *the corporate personhood* doctrine upheld by the US Supreme Court in the Citizens United decision is hard to miss (Hartmann 2010).

[4] *Indifference curves* map *consumer bundles* or *choice sets* of consumer goods that give the same satisfaction or *utility*. *Isoquants* map producer selections of *factor inputs* like labor and capital that (together) can produce the same output. If either consumers or producers could get to higher indifference or isoquant curves without going over their consumer or factor cost *budget constraints*, they would be able to get more utility or profit by being more *efficient* in their selections without reducing the utility or profit of any other consumer.

or exchange ratios that will *Pareto optimize* social welfare.[5]
Perfectly voluntary exchanges, that by definition (as they are voluntary) increase the utility or output of at least one agent without reducing them for any other agent, will produce an outcome that cannot be improved upon through a voluntary exchange as, if there were such a possibility, the exchange would have taken place. An *optimal* market system is *efficient* when it produces a state where there are no more *unrealized* voluntary exchange possibilities.

If this strikes you as a rather vacuous intellectual game, you may be right. But it serves a solid ideologically purpose. It projects an image of an economy as an ideal market that, through the operation of free and voluntary exchanges, arrives at a (very narrowly defined) *optimum* state that cannot be improved upon by free and voluntary exchanges.[6]

---

[5] Technically in a two consumer, two producer, two factor of production, two good model, in order for Pareto Optimality to hold, the ratio of the *marginal rates of substitution* between commodities for the two consumers, as determined by their demand preferences (i.e. the slopes of their respective indifference curves), must be equal to the ratio of the *marginal rates of product transformation*, as determined by the choice of technique along convex production isoquants that determine a *contract curve* of equalized *marginal rates of technical substitution*. All of these ratio equalities can be satisfied (subject to an arbitrary fixed constant multiplier or *numeraire*) if and only if price equals marginal costs in product markets and returns (wages and profits to labor and capital) equal marginal revenue products (of labor and capital) in factor markets (Mansfield 1994, Chap. 16–17.). This NC high theory persists in spite of the fact that a well-known critique of aggregate NC *production functions*, the "Cambridge Capital Controversy" conceded to by Paul Samuelson (1966), shows that the concept of *aggregate capital* cannot be defined until prices are determined, but according to NC theory prices cannot be derived without *marginal products of capital* that require defined measures of aggregate capital. See Nell (1980) for a good review of the related "re-switching debate" and Marglin (1984) for an alternative take on it.

[6] This is basic mainstream microeconomic theory as taught in college and high school textbooks and applied in *applications* of economics to law, utility regulation, and other fields and also in descriptions of what a market economy does in much of mainstream (especially in Conservative and Libertarian) political science. Interestingly, few current mainstream theoretical microeconomists continue to work on General Equilibrium Welfare Theory as numerous technical problems have arisen even under stringent NC assumptions (Dorman 2001). Many NC microeconomists now hold a *Game Theory* approach to microeconomics that (to my knowledge) does not even try to justify allocations as *welfare maximizing* in any sense (Gintis 2009). But regardless of what professional microeconomists work on or believe in, the precepts and conclusions of General Equilibrium Welfare Theory are hegemonic in textbooks, in political and legal discourse, and in the minds of public and *policy experts* (most of whom

PARETO "OPTIMALITY" AND "INITIAL ENDOWMENT" REDISTRIBUTION

At this point I expect that readers, especially those who have not been subjected to rigorous graduate training in economics, will immediately protest that this is no *optimality* at all!

What if Donald Trump is a *passive* owner of all of the businesses (so that they are still *perfectly competitive* with each other), who as owner of all of the capital and *renter* of all of the labor, receives all of the nonlabor income in the economy and spends it on an ever growing fleet of enormous yachts trying to outdo the current owners of the largest yachts in the world (Russian Billionaire Roman Abramovich, the President of the UAE, and the Vice President and Prime Minister of the UAE, respectively[7]), while due to the enormous free and voluntary competition for any kind of work in this economy (as, following NC assumptions, due to an abundance of labor relative to capital, the "marginal revenue product of labor" is very low), wages are extremely low and most people other than the Trump family are starving. How can this be construed as in any way *optimizing* social welfare?

To this, the committed NC has a ready answer etched into the brain circuitry of every student of mainstream economics. *Through a suitably chosen "initial allocation of endowments," any distributive outcome whatsoever can be arrived at through perfectly competitive markets under the conditions* delineated *above*. Presto! Let political scientists, sociologists, anthropologists, and other *soft* social scientists worry about values and distribution. Economists need not concern themselves with this. Instead they should worry about how to *optimize* markets, and thus maximize *efficiency*, without regard to initial (or final) distribution.[8]

---

are not professional economists) who have had any exposure to introductory economics courses, see for example (Mankiw 2008).

[7] https://en.wikipedia.org/wiki/List_of_motor_yachts_by_length. Accessed 8/14/2015.

[8] This is the conclusion of the "Second Fundamental Theorem of Welfare Economics." The first result alluded to above, that an ideal competitive market will generate a Pareto Optimal equilibrium is proved in the "First Fundamental Theorem of Welfare Economics." The Second Fundamental Theorem proves that a suitable allocation of initial endowments *can be found* that will produce *any* desired final market equilibrium allocation through an ideal competitive market process (Hahnel and Albert 1990). The third fundamental theorem proves that a free-market equilibrium *exists* for an idealized capitalist market economy similarly defined and under similar assumptions.

PRODUCTION IS *NOT* (EVEN HIGHLY IDEALIZED) CONSUMPTION

However, there is (at the very least) one major problem with all of this. This story has virtually nothing to do with real capitalist market economies—not even approximately under all of the presumed ideal assumptions and conditions. This is a *whole cloth* fabrication, or fairy tale—the precise choice of language probably depending on one's feelings about the ideological implications of this elaborate hoax. While no one disputes the need for simplifications and abstractions in modeling, for the resultant idealized construction to have any value it must have some relationship to the real phenomena being modeled—at least *at the limit* when approximate ideal assumptions are fulfilled. This idealization fails at the gate. It does not even get to first base.

There are numerous problems related to the unreality of simplifying assumptions—the *static* and *exogenous* nature of both the preference rankings and production choice sets, the assumptions of no externalities and no market power, the assumptions of no *indivisibilities* or *lumpiness* in production, of uniform smooth and continuous *convexity* of indifference curves and isoquants requiring diminishing returns, and of eventual rising marginal and average cost curves,[9] to name a few problems that have been highlighted by numerous critics (Hahnel and Albert 1990). Some of these can perhaps be considered useful PCFM simplifying assumptions, and others that are perhaps derivatives of these, but the core underlying ideological gambit behind this model is an attempt to shoehorn a capitalist *production system* into an idealized competitive voluntary equal-exchange barter system or *consumer market*.[10]

---

[9] As has been extensively discussed in Chap. 5, Sraffa's (1926) critique of the assumption that all production must exhibit long-run *diminishing returns*, which cites Alfred Marshall's (a founder of NC economics) more realistic analysis of production as possibly exhibiting increasing, constant, or diminishing returns, is well known. As substantial *fixed costs* generate *increasing returns* to scale, the critique in the text below in many ways follows this original Sraffian critique.

[10] This is of course a key part of the Marxist critique of capitalism as has been discussed in earlier chapters. Interestingly, the *transformation problem* of *orthodox* Marxist economics, somewhat analogously, creates irresolvable complications in deriving a practical prices-to-labor-value algorithm because of the heterogeneity of capital intensity in production, which mainstream economists readily acknowledge (Samuelson 1971). So both major forms of political economic ideology flounder on a plausible modeling of production but Marx's insights into the workings of capitalism as a class-based system of production and exploitation have been more *realistically*

The problem is that *production*, even under the most ideal competitive conditions does not fulfill the price equals marginal cost condition—not even remotely or approximately, because the real cost of *producing* something (just about anything) as opposed to *exchanging* something is not its *marginal*, or incremental cost, but rather the *total* cost of production that includes overhead or *fixed* costs such as plant, equipment, research and development, and *setup* costs that need to be paid for through the sale of the product. Businesses that are forced to price at marginal costs are typically facing *ruinous competition* and are not long for this world as their plant and equipment cannot be replenished even if it has been fully paid for in its current state.

Needless to say this is not a brilliant insight but rather an elementary fact of production discussed in every introductory microeconomics textbook. How can the enormous NC theoretical edifice be built on such a patently false premise? A claim that this is a *simplification* or *abstraction* makes no sense, as this assumption almost *never* holds in reality. This is just pure *make believe* mythology that should not be treated seriously—and in fact *is not* by most practicing NC economists—a point we discuss below.

PRODUCER PRICES ARE ALMOST ALWAYS *GREATER* THAN MARGINAL COST AND GENERALLY REGRESSIVE

In almost every case of real production:

$$\text{Price} > \text{marginal cost} \qquad (9.2)^{11}$$

Simply put, sales revenue and therefore prices must be high enough to cover *fixed costs* that have a marginal cost of zero as they do not increase as output increases, as well as *variable*, incremental, or marginal, costs of production. Prices must therefore almost always (except when fixed costs are zero or marginals costs increase very rapidly see below) be higher than marginal costs. And this deviation is not random, but systemic. Profit maximization implies that in the case of firms that produce more than one product, or that can sell the same product in relatively separable markets (perhaps under different brand names), almost all firms will attempt to take advantage of

(without unfounded abstractions and simplifications) modeled through "neo-Marxist" surplus theory constructions, see for example (Baiman 2006; Roemer 1988; Marglin 1984). As is shown below, similar efforts to construct a more realistic mainstream economic theoretical foundation end up as efforts to ideologically justify *immoral* outcomes.

[11] This is the case even if costs are defined to include so-called "normal profits" as they are in standard NC microeconomics.

relatively *price inelastic* consumers *or consumers that are less price sensitive* by raising their price markup above marginal cost higher for these consumers relative to the markup for products sold to *more price elastic* or price sensitive consumers.[12] For a monopoly firm, the *profit-maximizing* formula for this kind of *discriminatory* price setting is well known:

$$\frac{p_i - mc_i}{p_i} = \frac{1}{E_i} \qquad (9.3)$$

where p_i, mc_i, and E_i (all assumed positive) are the price, marginal cost, and price elasticity, respectively, for product i for a monopoly firm that produces multiple products (Chiang 1984, p. 365–9). The price over marginal-cost markup $\left(\frac{p_i - mc_i}{p_i} \right)$ will thus be *inversely* related to the price elasticity $\left(\text{as it is equal to } \frac{1}{E_i} \right)$. The higher the (positive) price elasticity E_i, which means that consumers are *more elastic* or *more price sensitive*, the lower the markup over marginal-cost.

Of course in *competitive* markets there will be constraints on the ability of firms to raise their markups but since they *have* to be able to cover their overhead costs which do not change as output increases and are therefore not included in marginal costs, no matter how competitive the sector prices, as noted above, will be higher than marginal costs and as all firms are biased toward raising them more for price inelastic products and less for price elastic products this systemic pattern will on average prevail in the overall economy.[13]

---

[12] The (positive) "Price Elasticity of Demand" is defined as the percentage increase in quantity demanded for every 1% decline in price, at a given price (P_i in text below).

[13] The only possible theoretical exception would be a *price-taking* firm with marginal costs that rise fast enough so that they are above average costs, and overhead costs that are low enough in normal production ranges such that the firm's producer surplus is adequate to fully cover its overhead (i.e. where a PCFM SDM model exists and works). As this is highly unlikely and occurs (if at all) only in a very small number of exceptional cases, we ignore it. In any case, the situation described in the text is actually a stronger than necessary claim for the refutation of the FTWE. As long as markups over marginal cost *are not uniform* (in their proportions) across products, the equal exchange premise of the General Theorems is violated and their outcome is vitiated. But there is no reason for these markups to be uniform and (9.3) suggests that these markups will be systemically biased as described, in the absence of highly unlikely countervailing conditions like inelastic markets being always more competitive than elastic markets and by just the right amount to perfectly offset (9.3).

Moreover, lower income consumers will spend a higher share of their income on *necessities* over which they have little or no *exit*, or *no-purchasing*, choice (e.g. public transportation, food, housing, heat, etc.) and therefore little price sensitivity (low elasticity), compared to higher income consumers who will purchase a larger share of *luxuries* (yachts, second homes, jewelry, fancy clothes, fine wine, etc.), which are more likely to be discretionary *purchases of choice* of goods and services with high price sensitivity (higher elasticity). Therefore, based on (9.3), goods for lower income consumers will have higher proportional markups over marginal cost, relative to competitive pressures, than goods for higher income consumers. Lower-income consumers will therefore, on average, pay more relative to marginal cost, than higher-income consumers.[14]

THE FTWE ARE FUNDAMENTALLY INVALID

So what happens if our erstwhile NC economist sets initial endowments based on the *Fundamental Welfare Theorems* (let us say for argument's sake) to *equalize* final distribution of resources? No matter all the other idealized assumptions, production pricing will immediately act to contravene this as consumers who happen to have a higher preference for low-elasticity products will lose income relative to consumers with a disproportionate preference for high-elasticity products. This in turn will cause income inequality to increase, as the low-income (low elasticity preference) consumers now devote their remaining income disproportionately to generally lower elasticity necessities and conversely for the preferences of high-elasticity consumers. Inequality in resource distribution will thus snow ball through *cumulative causation* undermining any hope of reaching an equalized final distribution of resources.[15]

The Fundamental Theorems in other words fundamentally fail—there is no, even approximate idealized competitive market economy, in which they can succeed. Pareto *efficient* voluntary market-driven discriminatory pricing mechanisms like (9.3) will undermine efforts to obtain the chosen

---

[14] Except, as noted in the previous footnote, under very unlikely circumstances reflecting highly unusual and specific conditions that would certainly be inadequate to support the *general* conclusions of the Fundamental Theorems.

[15] More generally, any deviation from a uniformly proportionate mark-up will cause the Fundamental Theorems to fail as then price will no longer correlate with marginal cost-see prior footnes.

equitable resource allocation based on initial endowment choices. The ideal *efficient* competitive markets that NC economics promotes as a key goal of neutral technocratic *amoral* economic *science* will impact *equity*. Even *Pareto efficiency* cannot therefore be a stand alone economic objective that can be divorced from moral or *equity* considerations.

BIBLIOGRAPHY

Baiman, R. (2006, Winter). Unequal exchange without a labor theory of prices: On the need for a global Marshall plan and a solidarity trading regime. *Review of Radical Political Economics, 38*(1), 71–89.

Chiang, A. C. (1984). *Fundamental methods of mathematical economics* (3rd ed.,). New York: McGraw Hill.

Dorman, P. (2001). Waiting for the echo: The revolution in general equilibrium theory and the paralysis in introductory economics. *Review of Radical Political Economics, 33*(1).

Gintis, H. (2009). *Game theory evolving: A problem centered introduction to modeling strategic interaction.* Princeton University Press.

Hahnel, R., & Albert, M. (1990). *Quiet revolution in welfare economics.* Princeton: Princeton University Press.

Hartmann, T. (2010). *Unequal protection: How corporations became "people" and how you can fight back* (2nd ed.,). San Francisco, CA: Berrett-Koehler Publisher.

Mankiw, N.G. (2008) *Principles of Microeconomics* (5th ed.). New York: Worth Publishers.

Mansfield, E. (1994). *Microeconomics: Theory and applications* (8th ed.). New York: W.W. Norton and Co..

Marglin, S. (1984). *Growth, distribution, and prices.* Cambridge: Harvard University Press.

Mas-Colell, Andreu, Michael D. Whinston, and Jerry R. Green. (1995). *Microeconomic Theory.* Oxford University Press.

Nell, E. J. (Ed.) (1980). *Growth, profits, and property: Essays in the revival of political economy.* Cambridge University Press.

Roemer, J. E. (1988). *Free to lose: An introduction to Marxist philosophy.* Cambridge: Harvard University Press.

Samuelson, P. (1966). A summing up. *The Quarterly Journal of Economics, 80*(4), 568–583.

Samuelson, P. (1971). Understanding the Marxian Notion of exploitation: A summary of the so-called transformation problem between Marxian values and competitive prices. *Journal of Economic Literature, 9*(2), 399–431.

Sraffa, P. (1926). The law of returns under competitive conditions. *Economic Journal, 36,* 535–550.

CHAPTER 10

From Amoral High Theory to Immoral Applied Theory

Surprisingly, given the substantial resources in time and energy that mainstream economics departments have historically required grad students to devote to general theorems of welfare economics (GTWE) *high theory* scholastics the vast majority of economists—basically all those who do not explicitly work on *General Equilibrium Welfare Theory*, pretty much ignore the theory discussed in Chap. 9 as *window dressing*. The main purpose of the GTWE appears to be to make mainstream economics look more like a natural science and serve as a useful gate keeper to select students who, after spending considerable time and energy plowing through the advanced mathematics necessary to derive these theorems, are more likely to become attached to their underlying ideological message.[1] Why else would one be required to spend so much time and effort on this?

The neoplatonic ideological message being implicitly conveyed is that, as these theorems are derived from dazzlingly fancy (for most economics students) mathematics, they must reflect some *deep* underlying *natural economic reality* common to all societies throughout history—a *timeless* and *apolitical* vision of how *normal* economies are supposed to work.

[1] In fact, though the fundamentals of General Equilibrium Welfare Theory are taught as bedrock economic principles in introductory and intermediate economics, public policy, law, political science, and other mainstream social science textbooks; most current theoretical NC microeconomists ignore General Equilibrium Welfare Theory, focusing instead on game theory applications that eschew any concern for "general welfare"—see footnote 6 in chapter 9.

© The Editor(s) (if applicable) and The Author(s) 2016
R.P. Baiman, *The Morality of Radical Economics*,
DOI 10.1057/978-1-137-45559-8_10

And even if, as may often be the case these days, GTWE theorems are *not* covered in detail even at the advanced graduate level, their *conclusions* that free markets are, under appropriate ideal conditions, *optimal* are repeated incessantly in NC textbooks at all levels and widely adhered to by even the most politically progressive NC economics.[2]

SOCIAL WELFARE OPTIMIZATION IN INTRODUCTORY NC ECONOMICS

Though useful and successful as a tool of ideological indoctrination, the GTWE theorems are *useless* for any kind of practical policy analysis as their assumptions never hold in any real world economic context. They, therefore, cannot justify, in any concrete and practical sense, the single minded focus on efficiency and competitive market exchange that characterizes NC economic "science." For this, a more practical and realistic *second best* theory is necessary.

This second more practical and more widely disseminated layer of the NC economics edifice begins, as every student of introductory economics knows, by defining consumer welfare as *consumer surplus* (CS), producer welfare as *producer surplus* (PS), and overall *social welfare* as the *sum* of CS and PS over individuals and businesses; where CS is defined as the area between the demand curve and the horizontal equilibrium price line, and PS is the area below the price line and above the producer's average total cost curve, as shown in Fig. 10.1 below.[3]

Both CS and PS are measured in dollars. Needless to say, this *work around* washes away the GTWE *noncomparability* assumptions from which the claim of amoral *separability* of equity and efficiency is derived. In this *second best* applied welfare economic world, not only can individual gains and losses be compared and added up (in terms of $ utils) but consumer welfare, measured as the sum of CS in dollars, can be, and is, weighted *equally* with the sum of profits or PS. This revisionist adaptation is not surprising as the high theory model of noncomparable *ordinal* utility is completely unworkable in practice where economic policies invariably involve *cost benefit analysis* or *tradeoffs*

---

[2] Consider for example Krugman's discussion of a carbon tax that, without a second thought, characterizes other noncarbon measures to address global warming as "*second best*" solutions (Krugman 2014).

[3] See also any standard introductory microeconomic text, for example Mankiw (2008), for further explanation.

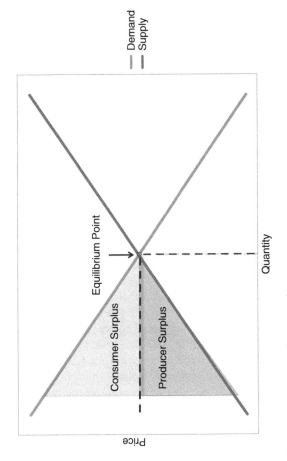

Fig. 10.1 SDM consumer and producer surplus

between winners and losers rather than gains for all. Real policy decisions almost always involve *costs* for which the Pareto optimality *gains for all* criteria is quite useless.

As discussed in Chap. 5, the sum of the areas of the CS and PS triangles is maximized in a simple idealized supply demand model (SDM) graph for a PCFM at the equilibrium price. As shown again in Fig. 5.6, in the SDM any *nonequilibrium* price P_{ne} will result in *deadweight loss* of CS plus PS relative to the PCFM SDM equilibrium price.

Thus, in the NC SDM view any form of *forced deviation* from the perfect market-equilibrium price through a mandated price floor, ceiling, or tax will result in *deadweight loss* or net loss of CS + PS (Mankiw 2008). In contrast, as explained in Chap. 5, in the demand and cost model (DCM), *political and institutional factors* are fundamental determinants of *static deadweight loss* that will result from any above-cost reallocation of CS to PS, see Fig. 5.12.

Advanced "Second Best" Applied NC Microeconomics

However, the simple SDM graphical exercise above which appears to support an *applied* welfare economics facsimile of the First Fundamental Theorem is more of a didactic exercise for introductory economics indoctrination purposes than a serious theory. For this to work as a justification of the *price equal marginal-cost* foundational equality of welfare economics (and this is how it is used in introductory texts—see Mankiw (2008)), it, like the high theory that it is supposed to represent, must *assume* that *perfectly competitive* firms price at marginal cost.[4] And this, as we have pointed out above, is a nonsensical assumption, even in the ad hoc applied welfare economics world of comparable dollar-valued CS and PS utils and, especially if the SDM model is, as has been pointed out in earlier chapters, fundamentally invalid and needs to be replaced by the DCM. Second best theory is the fall back theory of applied NC microeconomics precisely because it recognizes that marginal costs are *not*, in the real economy, equal to prices, so that a social welfare, or CS and PS, maximizing policy rule *other than* price equals marginal costs is practically necessary.

---

[4] This is necessary so that the assumption of *diminishing returns* or *increasing marginal costs* will generate an upward sloping supply curve. If, as the DCM shows, the supply curve does not exist, neither will the definitive market equilibrium point.

Applied NC microeconomics, or so-called second best theory attempts to do this by relying on the *Ramsey pricing theorem*. The claim is that, as Ramsey pricing theorem proves that market pricing maximizes the sum of equally weighed CS and PS, where CS is summed and equally weighted over households, market pricing, or "near marginal cost pricing," maximizes social welfare.[5]

The Ramsey pricing theorem shows that for any fixed level of PS, CS will be maximized when a firm pays for its overhead and other *nonmarginal* costs by raising price above marginal costs for its *i* products (or *i* separable markets) so that, following the notation of (9.3) in Chap. 9, with 0 < k < 1 (Ramsey 1927):

$$\frac{p_i - mc_i}{p_i} = k\frac{1}{E_i} \qquad (10.1)$$

If k is set to 1, it can be seen that (10.1) will be equivalent to (9.3). Voila! The profit-maximizing behavior described in (9.3) appears to maximize CS. Thus, *second best* theory (unlike the *first best* fundamental theorems) appears compatible with common sense, that is, the fact that prices are *above marginal cost* and that most firms are multiproduct (if not in actual products, at least in customized pricing and *brand differentiation* for different markets, e.g. airline ticket prices) producers with prices that will, depending on their market power, tend toward *inverse elasticity*, above marginal cost, pricing along the lines of (9.3) and (10.1).

Although it is not, like the high GTWE theory discussed in Chap. 9, based on the unrealistic and inapplicable assumptions of perfect competition, the Ramsey theorem is based on most of the standard assumptions of introductory NC microeconomic analysis with the sole (and critical) exclusion of the assumptions necessary in introductory NC microeconomics, making price equal to marginal cost.[6] Otherwise, in second best *applied* NC microeconomics, the terms social welfare and aggregate welfare, as in introductory NC Microeconomics, refer to *static* welfare measured

---

[5] Needless to say, this arbitrary weighting of CS and PS does not address issues of either *dynamic* efficiency over time, as opposed to purely *static* efficiency at one point in time, or the question of how and who should determine the proper level of investment and benefit from it, see later discussion.

[6] These include the assumptions of a PCFM composed of *price taking* firms that price at marginal cost along a rising, and above average-cost, marginal-cost curve.

in *cardinal utilitarian* terms as the unweighted dollar sums of CS and PS. Market shares, DCs, cost curves, products, and consumer preferences are all assumed fixed. Dynamic issues, such as technological change, and the proper level, allocation, and control of investment, as well as the distribution of benefits from it, are set aside. So are incentive issues and other externalities, which are central in other critical analyses.

Thus, some of the most essential features of markets are ignored, even as the approach is applied to real world policy decisions. This form of analysis is, therefore, strictly valid only for the short-term allocation of consumer goods and services with insignificant externalities. However, this is, nevertheless, an important allocation theory that deserves serious consideration by radical as well as NC economists as it is widely used by practitioners, and appears to offer fallback *second-best* support for the central ideological tenant of NC economics that *perfectly competitive* market pricing is welfare optimizing.

As has been noted above, the Ramsey, or *inverse-elasticity* pricing formula, stipulates that social efficiency is maximized when producers of multiple products, with below average-cost marginal costs (i.e. basically all producers) raise prices relatively higher above marginal cost for lower-elasticity products than for higher elasticity products. According to the Ramsey pricing Rule, social welfare will be maximized if such producers set the prices p_i of their products i so that[7]:

$$\frac{p_i - mc_i}{p_i} = k\frac{1}{E_i}$$

$$C(Q_1,...,Q_n) - \sum_i p_i Q_i = \delta_0 \qquad (10.2)$$

where δ_0 is a negative constant that fixes the overall level of positive profit for the firm, and $C(Q_1,...,Q_n)$ is a cost function for products Q_i (Baumol

---

[7] Another, closely related sales tax version of the Ramsey pricing *inverse-elasticity rule* stipulates that consumer welfare is maximized when *sales taxes* on different goods obey the inverse-elasticity rule so that, for every good, when cross-tax effects are negligible $t_i p_i = k/E_i$, where t_i is the sales tax on good i, p_i is the price of good i, k is a constant, and E_i is the own-price elasticity of demand of good; (Varian 1992, p. 412). Also, the simple own-price Ramsey pricing rule of (10.2) is strictly applicable only when "cross-price" effects are small or compensating. Baiman (2001) Appendix B derives a generalized "Progressive Ramsey pricing rule" for cases when cross-price effects are non-neglible or compensating that is analogous to the own-price progressive Ramsey Pricing Rule (10.6) discussed in this chapter.

1977, p. 516; Atkinson and Stiglitz 1980, p. 372). This formula can also be applied to producers of single commodities whose markets can be segmented by income or wealth by labeling products consumed in different markets as different products.

When elasticities are higher price increases will cause larger declines in consumer demand. Therefore, when trying to raise profits through price increases, producers will seek to limit reductions in demand by targeting higher relative price increases to lower-elasticity markets (see (9.3) above). *Since this standard profit-maximizing market-pricing strategy appears to generally follow the Ramsey inverse-elasticity pricing rule, as has been noted the Ramsey theorem seems to suggest that market-driven pricing is socially optimal even in imperfect oligopolistic markets.*

NC Second Best Theory Leads to Immoral Outcomes

As applied second best theory jettisons all pretense of purely ordinal non-comparable utility measures and, in fact, is most often used as a tool for *cost-benefit* economic impact analysis that purports to directly compare and assess private and public benefits and costs among businesses and households, it *cannot* be considered to be, in the GTWE sense, *amoral* or *strictly separable from equity or value judgments regarding economic impacts.* This in itself might be regarded as progress toward realism and practicality were it not for the perverse way in which second best theory evaluates equity.

A reasonable question at this point might be: "OK, we can understand why this applied welfare approach is no longer *amoral* but why is it necessarily *immoral?*" And the answer to this question would be that, second best theory is immoral because the solution that it offers in response to the critique discussed above (that almost no business can price at *marginal cost*) is immoral.

This is because lower-elasticity commodities are more likely to be *necessities* and have a larger share of lower income consumers. Conversely, higher-elasticity commodities are more likely to be discretionary *luxury* goods and have a larger share of higher income consumers. Raising prices more for lower elasticity than for higher-elasticity commodities and market segments will thus generally result in *regressive* pricing, which *increases prices over costs more for lower-income consumers than for higher-income consumers.* Progressive pricing, like progressive taxes, would do just the opposite. Since the Ramsey theorem supports this kind of generally regressive, market-pricing strategy that penalizes lower-income consumers who can least afford higher price increases, the most, and higher-income consumers who can most easily afford price increases, the least, it is a *generally perversely inequitable* pricing formula.[8]

Even if we disregard the equity question of whose welfare is being increased and whose is being reduced, the notion that Ramsey pricing increases aggregate social welfare appears counterintuitive. This is because regressive pricing, which includes higher price increases for lower-elasticity consumers and lower price increases for higher-elasticity consumers, would appear to reduce aggregate CS more than, for example, progressive price changes that did the opposite. If consumer welfare is identified with CS, as can be seen in Fig. 10.2 below, equivalent relative price increases will reduce CS more in a lower-elasticity market than in a higher-elasticity market.[9]

Ramsey pricing thus appears to coincide with the standard monopolistic *price discrimination* rule, stipulating that monopolistic multiproduct producers with above average-cost DCs and above marginal-cost average-cost curves can maximize profit by setting marginal cost equal to marginal revenue for each product. Under a set of assumptions equivalent to those used to derive (10.2), this implies that, for every product i (Chiang 1984, p. 356–359):

$$p_i(1 - \frac{1}{E_i}) = mc_i \qquad (10.3)$$

This confirms the fact that by exploiting the more restricted options or preferences of lower-elasticity consumers, producers can increase profit, and since in a static world increased profit can only come at the cost of reduced CS, it suggests that higher relative prices for lower-elasticity mar-

---

[8] Strictly speaking Ramsey pricing will be *regressive* and social pricing *progressive* only if own-price elasticities of demand are inversely correlated with income-wealth. As is explained in the text, this will often (but not always) be the case. However, the central point of this chapter, that equity must be explicitly taken into consideration in welfare evaluation and pricing, will be unaffected by the progressive or regressive *net* result of its incorporation.

[9] Figures 10.2 and 10.3 below, are for illustrative purposes only, as they refer to Demand Curves (DCs) for two products at similar prices and quantities demanded. Elasticities for DCs at different quantities and prices will not generally relate to each other in this way. However, since targeting lower-elasticity markets for higher relative price increases will lead to more (absolute) dollar valued CS loss than *progressive* or *flat* pricing, Ramsey pricing will generally result in aggregate CS, or welfare, loss, regardless of the slopes of the DCs in the region of the price increases.

kets will reduce rather than increase CS relative to more progressive pricing strategies. But the Ramsey pricing rule is a simple variant of the price discrimination formula, as a simple algebraic manipulation of (10.3) gives:

$$\frac{p_i - mc_i}{p_i} = \frac{1}{E_i} \qquad (10.4)$$

or, from (10.2), Ramsey pricing with k = 1. *The difference between unconstrained profit maximization and Ramsey pricing, therefore, is simply that, under Ramsey pricing, the revenue constraint prevents the firm from raising the overall average of its prices to profit-maximizing levels,* for non-monopoly, non-perfectly competitive, firms 0 < k < 1. Otherwise these formulas are exactly the same. The ratios between relative, above marginal cost, price increases for different products in (10.2) and (10.4) are identical. Standard monopolistic profit-maximization pricing strategy thus appears to maximize consumer welfare.

Ramsey Pricing Is Directly Linked to Immoral NC Economic Policy

The irony of the Ramsey pricing result has not gone unnoticed by NC economists. For example, in their classic Ramsey pricing article Baumol and Bradford note that:

This [Ramsey pricing] result is surely not immediately acceptable through intuition. It strikes us as curious, if for no other reason, because it seems to say that ordinary price discrimination might well set relative prices at least roughly in the manner required for maximal social welfare in the presence of a profit constraint. (Baumol and Bradford 1970, p. 267)

And then they offer the following confusing nonexplanation (Baumol and Bradford 1970, p. 267):

Since the objective of the [Ramsey pricing and profit maximizing pricing] can be described as the determination of the optimally discriminating set of prices needed to obtain the required profit, some degree of resemblance is perhaps to be expected. The case studied here is, thus, in a sense the obverse of the problem of profit maximizing price discrimination, and while the two solutions bear some qualitative resemblance, it can be shown that they may in fact differ substantially in quantity. [Brackets mine]

The problem with this explanation is that formulas (10.4) and (10.1) have more than a "qualitative resemblance"; they are mathematically *identical* up to a constant, and this constant is negligible from an economic point of view as only perfect monopolists will follow (10.4) precisely. All other price discriminating firms will practice *inverse-elasticity* pricing patterned on (10.1) up to a constant, so that the difference between (10.4) and (10.1) for most firms for practical purposes is inconsequential.

Moreover, when this theory really counts in terms of supporting policy decisions, theoretical subtleties regarding *qualitative* versus *quantitative* differences disappear, as, for example, in an Edison Institute funded white paper by three of the most prominent applied microeconomists of the time, Baumol, Joskow, and Kahn, that was submitted to the Federal Energy Regulatory Commission (FERC) in support of California's 1996 electricity deregulation. This was a deregulation disaster that led to skyrocketing rates and widespread blackouts and rationing that ultimately required a state bailout of the deregulated utilities even as their unregulated holding companies, including Enron, made off with billions (Vogel, 2000). The Elison Institute paper supported deregulation by positing in no uncertain terms an *equivalency* between *Ramsey pricing* for high fixed-cost oligopolistic markets and *marginal-cost pricing* for perfectly competitive markets (Baumol et al. 1994, p. 19, note 7)[10]:

> Economists have derived a formula for the (second best) efficient prices in these [average costs above marginal costs] circumstances; these are referred to as *Ramsey prices* (after their discoverer).
>
> Henceforth, *whenever we refer to prices set at marginal costs in this paper, we will mean either what the term literally implies, or, instead, we will be referring to Ramsey prices*, whatever is appropriate under the circumstances in question at that point in the discussion. [*italics* and brackets mine]

Baumol, Joskow, and Kahn again employ this Ramsey pricing-based marginal-cost pricing principle in a later section of this white paper subtitled paper on "allocative efficiency," where they argue that, in contrast to regulated utility-pricing regimes, competitive markets will exert pressure to achieve the

---

[10] The following discussion follows a more comprehensive presentation in Baiman (2001) p. 210–212.

afore mentioned "second-best" efficiencies of inverse-elasticity Ramsey-like pricing—although they (as noted in the cited footnote above) substitute the more palatable term "marginal-cost" pricing instead of the more accurate "Ramsey pricing" (Baumol et al. 1994, p. 23):

> Moreover, regulatory commissions have traditionally imposed price structures that grossly increased allocative inefficiencies. For example, if fixed costs (e.g. capital charges) were recovered from customers via a lump sum charge and variable or short run marginal (e.g. fuel) costs recovered in usage sensitive charges, *or if mark-ups or mark-downs from marginal costs were varied by category of customers roughly in inverse proportion to the elasticity of their demands, inefficient under-use or over-use of electricity would be reduced.* The adoption of such technically more efficient price structures has, however, been largely obstructed by the severe political difficulties they would raise, because they would essentially involve increased electric bills for the smallest, least mobile, customers; instead and for the same reason, regulators have often done the opposite imposing rate structures that subsidize the least elastic (e.g. residential) demand by the more-elastic (e.g. industrial) customers, *in direct violation of the dictates of allocative efficiency.*
>
> A more competitive order will exert pressures to minimize these distortions. It will tend to drive <u>average</u> prices closer to the long-run marginal cost of production; and by driving the prices currently paid by overcharged customers closer to the *marginal cost* of serving them, it will tend to undermine the cross-subsidizations (*italics mine*).

And the rest is history. Needless to say, I do not believe that Baumol, Bradford, Joskow, Kahn, or any other NC economists were assessed any portion of the cost of damages of this fiasco, nor have the official NC doctrines in leading economics journals and textbooks that support it been (to my knowledge) modified in any way, though the governor of California at the time (Democrat Gray Davis) lost his job in large part because of it (Lusvardi 2011).

NC "EQUITY NEUTRAL" ASSUMPTIONS CAUSE SECOND BEST THEORY'S IMMORAL OUTCOMES

Closer inspection reveals that the counterintuitive, and generally regressive, Ramsey pricing result is a direct consequence of the theoretically unjustifiable unweighted aggregation method used to derive it. Analysis of the different components of the standard Ramsey pricing maximand reveals that the driving factor behind this *welfare maximization subject to a profit constraint* exercise is *constrained profit loss minimization relative to welfare gain across market segments* (Baiman 2001). For any constant level of *profit*, when the absolute (dollar value) of CS for different segments is equally weighted, Ramsey pricing will maximize overall CS because the *extra CS loss* for lower-elasticity segments will be more than *offset* by the *reduction in profit loss or profit gain*, which comes from maintaining higher prices in these segments relative to higher-elasticity segments.

In other words, since CS is aggregated on a dollar-for-dollar basis, it becomes directly comparable to profit, which is aggregated in the same way. Flat aggregation of CS thus leads to a pricing rule that minimizes profit loss through the gouging of less elastic markets, even though this results in greater CS loss for these consumers, who will generally be the most hurt by these price increases. This is possible because, with a flat CS weighting scheme, the reduction in profit loss in lower-elasticity markets compared to higher-elasticity markets more than compensates for the increased CS loss by low-elasticity consumers; see Fig. 10.3 below.

The real issue is the CS loss. Referring to Fig. 10.3, the profit *loss penalty* relative to CS gain when prices are *reduced* is almost equal for low-elasticity consumers, but for high-elasticity consumers the profit loss *penalty* roughly half of CS gain. Therefore, to get the most CS gain with the least sacrifice of *fixed* profit, it is better to keep prices low in high-elasticity markets.

This explains the *Ramsey pricing paradox*. When CS is aggregated on a dollar-for-dollar basis just like profit, the profit constrained CS maximization behind the Ramsey pricing result, becomes profit loss minimization relative to CS gain, which regressively exploits the vulnerability of consumers with fewer options or preferences in exactly the same way that oligopolistic profit maximization does.

When firms face a profit constraint, and the inequitable effect of raising prices the most for the most vulnerable, and least for the most privileged, is *not* taken into account, a perversely regressive market-like pricing strategy, which exploits the most vulnerable and rewards the most secure, becomes *optimal*. A *reverse Robin Hood* strategy of robbing the poor to benefit the rich then increases over all CS. This is because the poor can be easily robbed and their greater loss of CS is more than made up for by the increased latitude thereby gained to increase CS by keeping prices low for the rich. This is true in spite of the fact that,

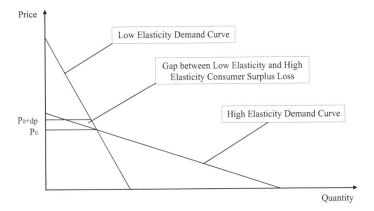

Fig. 10.2   Consumer surplus loss from price increases for high- and low-elasticity markets. *Note*: The price-elasticity values for these curves will correspond to their (inverted) slopes as they are both being measured at the same base price and quantity values

in the absence of a profit constraint, this kind of *price discrimination* will clearly result in a greater loss of CS, relative to more progressive, or even flat, pricing, as can be seen in Fig. 10.2 above, and as is evident in the derivation of (10.1) above. When profits are unconstrained the Ramsey theorem, which minimizes dollar profit loss per dollar CS gain, no longer applies. In this case price discrimination is more likely to simply increase overall profits and reduce overall CS (Fig. 10.2).[11]

A PROGRESSIVE SOCIAL PRICING RULE

As has been noted, the traditional Ramsey pricing derivation depends on an equal weighting of CS across individuals and an equal weighting of CS and PS. This allows for aggregation, which is necessary so that (10.2) can be interpreted as applying to social welfare. However, assuming that individual

---

[11] If the *Ramsey effect*, which increases CS for a fixed level of profit by reallocating it to high-elasticity segments, more than offsets the *price discrimination effect* which increases profits by reducing CS, aggregate unweighted CS might increase. In practice however, percentage profit increases from deregulation are generally large and will, therefore, most likely swamp *Ramsey effects*. Moreover, when CS is weighted before aggregation, *the net progressive social pricing rule* will generally work in a progressive direction eliminating this offset possibility, see text below and Baiman (2001).

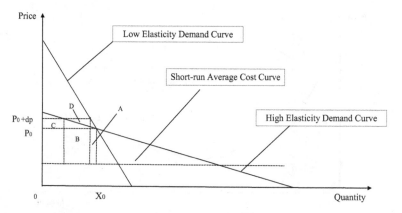

Fig. 10.3 Profit gain from price increase for high- and low-elasticity markets. *Note*: Profit gain for high-elasticity markets equals areas C – A – B. Profit gain from low-elasticity markets equals areas C + D – A

levels of CS are of equal marginal social benefit violates the common sense notion (and original Benthamite utilitarian philosophy) that marginal utility from income or wealth declines as income or wealth increases (Steinberg 1993). Unweighted aggregation of individual utilities can only be upheld through a, usually unacknowledged and unjustified, theoretically invalid and counterintuitive assumption that *consumers derive equal marginal utility from increases in CS regardless of their income or wealth status.*

On the relatively rare occasions when the inequity of this assumption is pointed out, the standard defense is that Ramsey pricing is an *equity neutral (post-transfer) Pareto efficient* rule in keeping with the "value-free" role of economic inquiry (Crew and Kleindorfer 1979, p. 12; Williamson 1966). The idea here is that, if winners (elastic consumers) compensated losers (inelastic consumers) for their losses, the resulting allocation would be Pareto efficient. Of course, such transfers will not occur voluntarily but they are theoretically possible through political programs. Within NC theory, equity issues such as income or wealth redistribution are, thus, generally viewed as political issues that lie outside the bounds of *neutral* technocratic economic theory.

Putting aside such theoretical apologetics, by any practical measure, Ramsey pricing result shows that far from being an equity neutral assumption, unweighted aggregation leads to clearly *regressive* pricing, which reduces static social welfare and long-run social efficiency. For example, a telephone service price change that resulted in a $100 decline in Donald Trump's telephone bill and $10 increases in the bills of nine low-income customers would increase aggregate CS and thus social welfare according to standard Ramsey pricing methodology. However in *real* economies, with oligopolistic markets and unequal distribution of income and wealth, this attempt to neglect *equity* and exclusively focus on *efficiency* is not possible (Kuttner 1984). Applying reasonable weights to Trump's gain and to the losses of the low-income consumers shows that aggregate weighted CS declines or that *efficiency* is *reduced* in this case along with *equity*.

Since interpersonal utility comparison *must* be made in order to aggregate CS it would seem eminently more reasonable to openly posit and justify a practical weighting scheme that would take declining average marginal utility of income into account, rather than assuming that social utility is an unweighted sum of individual utilities, directly contradicting the law of diminishing marginal utility of income.

When a utility weighting scheme like this is applied, it can be shown that social welfare, or in this context, weighted aggregate CS, will be maximized when prices for different products or segments obey the following *progressive social pricing* rule:

$$\frac{(p_i - mc_i)}{p_i} = \frac{1}{E_i}(\frac{\lambda - R_i}{\lambda}) \qquad (10.6)$$

where $E_i > 0$ is own-price demand elasticity for good i, $\lambda > 0$ is a constant Lagrange multiplier, and $\lambda - R_i > 0$ (Baiman 2001, p. 208).[12] And where following Feldstein (1972), R_i, defined as the "*distributional characteristic*" of good i, is a marginal utility of income-weighted, average of aggregate household

---

[12] Formulas (12–14, 372), (12:38; 378), (12–58, 388) and (15–25; 470) in Atkinson and Stiglitz (1980), and equation (6a) Feldstein (1972; 33), are equivalent or generalizations of (10.6) above. However, as is noted in the text below, these derivations are incomplete as, even though the consumer welfare maximand is clearly *convex* in price they do not include a demonstration that second order conditions necessary to *maximize* the Lagrangian are satisfied.

utility from the consumption of good i, as specified in Appendix A (Feldstein 1972, p. 33; Baiman 2001, (2.10), p. 207). Diminishing marginal utility from increases in income will cause R_i to be relatively greater, for goods consumed relatively more by low-income households than for high-income households, and lower when there is more demand from higher income consumers, who generally have a higher income elasticity of demand. As prices are lower relative to marginal costs for higher values of R_i, (10.6) generally, results in progressive pricing.[13]

MORE POLICY IMPLICATIONS

The progressive social pricing principle directly contradicts the mistaken but hegemonic NC view that market pricing is static welfare-maximizing. This doctrine has legitimated the wave of deregulation of many previously *price and entry* regulated industries (Kuttner 1996; Vietor 1994; Horwitz 1989). For example, in his influential text (alluded to above): *The Economics of Regulation*, Alfred Kahn, Cornell University economist and former chair of the Civilian Aviation Board (CAB) and Public Utilities Commissioner for New York State, writes:

> The central policy prescription of microeconomics is the question of price and marginal cost. If economic theory is to have any relevance to public utility pricing, that is the point at which the inquiry must begin. (Kahn 1993, p. 65)

As markets will tend to move prices toward marginal cost or near marginal cost, inverse-elasticity market pricing directly contradicts the progressive social pricing principle for static welfare maximization derived above. In particular, progressive social pricing for many social and physical infrastructure sectors, such as telecommunications, transportation, electricity, and other residential public utilities, and health care, education, cultural services, and other human services, which are of vital and increasing importance in developed and developing economies, is *more* rather than *less* efficient by standard microeconomic measures as it is more likely to increase properly weighted static social welfare.

For example, the intensely discriminatory pricing systems used by the deregulated US airline industry may represent a particularly extreme case of *static* consumer welfare *loss* due to market pricing. Moreover, in this case, there can be little doubt of the role that marginal-cost and near marginal-cost Ramsey pricing principles played in legitimating airline price

[13] See discussion in summary section of this chapter.

deregulation as the policy was supported by the chair of the CAB at that time, Alfred Kahn, author of the quote above (see also Kuttner 1996, pp. 255–270).

In this age of increasing reliance on unregulated market pricing, it is important to clarify the basic principles that support or do not support market pricing. The progressive pricing principle demonstrates that it is incumbent upon those who support deregulated market pricing to show that *dynamic* benefits from market pricing, where these may exist, will more than compensate for *static* welfare losses from the dismantling of regulated progressive social pricing where this has occurred. In this regard, it should be noted that as oligopolistic concentration ratios increase in the world economy, market-induced static welfare losses due to price discrimination can only increase. Analysis of the costs and benefits of market versus social pricing should also include the possible *loss* of long-term dynamic benefits due to lack of planning and regulation (Kuttner 1996).

Finally, it should also *not* be assumed that regulated progressive pricing is incompatible with *dynamic* market competition. The very successful Canadian "single payer" health care system is an example of a uniform price regulated system, which allows for competition over service *quality* while eliminating market-driven regressive pricing. It may also be possible to capture *both* static and dynamic pricing efficiency by implementing progressive social pricing systems that regulate *relative* pricing across products and market segments for producers that compete to have the lowest possible overall median or weighted average price and the highest possible quality.

IN SUMMARY

Ramsey pricing maximizes CS only when individual CS from consumers with different incomes or wealth are summed up *without weights* on a dollar for dollar basis *and* when this dollar sum of CS is also equally weighed with the dollar sum of PS (or revenue minus costs). With this kind of flat summing of CS and PS, as shown in Figures 10.2 and 10.3 above (See also Baiman(2000)):

(a) Price increases relative to average cost lead to larger PS or profit *gain* in low-elasticity markets relative to higher-elasticity markets.

(b) And the intuition that this will cause larger CS *loss* in low-elasticity markets relative to higher-elasticity markets *is* correct.

But standard Ramsey pricing provides an allocation, *not for maximizing an absolute level of CS, but rather for realizing a fixed level of PS or profit with the least possible loss of CS*. And the *counter intuitive* standard Ramsey pricing outcome is a result of the fact that:

(c) *Relative to PS gain*, CS loss in low-elasticity markets is *less* than in high-elasticity markets.

So that *if PS and CS are summed up without any weights in the same dollar units*, a given level of PS or profit, compared on a dollar to dollar basis with CS, can be realized with minimal CS loss (thus maximizing the CS remaining) by raising prices *higher* above marginal costs in low-elasticity markets than in high-elasticity markets.

So the *flat* dollar for dollar CS weighting scheme and equal dollar weighing of PS surplus in the Lagrangian objective function—see Appendix A, Equation (A5)—leads to a clearly *immoral* pricing formula that stipulates *higher* prices for generally lower income customers and *lower* prices for generally higher income customers. And this triumph of "second-best" *applied* practical NC microeconomic theory over regulatory common sense has directly supported catastrophic electricity price gouging in California and welfare *reducing* deregulation and NC neoliberal economic policy in general.[14]

Moreover, this problem with "second best" applied microeconomics has persisted in spite of the fact that a *moral* common sense short-term static allocation pricing theory has been available in theory for a long time. *A theoretically valid and available "progressive Ramsey pricing" rule based on a simple common sense weighing of consumer welfare benefits, or utils of CS, by income or wealth that, even if compared to an unweighted sum of PS, leads to an opposite but intuitive and common sense outcome of lower prices for generally low-income consumers and higher prices for generally higher-income consumers, has been available since at least 1972.*

Feldstein (1972), and Atkinson and Stiglitz (1980), both provided *progressive* Ramsey pricing formulations that are equivalent, or generalizations, of that provided in Baiman (2001, equation 2.13, p. 208), (Appendix, Equation (A6)). And though these demonstrations

---

[14] And similar, in terms of legitimating impact but more complex in the details "triumphs" of NC free market ideologically driven "efficient market theory" led to the even more catastrophic financial collapse of 2007 (Crotty 2011).

were incomplete, it is hard to imagine that they could not have been subsequently completed by these theorists or others.[15] In any case, Baiman (2001, Appendix A) provides a complete and definitive proof of the validity of the progressive Ramsey pricing formula by demonstrating in detail the validity of all of the necessary inequality conditions and proving that second order conditions hold.[16]

Why was the *progressive* Ramsey pricing formula ignored? One can only speculate that the utility sponsored Edison Institute was not about to fund a white paper discussing consumer welfare *loss* from *competitive market* pricing, and this kind of theory would not help bolster the endowments of business schools and economics departments.

There was one additional, neither stated nor proven, missing theoretical link in the earlier literature. Neither Feldstein, nor Atkinson and Stiglitz, proved that in practical cases *equity factors* will generally outweigh (narrowly conceived) *efficiency* factors in the *income weighted* Ramsey pricing formulations that they derived. However, this missing step has been proved—see Appendix A Equation (A7) (and Baiman (2002) for a complete derivation). *In fact, Baiman (2002) demonstrates that in almost every case, not only inverse-elasticity pricing, but even "flat" nonprogressive pricing is short-term welfare inefficient (See Appendix A, Equation (A7) and discussion following).*

It is important to note that this is not just an issue of utility regulation. If applied to the entire economy (as one firm that produces multiple products), the progressive social pricing result shows that once an overall level of profits is determined (based on a desired level of current consumption versus necessary investment for growth and future consumption) *optimal short-term static allocation can be best achieved through progressive rather than market-based pricing.*[17] This result thus flatly *contradicts* the practical

---

[15] Neither Feldstein, nor Atkinson and Stiglitz, provided a complete proof of the progressive Ramsey pricing formula as they did not demonstrate that all of the necessary inequalities hold or prove that *second order* conditions are satisfied—a gap that turns out to be nontrivial as the progressive welfare maximand on its own (without the constraint) in this case is *convex* rather than *concave* (Baiman 2000).

[16] Baiman (2000) proves that the concavity of the (PS) constraint outweighs the convexity of the welfare term so that the overall Lagranian maximand is concave—see previous footnote.

[17] In this more general application, *cross-price* effects, for the most part ignored in standard flat or progressive Ramsey pricing and for that matter in standard *marginal cost* theory as well, are likely to be more important. But though the formulas are more complex, Baiman (2001, Appendix B) shows that similar progressive pricing results hold with cross-price effects (with or without Slutsky symmetry).

second best effort to show that market prices maximize short-term social welfare. *Rather the progressive Ramsey pricing theorem shows that both market-led inverse-elasticity and even flat pricing are generally immoral, based on standard NC short-term welfare optimization criterion, as they both generally cause utility transfers from lower-elasticity (generally lower income) consumers to higher-elasticity (generally higher income) consumers.* And as shown above, the *high theory* "first best" effort to prove that market-based static allocation is optimally efficient based on supposedly *amoral* noncomparability assumptions, is also vacuous.

For the mathematically disposed, the key equations are provided in Appendix A (for detailed proofs see Baiman (2001, 2002)). The publication history of these papers is, I think, in itself an instructive example of the insularity and nonscientific dogmatic rigidity of mainstream economics.[18] However, readers who have had enough (or more than enough!) of these technical arguments may jump to the next section without any loss of continuity.

[18] As the subject matter of these papers directly addressed prior published papers by prominent mainstream economists and included the kind technical content highly encouraged in mainstream economics journals, with the intention of reaching broader exposure, I initially submitted them to a number of mainstream economics journals. However, after repeated cursory rejections that showed no evidence that any serious review had actually been conducted, even after appeals to the Editors challenging the specious arguments, when any were given at all, for rejection, as I was running out of time on a tenure decision (a common problem for younger and often more productive academics), I abandoned this futile effort *to bore from within*. This exercise was not entirely futile however as James Mirrlees, a "Nobel" prize winning Cambridge University microeconomist to whom I sent an early draft of the manuscript before submitting it for publication, did send me a thoughtful note advising me that *with the constraint*, the Lagrangian might be concave, which turned out to be the case. Joe Stiglitz, subsequently a "Nobel" prize winner, also sent me an encouraging note, and for the record, William Baumol also responded kindly to my inquiries on an earlier draft that did not include references to the Edison Institute paper that I had not yet discovered. I was grateful to be able to eventually publish these papers in the *Review of Radical Political Economics* (RRPE), and I think this example shows the importance of maintaining even just a small number of "heterodox" journals in economics like the RRPE though those of us who have served on the Editorial Boards of these renegade journals may sometimes wonder if our efforts to preserve this marginalized and ignored intellectual production served any useful purpose. I am also indebted to Vince Snowberger of the Colorado Public Utilities Commission, a fellow radical economist (and MIT alumnus, formerly at the University of Colorado at Boulder) who discovered an error in Equation 2.15 Baiman (2001, p. 208). This led to the corrected derivation of Equation (A7) Appendix A and Baiman (2002, Equation 5, p. 315).

BIBLIOGRAPHY

Atknson, A. B., & Stiglitz, J. (1980). *Lectures on public economics*. New York: McGraw Hill.

Baiman, R. (2000). Why the emperor has no clothes: The neoclassical case for price regulation. In B. Baiman, & D. Saunders (Eds.), *Political economy and contemporary capitalism: Radical perspectives on economic theory and policy*. New York: M. E. Sharpe.

Baiman, R. (2001). Why equity cannot be separated from efficiency: The welfare economics of progressive social pricing. *Review of Radical Political Economics, 33*, 203–221.

Baiman, R. (2002). Why equity cannot be separated from efficiency II: When should social pricing be progressive. *Review of Radical Political Economics, 34*, 311–317.

Baumol, William J. 1977. *Economic Theory and Operations Analysis*. Upper Saddle River, NJ: Prentice Hall.

Baumol, W. J., & Bradford, D. (1970, June). Optimal departures from marginal cost pricing. *American Economic Review, 60*(3), 265–283.

Baumol, William J., Joskow, Paul L., and Alfred E. Kahn. 1994. The Challenge for Federal and State Regulators: Transition from Regulation to Efficient Competition in Electric Power. December 4. Federal Energy Regulatory Commission (FERC) Docket no. RM 95-8-000.

Chiang, A. C. (1984). *Fundamental methods of mathematical economics* (3rd ed.,). New York: McGraw Hill.

Crotty, J. (2011, March). *The realism of assumptions does matter: Why Keynes-Minsky theory must replace efficient market theory as the guide to financial regulation policy*. Political Economy Research Institute (PERI), Working Paper 255.

Feldstein, M. (1972). Distributional equity and the optimal structure of public prices. *American Economic Review, 62*, 32–36.

Horwitz, Robert Britt. 1989.*The Irony of Regulatory Reform: The Deregulation of American Telecommunications*. Oxford University Press.

Kahn, A. E. (1993). *The economics of regulation*. Cambridge, MA: MIT Press.

Krugman, P. (2014, June 22). The big green test. *The New York Times*.

Kuttner, Robert. 1984. *The Economic Illusion: False Choices Between Prosperity and Social Justice*. Boston, MA: Houghton Mifflin.

Kuttner, R. (1996). *Everything for sale*. New York: Alfred A. Knopf.

Lusvardi, W. (2011). Bryson's troubled part in the California electric crisis. *California Watchdog*. Retrieved August 5, from http://www.calwatchdog.com/2011/08/05/brysons-troubled-part-in-ca-electricity-crisis/

Mankiw, N. G. (2008). *Principles of microeconomics* (5th ed.,). New York: Worth Publishers.

Ramsey, F. (1927). A contribution to the theory of taxation. *Economic Journal, 37*, 47–61.

Steinberg, I. S. (1993). Economics: Value theory in the spirit of Bentham. In B. Parekh (Ed.), *Jeremy Bentham: Critical assessments*. New York: Routledge.

Thoenig, J.-C., & Paradeise, C. (2014). Organizational governance and the production of academic quality: Lessons from two top U.S. research universities. *Minerva, 52*(4), 381–417.

Varian, H. R. (1992). *Microeconomic analysis* (3rd ed.,). New York: W. W. Norton.

Vietor, Richard H.K. 1994. *Contrived Competition: Regulation and Deregulation in America*. Harvard University Press.

Vogel, N. (2000, December 9). How California's consumers lost with electricity-deregulation. *Los Angeles Times*.

CHAPTER 11

The Morality of Radical Economics

Neoclassical (NC) economics is much more than an elaborate consumer welfare *bait and switch* from *amoral* in theory to *immoral* in practice operation. And the immorality of mainstream economics runs much deeper than the simple, though somewhat technically complex, issues of the proper weighing of consumer surplus (CS) and producer surplus (PS) discussed in earlier chapters. The deeper moral questions that a *moral* economics would address can, perhaps, best be concisely and schematically grasped by describing the following participatory exercise.[1]

Over the years, I have had the opportunity to lead many interactive participatory (5–50 person) workshops on the relationship between economics and values with US residents of varied age and background in college classes, Chautauqua and other activist workshops, nonprofit leadership training youth groups, public schools, Ethical Humanist Sunday School and adult retreats, Union for Radical Political Economics (URPE) camp workshops for kids, and Occupy Chicago mobilizations.[2] These workshops are built on an exercise called "Design Your Own Utopia" taken from a workbook for the second edition of a radical economics textbook, *Understanding Capitalism: Competition, Command, and Change* by Samuel Bowles and Richard Edwards (both founding members of URPE, the umbrella organization of radical economists in the USA), now in its third edition with

---

[1] Some of these topics have been discussed in Chap. 4. The following describes a participatory approach that develops these issues in a broader context.

[2] See: https://vimeo.com/43586469.

© The Editor(s) (if applicable) and The Author(s) 2016   253
R.P. Baiman, *The Morality of Radical Economics*,
DOI 10.1057/978-1-137-45559-8_11

Frank Roosevelt added as an author (Bowles et al. 2005). The workbook, long ago out of print, is listed as being authored by Mehrene Larudee, though Mehrene insists that it was actually a collective product of a group of University of Massachusetts at Amherst economics graduate students including herself.[3]

I start this exercise by handing out a copy of "Design Your Own Utopia" instructions (see Appendix B). I then divide participants into groups of 2–6 each and give each group a number or some other *neutral* name. I then ask each group to imagine that they are an elected leadership that has been asked to decide on an allocation of resources to be applied to working adults in their society based upon an omnipotent ability to measure six criteria. These criteria, described in the "Design Your Own Utopia" handout, with italicized short descriptors in parentheses added, are as follows:

- The value of the services or products that they produce (*productivity*);
- The amount of time and effort they spend (*effort*);
- The level of their need (*need*);
- The value of their property or wealth (*wealth*);
- The social status of their parents (e.g. "caste" or "nobility" level, or racial or ethnic background if this is tied to social status) (*social status*); and
- How much they have received as a result of luck (*luck*).

I then ask the group to make a *collective* decision as to how to allocate the currently produced resources of their society based on these criteria. As noted in the handout, each group thus needs to agree on a weighting scheme in the form of percentages that add up to 100 %. Each group is also asked to designate a spokesperson who will explain the rationale for the group's allocation scheme, though others in the group should feel free to comment on the spokesperson's summary. Groups have roughly half an hour (though it often takes less time than this) to come up with a collectively agreed upon scheme. If there are irreconcilable differences in the group, a *minority* report is acceptable. I strongly discourage groups from

[3] An excellent on-line "Instructor's Manual" for the third edition, with Arjun Jayadev listed as the author, that includes this exercise (on p. 37) is available at: sttpml.org/wp-content/uploads/2014/08/UnderstandingCapitalismInstructorsManual.pdf. UMass Amherst offers one of the five (as of 2012) radical or heterodox economics Ph.D. programs in the USA, the others are: The New School for Social Research in New York, The University of Missouri at Kansas City, The University of Utah, and American University in Washington D.C.

averaging individual choices as this method does not generally produce an outcome based on *collective* discussion and reasoning for a ranking of priorities, the development of which is the real point of the exercise.

In my experience, when working with adults and children age nine and older of many different backgrounds in the USA, most groups give the highest proportions of their resource allocation weights to the three criteria of (a) productivity, (b) effort, and (c) need, with sometimes, but less often, a significant allocation for (d) wealth, and almost always insignificant or zero allocations for (e) luck and (f) social status.

The miniscule or zero (f) allocation makes perfect sense as *social status* smacks of feudal inherited entitlement, an allocation factor that has been thoroughly discredited from the menu of *acceptable* claims on resources in the USA, a country with an over two-century dominant ideology of *anti-royalist* republicanism, more recently further enhanced by the Civil Rights, Women's Rights, and Gay Rights movements, all built on the legitimacy of the bedrock (classical) liberal principle of *blindness* with regard to race, gender, sexual orientation, parental or ethnoreligious background, and any other *identity* that might be related to *social status*, in the allocation of resources. This is not to say, of course, that the USA has in practical terms reached this liberal bourgeoisie nirvana but that, as a public *ideological* matter, this *principle* is well established.

Similarly, the small allocations given to (d) *luck* reflects a widespread sense that most resource allocation should, *at least in principle*, be justifiable or *deserved* based on some rationale that makes sense in terms of basic *values* and not simply a matter of *luck*.

Allocations for the four remaining criteria generally reflect more interesting and revealing choices. Groups typically place a great deal of weight on *productivity* and *effort*, placing these two criteria among the top two or three in terms of weight, from 20 to 50 % each.

Productivity is of course, at least in theory, the basic distribution criterion of a market economy where each factor of production (land, labor, and capital) is supposed to receive in accordance with what it produces, ignoring *land* and *capital* for the moment (see discussion below). This reflects the common and pervasively disseminated view of market transactions (in required high school economics classes, more subtly in college social science classes, and in the popular culture) as one of quid pro quo exchanges. These are said to be based on market values, so that the value of wages is equal to the worker's contribution to production, just as the price of a loaf of bread is *worth* the currency used to buy it, currency that could buy something else of equal value.

Interestingly, many groups give *effort* similar weight to productivity, reflecting an apparent desire to give a deserving *moral* rationale to the market. A fair number of groups will also give substantial weight to *need* in recognition that, after all, the economy is supposed to satisfy human need. Finally, more conservative groups, will give some weight, though generally not as much as is assigned to *productivity* or *effort*, to *property*.

When groups have completed deliberating, I ask the appointed spokesperson from each group to tell me the group's allocation scheme and provide a short rationale for it, with a particular focus on its rank ordering. For example, why did productivity get the *largest* weight, effort the *second* largest, and so on. I then write down the group's allocation for all to see in a column on a black board or poster board. If there is a *minority* report I write it down in a *subcolumn* for the same group. I try to concisely summarize the most important rationales when they differ from those that have already been offered in small phrases in relevant group columns. When all of the group allocations have been listed, I select the most extreme *Left Group*—the one with the highest allocations for need and effort and/or lowest for productivity and property—and conversely the most extreme *Right Group* with the opposite choices; see the four-group example in Table 11.1 below. I do not designate the groups as *Left* or *Right* to avoid immediate political labeling that might offend members of the groups and/or diminish open and constructive discussion.

I then begin to discuss these two allocation schemes usually starting with the *Right* group. For example, as in Table 11.1, with the group that chose 35 % weights for *productivity*, 35 % for *time and effort*, and another 8 % for property. My first question to the spokesperson for this group will often be to ask her to explain the group's large allocation for productivity. I ask her, and indirectly all participants, what makes a job more *productive?*

I note that though education, talent, and effort are always important, when looking at average *sector* productivity, a key factor is physical capital. For example, jobs in *retail services* will almost always be less *productive* than jobs in manufacturing.[4] In fact, I point out that the sector, or

---

[4] For the purposes of this discussion, I generally define *productivity* in the standard NC sense as *market valued* output per hour of labor, though discussions of the differences between *market* productivity defined in this way and *real* productivity that takes into account the actual human benefits of what is being produced (including distinctions between private and *public* goods and services, and market *externalities*) often come up and are good to engage in if there is time.

Table 11.1 "Design Your Own Utopia" Four-Group Example Outcome

Allocation criterion/ Group	1	2	3	4
Inherited social status	5 %	0 %	0 %	0 %
Luck	5 %	2 %	2 %	0 %
Need	30 %	38 % Output must satisfy needs	20 %	70 %
Productivity	30 % Need to produce something useful	20 %	35 %	0 %
Property or wealth	5 %	5 %	8 % The wealthy invest in growth for the future	0 %
Time or effort	25 %	35 %	35 %	30 % Effort should be rewarded
Sum of weights	100 %	100 %	100 %	100 %
Group			"Right" Group	"Left" Group

industry, that a person happens to work in often has more bearing on his or her *market productivity* and compensation than anything else. For example, across national economies, average market measured *value-added* wages in manufacturing are generally higher than value-added wages in retail services.[5] So although it makes sense that compensating productivity may be important for the economy as a *whole* (see discussion at end of chapter), it is less clear why it should have a large weight as an *individual* resource allocation factor.

[5] More extreme sector *productivity* differences can be drawn, as between workers in *finance*, for example, who receive greatly out-sized compensation and to whom are attributed enormous market-valued contributions, and *home-makers* who, in standard national income accounting, produce *zero* market-value added and who receive *no* compensation; see for example (Baiman 2014) and (Mutari 2000).

This productivity discussion offers a segue into a discussion of *effort*, as groups often have a difficult time distinguishing between productivity and effort, and have a tendency to conflate these two factors. Here I point out that though rewarding effort makes moral sense, effort is (on average) quite divorced from productivity in a market economy due to the sector value-added issue discussed above and because of vast differences in the innate talent and skills of persons making the effort. For example Michael Jordan and LeBron James can make millions from one lay-up for a basketball commercial that they can execute with very little effort. Of course, innate talent must typically be supplemented by training and education in order to generate, even narrowly defined, market-valued productivity. But this education and training is often easier, or at least more glamorous and interesting, than the hard work in less pleasant environments that is typically engaged in by the lowest-paid workers. For example, compare the work, including the time spent on education, of doctors, lawyers, and business executives, to that of janitors, farm workers, and retail clerks.

As discussed in Chap. 4, radical economist John E. Roemer makes a useful distinction between "internal" and "external" ownership (Roemer 1988). *Internal ownership* includes one's *innate* genetic, family, and social background, *as well as* one's formal education and training (or *human capital* in mainstream economic terms). In large measure due to *genetic endowment*, some people are intelligent, athletic, or beautiful, while others are less so. Ideal *liberal* (in the classic sense) market allocation that places a very large weight on equality of opportunity that allows one to realize one's *highest potential* in terms of *market productivity* of output ignores the *unequal ability* of all to succeed at this game, no matter how much *effort*.[6]

Finally to cap off discussion of *Right* group allocation, I introduce Milton Friedman's well-known designation of the dominant resource allocation criteria in a *capitalist* market economy (Friedman 1962, Chapter X, fifth sentence):

To each according to what he and the instruments he owns produces.

---

[6] See, for example, *Second Treatise on Government*, John Locke 1690, Barnes & Noble Publishing.

I point out that placing such a high value on productivity, as Friedman does, supports giving mostly *free reign* to competitive market outcomes of the sort that are imagined to result from *small-government free-market* capitalism.[7] But, notice that Friedman's criteria also includes a return to "the instruments that he owns," that is, *property* as a major resource allocation factor. And this comports with data on actually existing capitalist societies, particularly those *without* strong redistribution policies. For example, in the USA in the last 35 years 120.6 % of real family income for the top 10% gains from 1973 to 2008 went to the top 10 % of families so that average real family income for the bottom 90 % of families declined by –6.4% (Baiman 2011b). Moreover, the gains in real family income for the top 10 % are concentrated at the very top 0.01 % of families (9,000 families with incomes of over $9,141,190 in 2008) who on average increased their real income more than fivefold (544.8 %) over this period, and the Saez (2008) data on which this is based shows that in 2008 less than a fifth (18.4 %) of the income of these top 0.01 % families came from labor.[8]

But income from profit, dividends, interest, and rent, and a portion of capital gains income, that is, income from *income earning assets*, is generally, directly or indirectly, dependent on *labor*. Put more simply, in a capitalist market economy, a large component of income from the *things that you own* directly or indirectly includes the *labor*, or *output from rented labor time* (what Marx called "labor power") of *other* people. Distribution weights in existing capitalist market economies thus include, as an ideal, a large weight for productivity and, in practice, a large weight for property. As discussed in Chap. 4, though capitalist market economies no longer permit outright human *ownership*, or slavery, they are based on a wage-labor system that is, certainly in the most capitalist economies like the USA, without *codetermination* and other *stakeholder* corporate forms that have become common in Europe, undeniably *undemocratic* (Hill 2010, Chap. 3).

---

[7]Though, as discussed in Chap. 4, even in an ideal competitive market, there are substantial technical difficulties with actually equating value-added productivity with "factor" returns (wages, profits, and rents) due to the problem of assuming that "marginal" output is a good approximation of "average" output, similar to the marginal cost equal price conundrum discussed in chapters 9 and 10. (Schweickart 1993, Chap. 1).

[8]See data from Emmanuel Saez, Economics, University of California, Berkeley, Tables A7 and A8 at: http://www.econ.berkeley.edu/~saez/TabFig2008.xls. Based on this data, 44.8 % of all income of these top 0.01 % of filers came from capital gains, and 64 % of all their income exclusive of capital gains came profits, dividends, interest, and rent so that $(1 - 0.448) \times (1 - 0.64) = 0.184$ share of their income came from labor.

Workers in US corporations, and residents of the communities where they are based, do not have the right to vote for their managers or have any significant influence on company investment and other decisions in spite of the fact that these decisions typically have a much greater impact on *company workers* and local *communities* than on the mostly absentee stockholders who nominally "own" and are awarded all of the residual profits and capital gains income from the company.[9]

Some Right groups also assign a high value to *property*, with the standard justification that *savings* need to be encouraged so that they can be invested to support invention, innovation, and growth. In this case, as discussed in Chap. 4, I point out that the link between private wealth and savings under capitalism is a *social construction*. A tax (or "user fee" in Schweickart's (1993, 2011) model) could be levied to create a *social investment fund*. This fund could be managed by a system of decentralized public development banks that could use employment and, possibly, other *social indicators*, in addition to *private rate of return* for lending, or *savings allocation*, purposes. *Market socialists* like Roemer (1994) and Bowles and Gintis (1998), and nonmarket socialists like Pat Devine (1988), Albert and Hahnel (1991), and Ellman (2004), offer other schemes for *real* savings and lending, or for generating and allocating claims on investment resources.[10] All agree, however, that the conventional capitalist arrangement

---

[9] For a clear and systematic comparison of wage-labor to slavery and workplace democracy, see Archer (1995 , Chap. 2). For a comprehensive discussion of the benefi ts of economic democracy in relation to ca through appropriate institutional struct pitalism, including a review of examples of existing large-scale, fast-growing, and highly successful worker cooperatives like the Mondragon Cooperative Corporation in Spain, see Schweickart (1993, 2011) and Whyte and Whyte (1991).

[10] Though Bowles and Gintis express a concern about a possible excessive *risk adversity* public investment problem in a market socialist system, it would appear that this can be overcome through appropriate institutional structures given the Mondragon experience of extraordinarily rapid and successful entrepreneurship and innovation (Schweickart 1993, 2011; Whyte and Whyte 1991). The latter, in fact, emphasizes the much greater efficiency of the more *rational,* planned, *collective entrepreneurship* practiced by the Mondragon, compared to the large-scale waste of human and physical resources typical in conventional capitalist *individual risk-taking entrepreneurship*; and the environmental benefits of an *economic democracy* with locally rooted worker cooperatives more concerned about point of production environmental impact and better able to regulate the pace and allocation of growth to serve economic justice and environmental sustainability goals (Schweickart 1993, 2011). Though it should be noted that many commentators, including myself, believe that the *nonmarket* allocation mechanism proposed in Albert and Hahnel (1991) is unworkable (Baiman 1999).

that awards all of the residual benefits of production, and the power to dispose of this residual, to capitalists (Ellerman 2007) makes little sense. In addition, all agree that, as discussed in Chap. 7, awarding the power to *create* credit though *fractional reserve banking*, and the power to borrow and finance investment from financial savings based on the accumulation of these resources by wealthy individuals and families, is an historic *class society* anachronism that has no real economic or social justification. There are differences of opinion regarding the social benefits of different levels of private ownership and control of the *means of production*, ranging from a fairly large private ownership share by some who are concerned that too much social investment would be excessively *risk averse* (Bowles and Gintis 1998), to others who believe that allowing any scope for traditional market behavior will inevitably, through *endogenous preference formation*, nurture the excessively competitive and self-serving, morally undesirable, and individually and socially, destructive human behavior, that is characteristic of capitalism (Hahnel and Albert 1990). However, no market socialist believes that massively unequal private accumulation and inheritance of *income earning* assets and the control over human labor, and political power that directly and indirectly comes with this, serves any useful social purpose. In this sense, all agree with Piketty (2014) that "Patrimonial" capitalism undermines the most basic principles of fairness and democracy.

For our purposes, however, the major point is that the validity of the current social arrangement that results in a private *class monopoly* over savings and investment should not be taken as *natural*, or apologized for as *necessary* or *inevitable*, as it is in NC economics. This social arrangement should rather be *evaluated* from a *moral* economic perspective. This brings us to *Left Group* allocation criteria.

LEFT GROUP DISCUSSION

Left groups typically place high valuations on *need* and *effort*. These groups apparently hold the *bizarre* (sic!) view that the economy should support "human well-being" in Harris's terminology. Strange as this may seem, assume for the sake of argument that most people agree with this proposition. This view is probably best encapsulated by the age old socialist motto popularized by Marx[11]:

---

[11] *Critique of the Gotha Program*, Part 1 (Marx 1875). This was reportedly a well-known socialist slogan that may have originated with *utopian* socialist Luis Blanc (1851).

From each according to his ability, to each according to his need.

When stated in this way and contrasted with Friedman's market capital-ist motto, above, I have not found a single group object to my, fairly obvious, statement that this expression of socialist economic values expresses a higher moral standard than Friedman's earlier statement of the underlying values of a capitalist economy.

In fact, one group, at a 2002 Jim Hightower "Rolling Thunder Chautauqua" in Chicago, placed a 100 % valuation on *need* and zero on all other factors. Apparently a member of the group and well-known progressive and ex-Communist Party member from Hyde Park convinced the entire group to follow the socialist motto to the letter. If one interprets the exercise as narrowly applying only to *present* resource distribution, which is a fair interpretation, this makes perfect sense.

But the broader issue is whether the socialist ideal is at all *realistic* or feasible? Can resources be directly allocated with these goals in mind, or is this just a *pie in the sky* fantasy that, however laudable in theory, cannot usefully serve as a practical guide for direct resource allocation? This was, or has been taken as, Adam Smith's key point after all. Economic produc-tivity and growth is best secured by appealing to self-interest within *freely* competitive markets, not through altruistic moralizing and heavy handed government *intervention*. The real issue for Left groups is not their laud-able intentions but whether this idealism is naïve and misguided?

The answer in a nutshell is *no*. The entire history of economic thought from the time that humans began to realize that economic development is for the most a result of *human* activity[12] shows that social and eco-nomic *policy*, not a God in heaven (Yahweh), or a God on earth (the Free Market), is the key factor driving economic development.

Erik Reinert (2007) provides extensive evidence for this from centuries of economic *policy documents* generally not discussed in economic textbooks or academic treatises. Rienert's sources include documents on: fifteenth-century Tudor economic policy in England; polices of Giovanni Botero and Antonio Serra in Renaissance and post-Renaissance Italy in the late fifteenth and sixteenth centuries; policies of Barthelemy de Laffemas and Jean Baptiste Colbert in sixteenth- and seventeenth-century France; and Von Hornick in seventeenth-century Germany. Later in the 19th and 20th centuries Reinert's sources include: Fredrick List and the German Historical School; Marx and

---

[12] More precisely, human activity exclusive of natural forces beyond the powers of human anticipation or control. For better or worse, the impact of human activity has exponentially increased over millennia of recorded human history.

Schumpeter in Germany and Austria; Scmoller and Sombart in France; and, Alexander Hamilton, Daniel Raymond, M. & H. Carey, Veblen, the Institutional School, and Keynes, in the USA and the UK (Reinert 2007, Fig. 3, p. 33).

Eamonn Fingleton has similarly documented this in the modern period by analyzing the *Asian Model* of state-led economic development, originating with Japan and culminating with China (Fingleton 2008). Similarly, Ha Joon Chang shows that *all* currently developed countries, including most prominently the UK and the USA, consciously and deliberately employed extensive *mercantilist* trade policies that played a central role in their economic development, and successful modern developers like South Korea have done the same (Chang 2008). And Ian Feltcher provides extensive historical and empirical corroboration of this point with a particular focus on the history of US trade policy (Fletcher 2009).

Finally, Stephen Hill describes and extensively documents the critical role that far-reaching social, industrial, and trade policies have played in the most successful and well-off, in terms of almost every general indicator of *human well-being*, social democratic and *social market* societies. Based on these indicators, these countries, most prominently: Denmark, Sweden, Norway, and Germany, have among the most successful economies the world has ever known (Hill 2010). Hill focuses on the role of *workfare*, and environmental policies in these countries. He also highlights Germany's long-term quasipublic *middle-level* development bank financing and advanced training and education systems, jointly financed by industry, unions, and government, and policies being rolled out across Europe designed to foster democratic *stakeholder* (rather than *shareholder*) economies through *works council* and *codetermination* laws that mandate that, in large companies, a third or more of Corporate Boards of Directors must represent the workers at the company (Hill 2010, Chap. 3) (Geoghegan 2014).

As Reinert, Chang, Fletcher, and others have noted, when compared to this centuries-old record, current NC economic text book renditions portray a highly ideological, and mostly imaginary, economic history that has little relationship to the actual policies pursued by the most successful economies during their most successful periods of growth and development. For example, in mainstream economic texts the highly reviled *mercantilists* dominated economic policy in eighteenth-century Europe and the USA until losing out to NC free-market and free-trade policies that supported economic growth and development. But the actual historical record shows that NC theorists of classic liberal free-market thinking were in policy ascendency only during brief periods in the UK and USA *after* these and other advanced countries had already become world economic leaders, and these NC policies bear great responsibility for the subsequent *declines* of these economies (Marglin and Schor 1992). The *dominant* economic policies that were *actually deployed* by successful countries can only be gleamed from the real history of parliamentary and legislative debates and policy implementation, not from the now sanitized mainstream textbooks that espouse a rewritten ideological historical mythology.

Compared to this centuries-old *actual* world-wide record of economic history and history of economic thought, the elaborate and highly formalized NC *microeconomic* theory discussed in Chaps. 8, 9, and 10 the complementary, equally elaborate, and even more fanciful, NC *macroeconomic* constructions, ring hollow. These theories, from *comparative advantage* rationales for *free trade*; to *Chicago School rational choice* economics; to *Walrasian New Keynesian* doctrines; to *real business cycle theory, permanent income hypothesis*, and financial *efficient market theory* doctrines; have been selected as examples of the greatest achievement in economics science *high theory* by the economics "Nobel" prize committee.[13] But they have been shown, by the financial crash of 2008, and earlier in theory, for example, in a comprehensive review by Lance Taylor in *Reconstructing Macroeconomics* (Taylor 2004a), with a more summarized update in *Maynard's Revenge* (Taylor 2010), to be fantasies of the imagination, based on hypothetical and ad-hoc mathematical assumptions that have no bearing in the real world. Given the vacuity of both microeconomic and macroeconomic mainstream economics *high theory*, it is simply not possible to give this system of capitalist apologetics much credence as rational scientific inquiry, even it were based on a more humane system of values.

In fact, there are at least two eminently practical ways to increase the allocation of resources based on *need* and *effort*. Both have been tried and have been highly successful. Increased allocations for *effort* can be fostered through comprehensive wage and income distribution policies. Greater allocations based on *need* can be achieved through social programs (education, health care, fully socialized pension systems, human services, and culture) *that allocate resources away from markets* and toward *politically determined social need.*

---

[13] That is the committee that awards the Economics "Nobel," not the real Nobel Prize committee that awards Nobel prizes in natural science. The Economics Nobel Committee is sponsored by *Sweden's Central Bank.*

The most successful practitioners of *effort* rewarding policies have been the advanced Scandinavian *workfare* societies that have the highest labor force participation rates in the world. These countries have been able to markedly reduce inequality from labor income through high levels of unionization and, at least in the past, *solidarity wage* policies that have led to a greater equalization of pay for similar work regardless of employer profitability, and higher, more equitable pay for what would be largely low-wage service sector work in more market-oriented Anglo–US economies. Though these *solidarity wage* campaigns are now less successful than they were in the past, and "Meidner plan" originated *wage earner funds* do not own a majority of private sector shares as they would have if the original plan had been fully implemented, there is abundant evidence that due to policy-based redistribution of earnings, and strong centralized collective bargaining, income levels in these countries are more equitable and *effort* based (Huber and Stephens 2001).

Similarly, in terms of *need*, the advanced social democratic countries have the highest levels of social spending relative to their GDP's. This is funded through high, but progressive, levels of taxation; see Figs. 11.1 and 11.2 below. Scandinavian social spending funds a level of needs-based resource allocation that is hard to imagine in the U.S. Figure 11.2 below provides a detailed comparison.

These high levels of social spending and wages concretely reflect greater rewards for *effort* or labor and less for *property*; see Figure 11.3 below. This is particularly true if the often inferior health care, education, savings for retirement, and other costs paid for privately in the USA are compared to the more efficiently provided and generally higher quality public services paid for through taxes in the social democratic countries.

Finally, it is worth noting that Sweden recorded the highest GDP growth rate of all the advanced countries in 2012 (Krugman 2012)[14] and that the social democratic countries in general, unlike the more *free-market* Anglo–American societies, have generally been able to maintain advanced productive capacity and high-value competitive exports at a sufficient level to pay for their way in the world, and maintain and increase domestic living standards (Baiman 2010).

[14] See: http://www.nytimes.com/2012/02/27/opinion/krugman-what-ails-europe.html?_r=1.

Fig. 11.1 Public social expenditure as a percent of GDP OECD Countries 2014 (Source: OECD (2015), Social spending (indicator). doi: 10.1787/7497563b-en (Accessed on 23 September 2015))

Fig. 11.2 General government revenue as a percent of GDP OECD Countries 201 (Source: OECD (2015), General government revenue (indicator). doi: 10.1787/b68b04ae-en (Accessed on 23 September 2015))

Table 11.2   Rights of a Swedish citizen vs. the rights of a US citizen

	Sweden	USA
Parental leave	Parents are entitled to 480 days of paid parental leave when a child is born or adopted. For 390 of the days, parents are entitled to nearly 80 % of their normal pay. Benefits are calculated on a maximum monthly income of about $50,000. The remaining 90 days are paid at a flat rate. Those who are not in employment are also entitled to paid parental leave. Parental leave can be taken up until a child turns eight. The leave entitlement applies to each child (except in the case of multiple births), so parents can accumulate leave from several children. Outside the 480 paid days, parents in Sweden also have the legal right to reduce their normal working hours (and pay) by up to 25 % until the child turns eight.	All parents have the right to six weeks of unpaid leave to care for a newborn child. Some parents receive monetary assistance for a limited period of time if they are very poor.
Sick leave	First 14 days at 80 % of earnings. If still ill, up to 364 days over a 15-month period at 80 % of pay. An extension is possible for up to 550 days at 75 %, of pay covered by social insurance. For more serious illness, no formal maximum at 70 % of pay.	No legal guarantee of paid sick leave. Workers eligible for Social Security may receive medical disability payments but these are generally much less than prior earnings.
Vacations	Workers in Sweden are entitled to a paid annual leave of 25 working days or five weeks. They have a right to take at least four of these weeks consecutively, between June and August. They also receive "holiday pay" of 12 % of the wages they would have earned during their leave. Swedish law requires employers to allow workers to take paid leave for any days needed to fulfill union responsibilities. This leave is paid at the worker's normal salary (without additional holiday pay).	United States law offers no guarantees of paid leave. The only exceptions are for government contractors and subcontractors covered under the Davis-Bacon Act. Many workers get no paid vacation or sick leave.

(continued)

Table 11.2 (continued)

	Sweden	USA
Health care	All citizens receive high quality health care and dental care, with modest copayments up to a maximum copayment. Care is generally so good that even the wealthy use public health care.	Though the Affordable Care Act has increased coverage, roughly 10 % of US residents still have no health insurance. Most health insurance is provided by private for-profit companies so that health care is generally costly or of low quality for those without premium insurance plans. Those without insurance often go untreated for extended periods of time.
Education	Free education is provided for all citizens at all levels including college, vocational, and adult education (for people who want to explore new careers). Adult students receive time off from work and a stipend. Low-cost government subsidized loans are available, and often used, to help pay for student living expenses.	Free primary and secondary education is available to all citizens, with the quality varying widely depending on where one lives. People living in a poor school district generally receive an inferior education. Some limited funding is available for college students, but college is often beyond the reach of the poor and lower middle class. What funding is available is often in the form of loans, creating large debts for many students.
Job training	Free training is provided to all citizens who desire it. Those undergoing training receive a stipend from the Government.	Some training programs exist but they are limited in nature and usually only for the poor or unemployed. Trainees do not usually receive a stipend.
Employment	The Swedish government believes that every citizen has the right to meaningful work. Unemployed persons receive unemployment benefits, retraining, or a job in a public works project. Unemployment benefits are generous. Most unemployed Swedes received up to 80 % of their former salaries for their first 200 days of unemployment, and up to 70 % of their previous income for the next 100 days.	Some of the unemployed receive up to 6 months of unemployment benefits and job search assistance. During severe recessions, this can be extended, depending on state of residency, up to 99 weeks or longer. After this period, unemployment benefits are cut off. Unemployment benefits in the U.S. are generally between 40–50 % of previous pay.

(continued)

Table 11.2 (continued)

	Sweden	USA
Social security	All Swedish citizens receive a pension from the state which pays people at least 60 % of what they earned when they were working, or a guaranteed minimum amount if they did not work. The Swedish public pension system is funded through an 18.5 % payroll tax with a maximum income cap. For 90 % of workers this is topped off with another 3.5 % payroll tax to fund a private pension that tops off the public pension.	Most US citizens receive social security (SS), benefits but the payments are too little to live on. For example, for a worker who works until age 65–67 making average earnings, SS will provide about 36–40 % of earnings at retirement. SS is funded through a payroll tax of 12.4 % shared between employee and employer with a maximum income cap. Only 18 % of US private sector workers had private defined benefit pension plans in 2011, and in 2010, the median worker in the USA had only $2,500 in defined contribution IRA pension savings.
Housing	If Swedish citizens cannot afford a house, they are given a housing subsidy. Three million of 9.5 million Swedes live in rental housing, and over half of these live in public, municipally owned, housing. Sweden does not have a problem with homelessness due to the success of their housing and antipoverty programs, and they have almost no slums.	Some US citizens receive housing subsidies or a spot in public housing. But many citizens do not qualify for these benefits, and the USA has a significant number of homeless people. Every major US city has slums.

Sources: Multiple topics (Sackrey et al. 2013, p. 238–9); parental leave (Swedish Institute 2015); sick leave (Heymann et al. 2009); vacations (Ray et al. 2013); health care (Levy 2015); education (Phillips 2013); job training and employment (Cook 2008), (Savage, 2008), (Krugman, 2013); social security (Social Security 2013a, b; Morrissey 2013; Pizzigati 2013; Swedish Pensions Agency 2015); housing (Swedish Association of Public Housing 2015)

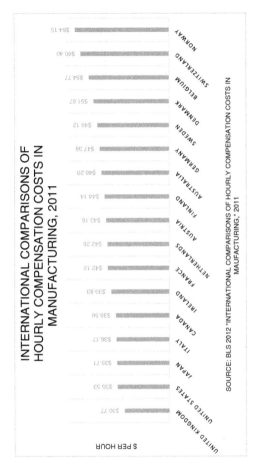

Fig. 11.3 International comparisons of hourly compensation costs in manufacturing, 2011 (Source: BLS 2012 "International Comparisons of Hourly Compensation Costs in Maufacturing," 2011)

BIBLIOGRAPHY

Albert, M., & Hahnel, R. (1991). *The political economy of participatory economics.* Princeton: Princeton University Press.

Archer, R. (1995). *Economic democracy: The politics of feasible socialism.* Oxford: Oxford University Press.

Baiman, R. (1999, Winter). Market socialism: The debate among socialists by David Schweickart, James Lawler, Hillel Ticktin, Bertell Ollman. *Science & Society, 63*(4), 518–522.

Baiman, R. (2010). Toward a new political economy for the U.S. *Review of Political Economics, 42*(3), 353–362.

Baiman, R. (2011). *Eisenhower era income tax rates on the upper 10 % of families would immediately erase the federal deficit.* Chicago Political Economy Group Working Paper 2011-2. Retrieved May, from http://www.cpegonline.org/workingpapers/CPEGWP2011-2.pdf

Baiman, R. (2014). Unequal exchange and the Rentier economy. *Review of Radical Political Economics, 46*(4) 536–557.

Blanc, L. (1851). In C. Joubert (Ed.), *Plus de Girondins.* Paris: Passage Dauphine.

Bowles, S., Gintis, H., & Wright E.O. (1998). *Recasting Eqalitarianism: New Rules for Communities, States and Markets.* NY: Verso Press.

Bowles, S., Edwards, R., & Roosevelt Jr., F. (2005). *Understanding capitalism: Competition, command, and change.* New York: Oxford University Press.

Chang, H.-J. (2008). *Bad Samaritans: The myth of free trade and the secret history of capitalism.* New York: Bloomsbury Press.

Chomsky, N. (2006). *Language and mind* (3rd ed.). Cambridge: Cambridge University Press.

Chomsky, N. (2007). Of minds and language. *Biolinguistics.*

Chomsky quoting Jacob, Jacob, François. (1977). Evolution and tinkering. *Science,* 196(1), 161–171.

Cook, B. (2008). *National, regional and local employment policies in Sweden and the United Kingdom.* Working Paper No. 08–05. October. Centre of Full Employment and Equity (COfFEE). Retrieved from http://e1.newcastle.edu.au/coffee/pubs/wp/2008/08-05.pdf

Devine, P. (1988). *Democracy and economic planning: The political economy of a self-governing society.* Boulder: Westview Press.

Ellerman, D. (2007). On the role of capital in "capitalist" and in labor-managed firms. *Review of Radical Political Economics, 39*(1), 5–26.

Ellman, M. (2004). Economic lessons from the transition: The basic theory re-examined. *Comparative Economic Studies, 46*(4), 570–571.

Fingleton, E. (2008). *In the Jaws of the Dragon: America's fate in the coming era of Chinese Dominance.* New York: St. Martin's Griffin.

Fletcher, I. (2009). *Free trade doesn't work: Why America needs a tariff.* Washington, DC: U.S. Business & Industry Council.

Friedman, M. (1962). *Capitalism and freedom*. Chicago: University of Chicago Press.

Geoghegan, T. (2014). *Only one thing can save us: Why America needs a new kind of labor movement*. New York: The New Press.

Hahnel, R., & Albert, M. (1990). *Quiet revolution in welfare economics*. Princeton: Princeton University Press.

Heymann, J., Rho, H. J., Schmitt, J., & Earle, A. (2009, May). *A comparison of paid sick day policies in 22 countries*. Center for Economic and Policy Research (CEPR).

Hill, S. (2010). *Europe's promise: Why the European way is the best hope in an insecure age*. Berkeley: University of California Press. Dec. 3.

Huber, E., & Stephens, J. (2001). *Development and crisis of the welfare state: Parties and policies in global markets*. Chicago: University of Chicago Press.

Krugman, P. (2012, February 28). What ails Europe?. *The New York Times*.

Krugman, P. (2013, December 3). The Punishment Curve. *The New York Times*.

Levy, J. (2015). *In U.S., uninsured rate dips to 11.9 % in first quarter*. Gallup Well-Being. Retrieved April 13, from http://www.gallup.com/poll/182348/uninsured-rate-dips-first-quarter.aspx

Locke, J. (1690). *Second treatise on government*. New York: Barnes & Noble Publishing.

Marglin, S., & Schor, J. (1992). *The golden age of capitalism: Reinterpreting the post-war experience*. Oxford: Clarendon Press.

Marx, K. (1875). *Critique of the Gotha program*. Moscow: Progress Publishers, Republished 1970.

Morrissey, M. (2013). *Private-sector pension coverage fell by half over two decades*. Economic Policy Institute Working Economics Blog. Retrieved January 11, from http://www.epi.org/blog/private-sector-pension-coverage-decline/

Mutari, E. (2000). A primer on feminist political economy. In B. Baiman, & D. Saunders (Eds.), *Political economy and contemporary capitalism: Radical perspectives on economic theory and policy*. New York: M. E. Sharpe.

Phillips, M. (2013). The high price of a free college education in Sweden. *The Atlantic*. Retrieved May 31, from http://www.theatlantic.com/international/archive/2013/05/the-high-price-of-a-free-college-education-in-sweden/276428/

Piketty, T. (2014). *Capitalism in the twenty-first century*. Cambridge, MA: The Belknap press of Harvard University Press.

Pizzigati, S. (2013). "Remember when people had pensions?" Too much: A commentary on excess and inequality. *Featured News*. Retrieved September 7, from http://toomuchonline.org/remember-when-people-had-pensions/

Ray, R., Sanes, M., & Schmitt, J. (2013). *No vacation nation revisited*. Center for Economic and Policy Research (CEPR). Retrieved May, from http://www.cepr.net/documents/publications/no-vacation-update-2013-05.pdf

Reinert, E. (2007). *How rich countries got rich and why poor countries stay poor*. New York: Public Affairs.

Roemer, J. E. (1988). *Free to lose: An introduction to Marxist philosophy*. Cambridge: Harvard University Press.

Roemer, J. E. (1994). *A future for socialism*. Cambridge: Harvard University Press.

Sackrey, C., Schneider, G., & Knoedler, J. (2013). *Introduction to political economy* (7th ed.,). Boston: Dollars and Sense.

Saez, Emmanuel. (2008). University of California, Berkeley, Tables A7 and A8. Retreived from: http://www.econ.berkeley.edu/ ~ saez/TabFig 2008.xls.

Savage, J. (2008). How does Swedish Unemployment Insurance Work. *The Local, se.* Sept. 5.

Schweickart, D. (1993). *Against capitalism: Studies in Marxism and social theory*. Cambridge University Press.

Schweickart, D. (2011). *After capitalism* (2nd ed.,). Lanham: Rowan & Littlefield.

Social Security. (2013a). *Social security programs throughout the world: The United States of America*. Social Security Administration (SSA) and The International Social Security Association (ISSA). Retrieved from http://www.ssa.gov/policy/docs/progdesc/ssptw/2012-2013/americas/united-states.pdf

Social Security. (2013b). *Social security programs throughout the world: Sweden*. Social Security Administration (SSA) and The International Social Security Association (ISSA). Retrieved from http://www.ssa.gov/policy/docs/progdesc/ssptw/2012-2013/europe/sweden.pdf

Swedish Association of Public Housing. (2015). *Public housing in Sweden*. Web publication accessed 8/31/15: http://www.sabo.se/om_sabo/english/Sidor/Publichousing.aspx

Swedish Institute. (2015). *10 things that make Sweden family friendly*. Web publication: https://sweden.se/society/10-things-that-make-sweden-family-friendly/. Dated 2013–2015. Accessed 8/30/2015.

Swedish Pensions Agency. (2015). *How you earn your retirement pension*. Web Publication accessed 8/31/2015: http://www.pensionsmyndigheten.se/HowYouEarnYourRetirementPension_en.html

Taylor, L. (2004a). *Reconstructing macroeconomics: Structuralist proposals and critiques of the mainstream*. Cambridge, MA: Harvard University Press.

Taylor, Q. P. (2004b, Winter). An original omission? Property in Rawls's political thought. *The Independent Review, VII*(3), 387–400.

Taylor, L. (2010). *Maynard's revenge: The collapse of free market economics*. Cambridge, MA: Harvard University Press.

Whyte, W. F., & Whyte, K. K. (1991). *Making Mondragon: The growth and dynamics of the worker cooperative complex*. Ithaca: Cornell University Press.

CONCLUSION

Orienting an economy toward human need and effort in a way that satisfies human needs induces more socially productive economic activity is a perfectly practical goal. The problem for mainstream NC economists is that this is a fundamentally value-based or moral goal that *cannot* be derived from an amoral or immoral theoretical apparatus.

If economists began to view themselves properly again as *moral philosophers* deriving best practices from widely understood and agreed upon moral values conducive to *human well-being*, based on evidence from societies and economies that have been most successful at this, rather than trying to explain away success that does not fit NC ideological precepts, the profession could rise above its current lap-dog apologetic status and become the vital and essential moral social science that humanity in the early twenty-first century so desperately needs.

Such an economics would forthrightly condemn, as the best of the classical political economists such as Smith, Ricardo, Marx, Veblen, George, and Keynes did, *unearned income* for unproductive *rentier* activity and rewards for the already obscenely wealthy that serve no social purpose, arguing that resources should be directed toward real needs, with motivational resources for productive effort that are just sufficient to induce such effort and not more (Baiman 2014). Can there really be any morally justifiable argument against minimizing the advantages of inherited external ownership (or wealth) and reducing, as much as possible, the advantages of inherited *internal ownership* (or genetic endowment) subject to supporting overall productivity and well-being with optimal but not excessive incentives for entrepreneurship, discovery, and the cultivation and utilization of individual skills and talents to benefit others? (Roemer 1988). Can one really make a moral case that some humans should be able to control and benefit from the labor of armies of other, often low paid and impoverished, people because they can directly or indirectly afford to *rent* their labor, while these workers (who are generally better off than the masses of *unemployed*—another indispensable component of neoliberal capitalism—with no formal income at all) have no alternative but to *sell* their labor to them?[1] Is there any question that such an economics as a branch of *scientific moral social philosophy* would be strongly supportive of social democracy, democratic socialism, and ideal communism as feasible within a democratic society?

The only way that the current *capitalist* ("to each according to what they and the instruments they own – including the labor of other people – produce"), as opposed to *democratic socialist* ("from each according to their ability, and to each according to their need,"), economics can be justified is through an *ends justifies the means* argument common to NC economics and conservative thought more generally. This is the 18th century Adam Smith rationale that postulates that self-interest and the use of the labor of others for one's own gain is justified because, though it is based on patently unethical, undemocratic, and exploitative relationships, *it delivers the goods*. The claim is that capitalism fosters innovation, growth and prosperity that supports *human well-being* and *political democracy, overall and in the long run,* and there is no other practical economic system that will do this.

But even if this, *means justify the ends,* thinking were supportable,[2] where is the evidence for this particular claim that evil produces good?

The Chinese *market opening* cannot, for example, be used as a good historical example as China is practicing its own—highly politically repressive (see Fingleton 2008; Mann 2007; Navarro 2008)—version of the *Asian*

---

[1] That is can undemocratic class power based on ownership of capital and the *renting* of *labor be justified?* This is the pretence of NC economics, though, as discussed in chap. 4, it is hard to see how labor or *labor power* can be separated from the will and well-being of the humans who deploy it (Ellman 2004).

[2] Hahnel and Albert (1990), for example, make a strong case that capitalist individualist and competitive *means* that sanction the human exploitation of other humans, or *the treatment of others as means and not ends* for those with a Kantian bent, reinforce the worst aspects of human behavior and thus produce *ends* that, however *prosperous* in market-based consumer-values terms, generate increasingly brutal and barbaric societies that tolerate widespread exploitation, poverty, and inequality, and undermine the most valuable aspects of human behavior and life in general.

Model of *state capitalism* that is not free-market capitalism and, certainly, not a good example of an *advanced* democratic economy and society like those of Northern Europe and the Mondragon Cooperatives, which also provide direct *existing* highly successful counter examples to the claim that *there is no alternative* (TINA) to capitalism (Schweickart 1993, 2011).

The collapse of Soviet style *central planning* cannot be used as supporting evidence, as the most advanced and successful capitalist Social Democracies do *not* attempt to do away with markets, but rather try to tightly constrain, regulate, and guide them through political means to directly serve the goal of human well-being. And by almost every indicator—empowerment of women, political participation, the breadth and depth of public political debate, and the empowerment of citizens rather than money—these societies are much *more* democratic than the USA and the UK (Hill 2010, Part Five).

So a properly moral *mainstream economics* would be a *democratic socialist* (neo-Marxist, Left post-Keynesian, radical political economics) economics, rather than the current NC *capitalist* economics. And this kind of economics would not be, and is not, an *ideology* but a true *economic science* based on a generally accepted, scientifically grounded, basic understanding of what is good for human well-being—satisfying need, rewarding effort, caring for the environment, and fostering economic democracy—unlike the *truly ideological* mainstream or NC economics that now masquerades as *amoral* economic science, but is based on, and attempts to justify, morally unsupportable capitalist values like the sanctioning of *rentier* exploitation.[3]

Economics cannot be a *value-free* natural science, as it is inherently a *moral* science. The real question is whether it should be based on scientifically supportable moral values that foster human well-being, or be a thinly disguised system of capitalist apologetics that pretends to be amoral. Only the former, that is democratic socialist economics—referred to as *radical political economics* in the USA and UK—can be justified as scientific in the sense that it explicitly attempts to improve social and human well-being based on widely shared values of social equity, democracy, and solidarity,

---

[3] As the most forthright NC's will occasionally openly admit. For example, a fellow member of the Ethical Humanist Society of Chicago (a person who is thus otherwise publicly committed to secular humanistic values) and faculty member of the University of Chicago Business School once stated in a public debate with me on these issues, that: "Of course, my job is to promote capitalism."

rather than pretending to be amoral but in practice functioning as a fundamentally *immoral legitimation theory* for capitalism.

What purpose does the persistence of extraordinary levels, for a wealthy and advanced economy, of clearly unmet human needs and aspirations, due to poverty, unemployment, lack of health care and educational opportunity, housing, and even food, serve, even as unheard of wealth and economic and political power is showered on a tiny minority and their families and heirs?

Is there any way to reasonably justify this kind of late-capitalist, *rentier-based*, global neofeudalism?

There is not. There is no reason and no excuse for us not to do better.

Only by sticking its collective head in the sand and refusing to allow basic human morality to *intrude* in any way, can mainstream neoclassical economic thinking pretend that the current, largely unfettered, market capitalist status quo is justifiable.

APPENDIX A

Consider an enterprise that produces q_i = 1, 2, 3, ...n goods and sells them at prices p_i to households with income y who buy $q_i(p_1, ..., p_n, y)$ and have consumer surplus $S(p_1, ..., p_n, y)$. If N denotes the total number of households in the market, $f(y)$ the relative density function for the numeric share of households by income, and $u'(y)$ marginal social utility of household income (assumed to decline with increasing income/wealth), then aggregate consumer welfare, or total weighted consumer surplus, W, will be (Baiman 2001, (2.2), p. 206):

$$W = N \int_0^\infty S\left(p_1, ..., p_n, y\right) u'\left(y\right) f\left(y\right) dy \qquad (A1)$$

And aggregate consumption of good i will be (∞ could be replaced with maximal income $\hat{y}$, but ∞ is the value that is used in the papers) (Baiman 2001, (2.3), p. 206):

$$Q_i = N \int_0^\infty q_i\left(p_1, ..., p_n, y\right) f\left(y\right) dy \qquad (A2)$$

Following Feldstein we define the *distributional characteristic* of good i as the marginal utility of income weighted, average of aggregate household utility from the consumption of good i (Feldstein 1972, p. 33) (Baiman 2001, (2.10), p. 207):

$$R_i = \frac{N}{Q_i} \int_0^\infty q_i(y) u'(y) f(y) dy \qquad (A3)$$

Diminishing marginal utility from increases in income will cause R_i to be greater for goods consumed relatively more by low-income households for which $u'(y)$ is larger than for goods with a relatively larger share of high-income consumers for which $u'(y)$ is smaller. In other words, the greater the income elasticity of demand, that is the more demand there is from higher income consumers, the lower the value of R_i.

For constant income elasticity of demand household consumption, $q_i(y) = b_i y^{\alpha_i}$, with marginal utility of income $u'(y) = y^{-\eta}$ where η is a policy determined elasticity of marginal utility of income with respect to income, and lognormal income distribution with $\overline{Y} = \text{mean of } \log(y)$ and variance $\sigma_{\overline{Y}}^2$, Feldstein estimates that (Feldstein 1972, p. 35)[4]

$$R_i = \exp\left[-\eta \overline{Y} + \left(\frac{1}{2}\right)\left(\eta^2 - 2\alpha_i \eta\right)\sigma_{\overline{Y}}^2 \right] \qquad (A4)$$

Note that according to (A4) for any given positive value of η (assuming similar variances $\sigma_{\overline{Y}}^2$), goods with higher income elasticities of demand α_i, and goods whose consumers have higher average incomes $\overline{Y}$ will have lower R_i.

Subject to these definitions, Baiman (2001, p. 208 and 206, Eqs. 2.13 and 2.5) provides a complete proof that, when cross-price effects are negligible,[5] total weighted CS, or W in (A1), is maximized subject to[6].

$$C(Q_1,\ldots,Q_n) - \sum_i p_i Q_i = \delta_0 \qquad (A5)$$

where δ_0 is a (negative) constant that fixes the overall level of (positive) profit for the firm when the *Progressive Ramsey Pricing* formula:

---

[4] Baiman (2001; 216; Footnote 19) mistakenly adds a constant to this formula. This, however, does not affect the subsequent derivations.

[5] See (Baiman 2001, Appendix B) for analogous but more complex formulas when cross-price effects are not negligible.

[6] Specifying the profit constraint in this way is necessary for a positive Lagrangian multiplier $\lambda > 0$ in Eq. (A6) below—see (Baiman 2001, p. 215–6, Footnote 17).

$$\frac{\left(p_i - mc_i\right)}{p_i} = \frac{1}{E_i}\left(\frac{\lambda - R_i}{\lambda}\right) \tag{A6}$$

is satisfied, where $E_i > 0$ is (defined as positive) own price demand elasticity for good i, $\lambda > 0$ is a constant Lagrange multiplier, and $\lambda - R_i > 0$ (Baiman 2001, p. 208).[7] Note that Eq. (A6) reverts back to the standard *flat* Ramsey pricing formula (10.1) when income distributions of customers of product segments i are identical (so that the parameters in Eq. (A4) are equal across product segments i), or when the marginal utility of income does not decline ($\eta = 0$), as in both of these cases from Eq. (A4) $R_i = c = $ constant, so that:

$$\frac{\left(p_i - mc_i\right)}{p_i} = \frac{1}{E_i}\left(\frac{\lambda - R_i}{\lambda}\right) = \frac{1}{E_i}\left(\frac{\lambda - c}{\lambda}\right) = \frac{1}{E_i}k$$

Where k is constant across all goods i: $k = \left(\frac{\lambda - c}{\lambda}\right)$.

Finally, (Baiman 2002, Equation 5, p. 315) determines when Eq. (A6) stipulates that CS maximization requires "progressive pricing" *in the usual sense* that prices relative to marginal costs for goods consumed more by lower income consumers are lower than prices relative to marginal costs for goods consumed more by higher income consumers. This is not obvious from Eq. (A6) as there may be cases in which the Ramsey inverse-elasticity *efficiency* effect may override the direct-elasticity *equity* effect whereby a larger R_i (generally corresponding to a lower E_i) produces a lower $(p_i - mc_i)/p_i$.

The question is when does $R_i/R_j > 1$ imply that: $(p_i - mc_i)/p_i < (p_j - mc_j)/p_j$, or: $\hat{p}_i < \hat{p}_j$? (where $\hat{p}_i = \left(p_i - mc_i\right)/p_i$ for all i). It turns out that the necessary and sufficient condition for this is that (Baiman 2002, Eq. (5), p. 315)[8]:

---

[7] Formulas (12–14, 372), (12:38; 378), (12–58, 388) and (15–25; 470) in Atknson and Stiglitz (1980), and Feldstein (1972; 33) Eq. (6a), are equivalent, or generalizations, of Eq. (A6) above. However, as is noted in the text above, these derivations are incomplete as, even though the consumer welfare term in the maximand is clearly *convex* in price, they do not include a demonstration that second order conditions requiring that the *constrained* maximand, including (A5), be *concave* in price. This proof is necessary to *maximize* the Lagrangian.

[8] Note that Eq. (2.15) in (Baiman 2001; 208) is erroneous. Equation (5) in (Baiman 2002: 315) is the correct replacement formula. This error was pointed out by Vincent Snowberger – see Baiman (2002) Footnote 2.

$$\frac{1}{\hat{p}_i} - E_i < \frac{R_i}{R_j}\left(\frac{1}{\hat{p}_i} - E_j\right) \tag{A7}$$

The following are different ways in which weighted CS maximization requires that prices be "*progressive in the usual sense*" or that $R_i/R_j > 1$ imply that $\hat{p}_i < \hat{p}_j$ for all products i of a monopolistic single *firm*, or entire economy, operating under a fixed profit constraint:

(a) when $E_i \geq E_j$, for example when price elasticities of demand in normal price ranges for products consumed more by lower-income consumers are greater or equal to those products consumed more by higher-income consumers, *progressivity in the usual sense* always holds. In particular, if $E_i \approx E_j$ can be approximated by a constant elasticity E *progressivity in the usual sense* always holds.

(b) When $E_i < E_j$ (the most interesting case), if E_i does not get *too small* relative to (R_i/R_j) and E_j as determined by Eq. (A7), *progressivity in the usual sense* holds. It turns out that, given the very unequal income and wealth distributions of capitalist economies, even when E_i is *substantially lower* than E_j, Eq. (A6) has to stipulate a very high markup over marginal-costs $\hat{p}_i$ before Eq. (A7) is violated, *so that even in this case, Eq. (A6) will generally dictate that "pricing progressivity in the usual sense" must be followed if (static) welfare optimality is to be obtained*. This can be demonstrated as follows.

Using Eq. (A4) above, for any policy determined $\eta > 0$, conservatively assuming consumers of goods i and j have roughly equal *income* elasticities of demand α_i, and that the distribution of household incomes of these consumers have roughly equal variance $\sigma_{\overline{Y}}^2$, we have:

$$\frac{R_i}{R_j} = \frac{\exp\left(-\overline{Y}_i\right)}{\exp\left(-\overline{Y}_j\right)}$$

But since for a log normal distribution the actual mean $\overline{y}$ has the following relationship to the mean of log(y), or $\overline{Y}$,

$$\bar{y} = \exp\left(\bar{Y} + \frac{\sigma_{\bar{y}}^2}{2}\right)$$

Under the assumption of roughly equal variance:

$$\frac{R_i}{R_j} = \frac{\bar{y}_j}{\bar{y}_i}$$

Where $\bar{y}_i$ are the actual means (not the log means) of household incomes for consumers of goods i and j, respectively.

So if we assume that good i is consumed mostly by consumers in the two *lowest* quintiles of household income (quintiles 4 and 5), which in 2006 (in 2007 dollars) had an average after-tax income of $20,200, and good j is consumed mostly by consumers in the second highest quintile of household income (quintile 2) with average after tax income of $74,700 (Wolff 2010, p. 46), we have:

$$\frac{R_i}{R_j} = \frac{R_{4-5}}{R_2} = \frac{\$74,700}{\$20,200} = 3.698$$

So that in this case, even if $E_2 = 1$ and $E_{4.5} = 0.5$, from Eq. (A7): for welfare maximization, prices for goods i and j will to be *progressive in the usual sense* as long as:

$$\overline{P_{4-5} < 0.84}$$

So that as long as the markup over marginal cost for good i is less than $5.25 = 1/(1-0.84)-1$, or 525%, prices for goods i and j will to be progressive in the usual sense. Thus in most cases, for static welfare maximization, even with large price elasticity differences, static consumer welfare maximizing prices will be *progressive in the usual sense*.

If we do the same calculation using 2007 *wealth* distribution (Wolff 2010, p. 46), we have (again in 2007 dollars)[9]:

$$\frac{R_i}{R_j} = \frac{R_{4-5}}{R_2} = \frac{\$291,000}{\$2,200} = 132.3$$

And:

$$\overline{p_{4-5} < 0.96}$$

So that as long as the markup over marginal cost for good i is less than 24 = $(1/(1-0.96))-1$, or 2,400%, prices for goods i and j need to be progressive in the usual sense. Thus *in almost every case*, for static welfare maximization, even with large price elasticity differences, prices will be progressive in the usual sense.

(c) Finally, Eq. (A7) provides a condition for the static welfare optimality of *flat* markup pricing under the (usual) downward sloping demand curve, average-costs higher than marginal-costs, conditions. In this case

$\hat{p}_i = \hat{p}_j$ is welfare optimal *if and only if* $1/\hat{p}_i - E_i = R_i / R_j \left(1/\hat{p}_i - E_j \right)$

holds. This can be derived from Eq. (A7) with equalities instead of inequalities (Baiman 2002; 316). *Thus, in almost every case, even flat marginal pricing, not to mention "standard" Ramsey "inverse-elasticity" regressive pricing, is suboptimal.* Thus even a modification of the NC "inverse elasticity" Ramsey pricing doctrine encapsulated in (10.1) that stipulated that static welfare maximization occurs when prices *are proportional* to marginal cost would be wrong in any market where average costs are higher than marginal costs, that is, *in almost all markets.*

---

[9] I am using (Wolff 2010) household income distribution data so that income and wealth data come from the same source.

Appendix B

Design Your Own Utopia[10]

Assume that you are a member of an Executive Committee of elected representatives with the power to restructure your nation's economy so that it allocates economic resources to working adults in a way that is as fair to individuals, and as beneficial to society, as possible. Assume also that your committee is *omnipotent* in the sense that it has detailed knowledge that allows for an accurate measurement of the level of each of the criteria below for each working adult. In other words assume that you have yearly data for all the people in your country (remember, you are omnipotent!) that measures:

(a) The value of the services or products that they produced.
(b) The amount of time and effort they spent.
(c) Their level of need.
(d) The value of their property or wealth.
(e) The social status of their parents (e.g. "caste" or "nobility" level; or racial or ethnic background if this is tied to social status.)

[10] Adapted from an Instructor's Manual edited by Mehrene Larudee for the 2nd edition of an introductory economics text: *Understanding Capitalism* by Samuel Bowles and Richard Edwards (1993: New York, Harper Collins). A new 2005 third edition of this text has been published by Oxford University Press with Frank Roosevelt added as a coauthor. Jayadev (2014) is listed as the author of an Instructor's Manual for the 3rd edition of this text (Bowles et al. 2005) that includes a similar exercise.

(f) How much they have received as a result of luck.

Given this data, you want your staff (who will work out all the details of *how* to do this) to set up an economy that will allocate resources based on the criteria listed below with weights, or levels of importance, given to each criteria so that the sum of the weights adds up to 100 %. You also want to be able to explain your choice of weights to your staff.

Criteria for allocating resources	Weight or importance
(a) Inherited social status	____
(b) Luck	____
(c) Need	____
(d) Productivity	____
(e) Property or wealth	____
(f) Time or effort	____
Sum of weights:	100 %

BIBLIOGRAPHY

Albert, M., & Hahnel, R. (1991). *The political economy of participatory economics.* Princeton: Princeton University Press.

Allen, B. W., Doherty, N. A., Weigelt, K., & Mansfield, E. (2013). *Managerial economics: Theory, applications, and cases* (8th ed.,). New York: W.W. Norton.

Anderberg, D., Rainer, H., Wadsworth, J., & Wilson, T. (2013). Unemployment and domestic violence: Theory and evidence. *Forschungsinstitut zur Zukunft der Arbeit Institute for the Study of Labor* (IZA). Discussion Paper No. 7515. Retrieved July, from http://ftp.iza.org/dp7515.pdf

Appelbaum, B. (2015, January 9). Windfall for taxpayers coming to end. *New York Times.*

Archer, R. (1995). *Economic democracy: The politics of feasible socialism.* Oxford: Oxford University Press.

Arrighi, G. (2005). Hegemony unravelling I and II. *New Left Review, 32*(33), March, April, May and June.

Arrow, K. (1951/1963). Social choice and individual values (2nd ed.). New Haven: Yale University Press.

Arrow, K., & Bowles, S. (Eds.) (2000). *Meritocracy and economic inequality.* Princeton: Princeton University Press.

Atknson, A. B., & Stiglitz, J. (1980). *Lectures on public economics.* New York: McGraw Hill.

Backhouse, R. E. (2006). *Economics since the Second World War.* University of Birmingham. Retrieved March, from http://www.grammatikhilfe.com/CPNSS/events/Abstracts/HIstoryofPoswarScience/Econsince1945.pdf

Baiman, R. (1997). A proposal for Democratic Constitutional Reform in Cuba. Presented June 17, 1997, at the *VII Enceunetro en Holguin con Filosophos Norteamericanos,* Universidad de Holguin, Cuba, and on June 23, 1997, at the

© The Editor(s) (if applicable) and The Author(s) 2016
R.P. Baiman, *The Morality of Radical Economics,*
DOI 10.1057/978-1-137-45559-8

IV Conferencia Internacional de Ciencias Sociales y Humanisticas, Universidad de Camaguey, Cuba.

Baiman, R. (1999, Winter). Market socialism: The debate among socialists by David Schweickart, James Lawler, Hillel Ticktin, Bertell Ollman. *Science & Society, 63*(4), 518–522.

Baiman, R. (2000). Why the emperor has no clothes: The neoclassical case for price regulation. In B. Baiman, & D. Saunders (Eds.), *Political economy and contemporary capitalism: Radical perspectives on economic theory and policy.* New York: M. E. Sharpe.

Baiman, R. (2001). Why equity cannot be separated from efficiency: The welfare economics of progressive social pricing. *Review of Radical Political Economics, 33,* 203–221.

Baiman, R. (2002). Why equity cannot be separated from efficiency II: When should social pricing be progressive. *Review of Radical Political Economics, 34,* 311–317.

Baiman, R. (2006, Winter). Unequal exchange without a labor theory of prices: On the need for a global Marshall plan and a solidarity trading regime. *Review of Radical Political Economics, 38*(1), 71–89.

Baiman, R. (2010a, September). Toward a new political economy for the U.S. *Review of Radical Political Economics, 42*(3), 353–362.

Baiman, R. (2010b). The infeasibility of free trade in classical theory: Ricardo's comparative advantage parable has no solution. *Review of Political Economy, 22*(3), 419–437.

Baiman, R. (2014). Unequal exchange and the Rentier economy. *Review of Radical Political Economics, 46*(3), 353–362.

Baiman, R. (2011b). *Eisenhower era income tax rates on the upper 10 % of families would immediately erase the federal deficit.* Chicago Political Economy Group Working Paper 2011–2. Retrieved May, from http://www.cpegonline.org/workingpapers/CPEGWP2011-2.pdf

Baiman, R. (2012a). *Self-adjusting "free trade": A generally mathematically impossible outcome.* Available from author, submitted for publication.

Baiman, R. (2012b). *A 2012 May Day manifesto: 'Left Structuralism' versus 'LiberalCyclicalism',* May. Chicago Political Economy Group (CPEG), see: http://www.cpegonline.org/documents/MayDayManifesto.pdf

Baiman, R. (2015a). *The Taylor/Piketty four fundamental laws: A radical/post-Keynesian Macroeconomic Consensus?,* January. Unpublished paper available from the author.

Baiman, R. (2015b). National Note. *CPEG Notes* (Vol. 1, Issue 2). Retrieved March, from http://www.cpegonline.org/wp-content/uploads/2015/06/Vol-I-No-2-CPEG-Notes-FINAL-May-2015a.pdf

Baiman, R. (2016a). The limits of free trade in neoclassical theory: From Hecksher-Ohlin to unequal exchange. Chapter in forthcoming *The Global Free Trade*

Error: The Infeasibility of Ricardo's Comparative Advantage Theory, by R. Baiman. New York: Routledge.

Baiman, R. (2016b, January). Globally sustainable and balanced International TradeBased on Exchange-Rate adjustment is mathematically unstable and therefore economically infeasible. Chapter in forthcoming *The global free trade error: The infeasibility of Ricardo's comparative advantage theory*, by R. Baiman. New York: Routledge.

Baumol, W. J., & Bradford, D. (1970, June). Optimal departures from marginal cost pricing. *American Economic Review*, 60(3), 265–283.

Bentham, J. (1818). Church of Englandism and its catechism examined. Published by Jeremy Bentham. London.

Blanc, L. (1851). In C. Joubert (Ed.), *Plus de Girondins*. Paris: Passage Dauphine.

Blecker, R. (1999). *Taming global finance*. Washington, DC: Economic Policy Institute.

Blinder, A. S., Canetti, E., Lebow, D., & Rudd, J. B. (1998). *Asking about prices: A new approach to understanding price stickiness*. New York: Russel Sage Foundation.

Boulding, K. (1969). *American Economic Review*, 59(1), 1–12.

Bowles, S., & Gintis, H. (1993). A political and economic case for the democratic enterprise. *Economics and Philosophy*, 9, 75–100.

Bowles, S., & Gintis, H. (2008). The evolutionary basis of collective action. In D. A. Wittman, & B. R. Weingast (Eds.), *The Oxford handbook of political economy*. Oxford: Oxford University Press.

Bowles, S., Gintis, H., & Wright, E. O. (1998). *Recasting egalitarianism: New rules for communities, states, and markets*. London: Verso Press.

Bowles, S., Edwards, R., & Roosevelt Jr., F. (2005). *Understanding capitalism: Competition, command, and change*. New York: Oxford University Press.

Carlsen, L. (2013, November 24). Under NAFTA Mexico suffered and the U.S. felt it's pain. *New York Times*.

Carnevlae, A., & Strohl, J. (2010). *Rewarding strivers: Helping low-income students succeed in college*. New York: The Century Foundation Press.

Chang, H.-J. (2002). *Kicking away the ladder: Development strategy in historical perspective*. London: Anthem Press.

Chang, H.-J. (2008). *Bad Samaritans: The myth of free trade and the secret history of capitalism*. New York: Bloomsbury Press.

Chase, E. P. (2000). The P-R-I-C-E of full employment, by Elmer P. Chase. In B. Baiman, & D. Saunders (Eds.), *Political economy and contemporary capitalism*. M.E. Sharpe.

Chiang, A. C. (1984). *Fundamental methods of mathematical economics* (3rd ed.,). New York: McGraw Hill.

Coase, R. H. (1960). The problem of social cost. *Journal of Law and Economics*, 3(1), 1–44.

Colander, D. (1994). *Macroeconomics* (2nd ed.,). New York: Irwin/ McGraw-Hill.

Colander, D. (1998). *Macroeconomics* (3rd ed.,). New York: McGraw-Hill.

Colander, D., & Landreth, H. (1998). Political influence on the textbook Keynesian revolution: God, man and Lorie Tarshis at Yale. In O. F. Hamouda & B. B. Price (Eds.), *Keynesianism and the Keynesian revolution in America: A memorial volume in Honour of Lorie Tarshis* (pp. 59–72). Cheltenham: Edward Elgar. Conn, Matt. 2004.

Conn, M. (2004, March 24). Loyalty Day celebration set for return to Medford. *The Wausau Daily Herald*.

Cook, B. (2008). *National, regional and local employment policies in Sweden and the United Kingdom*. Working Paper No. 08–05. October. Centre of Full Employment and Equity (COfFEE). Retrieved from http://e1.newcastle.edu. au/coffee/pubs/wp/2008/08-05.pdf

Cozzi, G., McKinley, T., & Michell, J. (2014). Can conventional macroeconomic models prevent persistent stagnation in the European Union. Policy Brief No. 5, *Center for Development Policy and Research* (CDPR). Retrieved from http:// www.feps-europe.eu/assets/b2ba4b96-ba66-4f87-aeaf-d91bd91e1eed/201411-pb5-cozzi-mckinley-michellpdf.pdf

Cripps, F., & Godley, W. (1976, November). A formal analysis of the Cambridge Economic Policy Group Model. *Economica (New Series), 43*(172), 335–348.

Crotty, J. (2011, March). *The realism of assumptions does matter: Why Keynes-Minsky theory must replace efficient market theory as the guide to financial regulation policy*. Political Economy Research Institute (PERI), Working Paper 255.

Daly, H. (1997). *Beyond growth*. Boston: Beacon Press.

Democracy at Work. (2013). Website data updated January 10, 2013. Accessed February 12, 2015 from http://www.democracyatwork.info/studies/ mondragon/

Devine, P. (1988). *Democracy and economic planning: The political economy of a self-governing society*. Boulder: Westview Press.

Dobb-Frank Wall Street Reform and Consumer Protection Act. (2010). Retrieved January 5, from http://www.cftc.gov/ucm/groups/public/@swaps/documents/file/hr4173_enrolledbill.pdf. Downloaded 8/27/2015.

Dorman, P. (2001). Waiting for the echo: The revolution in general equilibrium theory and the paralysis in introductory economics. *Review of Radical Political Economics, 33*(1).

Dornbusch, R., Fischer, S., & Samuelson, P. (1977). Comparative advantage, trade, and payments in a Ricardian model with a continuum of goods. *American Economic Review, 67*(5), 823–839.

Duke, N. (2000). For the rich it's richer: Print experiences and environments offered to children in very low- and very high-socioeconomic status first-grade classrooms. *American Educational Research Journal, 37*(2), 441–478.

Dumenil, G., & Levy, D. (2004). *Capital Resurgent.* Cambridge, MA: Harvard University Press.

Dymski, G., Epstein, G., & Pollin, R. (1993). *Transforming the U.S. financial system: Equity and efficiency for the 21st century.* New York: M. E. Sharpe.

Eatwell, J., & Taylor, L. (2000). *Global finance at risk.* New York: New Press.

Ellerman, D. (1992). *Property and contract in economics: The case for economic democracy.* Cambridge, MA: Basil Blackwell Publishers.

Ellerman, D. (2007). On the role of capital in "capitalist" and in labor-managed firms. *Review of Radical Political Economics, 39*(1), 5–26.

Ellman, M. (2004). Economic lessons from the transition: The basic theory re-examined. *Comparative Economic Studies, 46*(4), 570–571.

Erixon, L. (2008). *The Rehn-Meidner plan: It's rise, challenges, and survival.* Stockholm: Department of Economics, Stockholm University.

Evans, D. (2008). *FDIC may need $150 billion bailout as more banks fail (Update3).* New York: Bloomberg News. Retrieved September 25, from http://www.bloomberg.com/apps/news?sid=amZxIbcjZISU&pid=newsarchive

Feldstein, M. (1972). Distributional equity and the optimal structure of public prices. *American Economic Review, 62,* 32–36.

Felkerson, J. (2011). *$29,000,000,000,000: A detailed look at the Fed's bailout by funding facility and recipient.* Levy Institute Working Paper #698. Retrieved December, from http://www.levyinstitute.org/pubs/wp_698.pdf

Ferber, M. A., & Nelson, J. A. (Eds.) (1993). *Beyond economic man: Feminist theory and economics.* Chicago: University of Chicago Press.

Findlay, R. (1995). *Factor proportions, trade, and growth.* Cambridge, MA: MIT Press.

Fingleton, E. (2008). *In the Jaws of the Dragon: America's fate in the coming era of Chinese Dominance.* New York: St. Martin's Griffin.

Fletcher, I. (2009). *Free trade doesn't work: Why America needs a tariff.* Washington, DC: U.S. Business & Industry Council.

Friedman, M. (1953). *Essays in positive economics.* Chicago: University of Chicago Press.

Friedman, M. (1962). *Capitalism and freedom.* Chicago: University of Chicago Press.

Friedman, M. (1963). *Inflation causes and consequences.* New York: Asia Publishing House.

Friedman, H. (2012). The American myth of social mobility. *Huffington Post.* Retrieved July 16, from http://www.huffingtonpost.com/howard-steven-friedman/class-mobility_b_1676931.html

Gailbraith, J. K. (2014, Spring). Kapital for the twenty first century?. *Dissent.*

Garbade, K. D. (2014). *Direct purchases of U.S. treasury securities by Federal Reserve Banks.* Federal Reserve Bank of New York Staff Reports No. 684.

Geoghegan, T. (2014). *Only one thing can save us: Why America needs a new kind of labor movement*. New York: The New Press.

Georgescu-Roegen, N. (1999). *The entropy law and economic processes*. iUniverse Inc.

Gilens, M., & Page, B. I. (2014, September). Testing theories of American politics: Elites, interest groups, and average citizens. Perspectives on Politics, 12(3), 564–581.

Ginsburg, H. (1982). How Sweden combats unemployment among young and older workers. *Monthly Labor Review, 105*(10), 22–27.

Gintis, H. (2009). *Game theory evolving: A problem centered introduction to modeling strategic interaction*. Princeton University Press.

Godley, W., & Lavoie, M. (2007). *Monetary economics: An integrated approach to credit, money, income, production and wealth*. New York: Palgrave Macmillan.

Godley, W., Izurieta, A., & Zezza, G. (2004, August). Prospects and policies for the U.S. economy. In *Strategic analysis*. New York: Levy Institute at Bard College.

Goldsmith, A., & Diette, T. (2012). Exploring the link between unemployment and mental health outcomes. *American Psychological Association SES Indicator*. Retrieved April, from http://www.apa.org/pi/ses/resources/indicator/2012/04/unemployment.aspx

Goodwin, D. (2001). The way we won: America's economic breakthrough during World War II. *American Prospect*. Retrieved December 19, from http://prospect.org/article/way-we-won-americas-economic-breakthrough-during-world-war-ii

Goodwin, N., Nelson, J. A., & Harris, J. (2009). *Macroeconomics in context*. Armonk: M. E. Sharpe.

Gordon, R. (2012). *Is U.S. economic growth over? Faltering innovation confronts the six headwinds*. NBER Working Paper No. 18315. Retrieved August, from http://www.nber.org/papers/w18315

Gould, E. (2015). *2014 continuous a 35 year trend of broad based wage stagnation*. February 19. Issue Brief #393. Washington, DC: Economic Policy Institute.

Granqvist, R., & Lind, H. (2004, Fall). Excess burden of an income tax: What do mainstream economists really measure?. *Review of Radical Political Economics, 37*(4).

Habermas, J. (1975). *Legitimation crisis*. Boston: Beacon Press.

Habermas, J. (1990). *Moral consciousness and communicative action* (C. Lenhardt & S. W. Nicholsen, Trans.) Cambridge, MA: The MIT Press.

Hahnel, R., & Albert, M. (1990). *Quiet revolution in welfare economics*. Princeton: Princeton University Press.

Hancock, K. (2013). *Australian wage policy: Infancy and adolescence*. Adelaide: University of Adelaide Press.

Hanlon, S. (2011, May 5). Big oil's misbegotten tax gusher: Why they don't need $70 billion from taxpayers amid record profits. *Think Progress*.

Harkinson, J. (2009). How the Nation's Only State-Owned Bank became the Envy of Wall Street, March 27. *Mother Jones.*

Harris, S. (2010). *The moral landscape: How science can determine human values.* New York: Free Press.

Harris, N. B. (2014). The chronic stress of poverty: Toxic to children. *The Shriver Report.* Retrieved January 12, from http://shriverreport.org/the-chronic-stress-of-poverty-toxic-to-children-nadine-burke-harris/

Hartmann, T. (2010). *Unequal protection: How corporations became "people" and how you can fight back* (2nd ed.,). San Francisco, CA: Berrett-Koehler Publisher.

Harvey, D. (2003). *The new imperialism.* New York: Oxford University Press.

Harvey, D. (2007). *A brief history of neoliberalism.* New York: Oxford University Press.

Heilbroner, R. L. (1992). *The worldly philosophers: The lives, times and ideas of the great economic thinkers* (6th ed.,). New York: Touchstone/Simon & Schuster.

Helper, S., Krueger, T., & Wial, H. (2012). *Why does manufacturing matter? Which manufacturing matters? A policy framework.* February. Brookings Metropolitan Policy Program.

Heymann, J., Rho, H. J., Schmitt, J., & Earle, A. (2009, May). *A comparison of paid sick day policies in 22 countries.* Center for Economic and Policy Research (CEPR).

Hill, S. (2010). *Europe's promise: Why the European way is the best hope in an insecure age.* Berkeley: University of California Press.

Hill, R., & Myatt, T. (2010). *The economics anti-textbook: A critical thinkers guide to micro-economics.* Halifax and London: Fernwood Publishing and Zed Books.

Hirschman, A. O. (1970). *Exit, voice, and loyalty: Responses to decline in firms, organizations, and states.* Cambridge, MA: Harvard University Press.

Howard, A. (2009). "Codetermination" from website of American Studies at the University of Virginia. http://xroads.virginia.edu/~ma98/pollklas/thesis/codetermination.html. Last updated 9/01/2009. Accessed 26 Aug 2015.

Huber, E., & Stephens, J. (2001). *Development and crisis of the welfare state: Parties and policies in global markets.* Chicago: University of Chicago Press.

Hume, D. (1742). *Essays, moral, political, and literary* (Republished 1987). Indianapolis: Liberty Fund Inc.

Inman, P. (2015). Where did the Greek bailout money go? *The Guardian.* Retrieved June 29, from http://www.theguardian.com/world/2015/jun/29/where-did-the-greek-bailout-money-go

Isaacs, J. (2008). *International comparisons of economic mobility.* PEW/Brookings report based on 1998–2001 data from the International Social Survey Program. Retrieved from http://www.brookings.edu/~/media/research/files/reports/2008/2/economic%20mobility%20sawhill/02_economic_mobility_sawhill_ch3.pdf

Jayadev, A. (2014). *Instructors manual for 3rd edition of understanding capitalism by Bowles, Edwards, and Roosevelt.* University of Massachusetts at Boston. Retrieved from

http://sttpml.org/wp-content/uploads/2014/08/UnderstandingCapitalism
InstructorsManual.pdf

Kahn, A. E. (1993). *The economics of regulation*. Cambridge, MA: MIT Press.

Kahneman, D. (2011). *Thinking fast and slow*. New York: Macmillan.

Kalecki, M. (1971). *Selected essays on the dynamics of the capitalist economy*. Cambridge: Cambridge University Press, Cambridge, U.K.

Kant, E. (1785). *Groundwork of the metaphysics of morals*. Cambridge University Press (2012). Cambridge, U.K.

Keen, S. (2011). *Debunking economics* (2nd ed.,). Pluto Press, London, U.K.

Keynes, J. M. (1924). *A tract on monetary reform*. London: Macmillan and Co. Ltd..

Keynes, J. M. (1936). *The general theory of employment, interest, and money*. London: Macmillan/Cambridge University Press.

Kiefer, D., & Rada, C. (2014). Profit maximizing goes global: The race to the bottom. *Cambridge Journal of Economics*, First published online September 29, 2014.

Kim, J. (2011). How modern banking originated: The London goldsmith bankers' institutionalization of trust. *Economic History*, 53(6) 939–959.

Klein, N. (2008, June 24). *Shock doctrine: The rise of disaster capitalism* (1st ed.). New York: Macmillan/Picador.

Klein, N. (2014). *This changes everything*. New York: Simon & Schuster.

Kochhar, R., Fry, R., & Taylor, P. (2011). *Wealth gaps rise to record highs between whites, blacks, hispanics*. Pew Research Social & Demographic Trends. Retrieved from http://www.pewsocialtrends.org/2011/07/26/wealth-gaps-rise-to-record-highs-between-whites-blacks-hispanics/

Kornai, J. (1986). The soft budget constraint. *Kyklos, 39*, 3–30.

Kornai, J., Haggard, S., & Kaufman, R. R. (2001). *Reforming the state: Fiscal and welfare reform in post-socialist countries*. Cambridge: Cambridge University Press.

Koshiro, K. (1984, August). Lifetime employment in Japan: Three models of the concept. *Monthly Labor Review, 107*, 34–35

Krashen, S. (2002). Poverty has a powerful impact on educational attainment, or, don't trust Ed trust. *Substance*. Retrieved February, from http://www.fairtest.org/poverty-has-powerful-impact-educational-attainment-or-dont-trust-ed-trust

Krassa, M., & Radcliff, B. (2014). Does a higher minimum wage make people happier. *Washington Post*. Retrieved May 14, from http://www.washington-post.com/blogs/monkey-cage/wp/2014/05/14/does-a-higher-minimum-wage-make-people-happier/

Krugman, P. (1996). Ricardo's difficult idea. Published on MIT website: http://web.mit.edu/krugman/www/ricardo.htm. Downloaded 8/272015.

Krugman, P. (2012a). Where the productivity went. *The New York Times*. Retrieved April 28, from http://krugman.blogs.nytimes.com/2012/04/28/where-the-productivity-went/

Krugman, P. (2012b, February 28). What ails Europe?. *The New York Times.*
Krugman, P. (2014, June 22). The big green test. *The New York Times.*
Krugman, P. (2015a). TPP at the NABE. *The New York Times.* Retrieved March 11, from http://krugman.blogs.nytimes.com/2015/03/11/tpp-at-the-nabe/
Krugman, P. (2015b). The case for cuts was a lie, why does Britain still believe it?: The austerity delusion. *The Guardian.* Retrieved April 29, from http://www.theguardian.com/business/ng-interactive/2015/apr/29/the-austerity-delusion
Kuttner, R. (1996). *Everything for sale.* New York: Alfred A. Knopf.
Larudee, M. (1993). *Instructor's manual for the 2nd edition of understanding capitalism by Samuel Bowles and Richard Edwards.* New York: Harper Collins.
Lavoie, M. (2005). A Primer on Endogeneous Credit Money in *Modern Theories of Money: The Nature and Role of Money in Capitalist Economics.* Cheltenham, U.K.: Edward Elgar.
Lavoie, M. (2009). *Introduction to post-Keynesian economics.* New York: Palgrave Macmillan.
Lee, F. (1998). *Post Keynesian price theory.* Cambridge: Cambridge University Press.
Lerner, A. P. (1944). *The economics of control.* New York: Macmillan.
Levy, J. (2015). *In U.S., uninsured rate dips to 11.9 % in first quarter.* Gallup Well-Being. Retrieved April 13, from http://www.gallup.com/poll/182348/uninsured-rate-dips-first-quarter.aspx
Locke, J. (1690). *Second treatise on government.* New York: Barnes & Noble Publishing.
Loth, R. (2015). *The greatest investors: George Soros.* From Investopedia website. Retrieved from http://www.investopedia.com/university/greatest/georgesoros.asp. Downloaded 8/27/2105.
Lusvardi, W. (2011). Bryson's troubled part in the California electric crisis. *California Watchdog.* Retrieved August 5, from http://www.calwatchdog.com/2011/08/05/brysons-troubled-part-in-ca-electricity-crisis/
MacEwan, A. (1999). *Neo-Liberalism or democracy?* New York: Zed Books.
Malthus, T. R. (1798). *An essay on the principle of population.* London: J. Johnson is St. Paul's Church Yard.
Mankiw, N. G. (2008). *Principles of microeconomics* (5th ed.,). New York: Worth Publishers.
Mann, J. (2007). *The China fantasy: How are leaders explain away Chinese repression.* New York: Viking.
Mansfield, E. (1994). *Microeconomics: Theory and applications* (8th ed.,). New York: W.W. Norton and Co..
Marglin, S. (1984). *Growth, distribution, and prices.* Cambridge: Harvard University Press.
Marglin, S., & Schor, J. (1992). *The golden age of capitalism: Reinterpreting the post-war experience.* Oxford: Clarendon Press.
Marshall, A. (1890). *Principles of economics.* London: Macmillan and Co.

Marx, K. (1859). *A contribution to the critique of political economy. Preface.* Moscow: Progress Publishers, 1977.

Marx, K. (1863). *Theories of surplus value.* Moscow: Progress Publishers.

Marx, K. (1867). *Capital* (Vol. I). Moscow: Progress Publishers.

Marx, K. (1875). *Critique of the Gotha program.* Moscow: Progress Publishers, Republished 1970.

Marx, K. (1984). In F. Engels (Ed.), *Capital* (Vol. III). London: Penguin, First published 1894.

Marx, K., & Engels, F. (1848). *Manifesto of the Communist Party.* Marx/Engles Selected Works Vol. I (1969). Moscow: Progress Publishers.

Mill, J. (1808). *Commerce defended. An answer to the arguments by which Mr. Spence, Mr. Cobbett, and Others, have attempted to Prove that Commerce is not a source of National Wealth.* London: C. and R. Baldwin.

Mills, G. T., & Rockoff, H. (1983). Business attitudes toward wage and price controls in World War II. *Business and Economic History, 12.*

Minsky, H. (1982). *Can it happen again?: Essays on instability and finance.* Armonk: M. E. Sharpe.

Mirowski, P. (2001). *Dream machines: Economics becomes a Cyborg science.* Cambridge University Press.

Morrissey, M. (2013). *Private-sector pension coverage fell by half over two decades.* Economic Policy Institute Working Economics Blog. Retrieved January 11, from http://www.epi.org/blog/private-sector-pension-coverage-decline/

Mutari, E. (2000). A primer on feminist political economy. In B. Baiman, & D. Saunders (Eds.), *Political economy and contemporary capitalism: Radical perspectives on economic theory and policy.* New York: M. E. Sharpe.

Navarro, P. (2008). *The coming China wars: Where they will be fought and how they can be won.* London: FT Press.

Nell, E. J. (1967). Theories of growth and theories of value. *Economic Development and Cultural Change, 16,* 15–16.

Nell, E. J. (Ed.) (1980). *Growth, profits, and property: Essays in the revival of political economy.* Cambridge University Press.

Nell, E. J. (1992). *Transformational growth and effective demand.* New York: New York University Press.

Nell, E. J. (1996). *Making sense of a changing economy.* London and New York: Routledge.

Nell, E. J. (1998). *The general theory of transformational growth.* New York: Cambridge University Press.

Nell, E. J. (2006). The simple theory of aggregate demand. *Cambridge Journal of Economics, 30*(4).

Neuman, S., & Celano, D. (2001). Access to print in low-income and middle-income communities. *Reading Research Quarterly, 36*(1), 8–26.

OECD. (2010). *Economic policy reforms going for growth.* Retrieved from http://www.oecd.org/tax/public-finance/chapter%205%20gfg%202010.pdf

Oil Change International. (2015). Front page of website downloaded 8/27/15: http://priceofoil.org/thepriceofoil/global-warming/

Palley, T. I. (2008a). Keynesian models of deflation and depression revisited. *Journal of Economic Behavior & Organization, 68*(1), 167–177.

Palley, T. I. (2008b). *Endogenous money: Implications for the money supply process, interest rates, and macroeconomics.* August. Political Economy Research Institute (PERI), Working Paper 178. Retrieved from http://scholarworks. umass.edu/cgi/viewcontent.cgi?article=1149&context=peri_workingpapers

Palley, T. I. (2013a). *Money, fiscal policy, and interest rates: A critique of Modern Monetary Theory.* Author's working paper. Retrieved January, from http://www.thomaspalley.com/docs/articles/macro_theory/mmt.pdf

Palley, T. I. (2013b). *Gattopardo economics: The crisis and the mainstream response of change that keeps things the same.* Working Paper 112, Institut für Makroökonomieund Konjunkturforschung Macroeconomic Policy Institute. Retrieved April, from http://www.boeckler.de/pdf/p_imk_wp_112_2013.pdf

Parramore, L. (2015). What Thomas Piketty and Larry summers don't tell you about income inequality. Institute for New Economic Thinking and *Huffington Post.* Retrieved February 6, from http://www.huffingtonpost.com/lynn-par-ramore/what-thomas-piketty-and-l_b_6630688.html

Phillips, M. (2013). The high price of a free college education in Sweden. *The Atlantic.* Retrieved May 31, from http://www.theatlantic.com/international/archive/2013/05/the-high-price-of-a-free-college-education-in-sweden/276428/

Pieper, U., & Taylor, L. (1998). *The revival of the liberal creed: The IMF, The World Bank, and Inequality in a Globalized Economy.* New York: CEPA Working Paper Series 1, WP 4. Retrieved January, from http://www.economicpolicyre-search.org/scepa/publications/workingpapers/1998/cepa0104.pdf

Piketty, T. (2014). *Capital in the twenty-first century.* Cambridge, MA: The Belknap Press of Harvard University Press.

Pizzigati, S. (2013). "Remember when people had pensions?" Too much: A commentary on excess and inequality. *Featured News.* Retrieved September 7, from http://toomuchonline.org/remember-when-people-had-pensions/

Polanyi, K. (1944). *The great transformation.* New York: Beacon.

Porter, M. (1990). The Competitive Advantage of Nations. *Harvard Business Review,* March/April 68(2), 73–91.

Ramsey, F. (1927). A contribution to the theory of taxation. *Economic Journal, 37,* 47–61.

Rawls, J. (1971). *A theory of justice.* Cambridge, MA: Harvard University Press.

Ray, R., Sanes, M., & Schmitt, J. (2013). *No vacation nation revisited.* Center for Economic and Policy Research (CEPR). Retrieved May, from http://www.cepr.net/documents/publications/no-vacation-update-2013-05.pdf

Reardon, S. F. (2013). No rich child left behind. *New York Times.* Retrieved April 13, from http://opinionator.blogs.nytimes.com/2013/04/27/no-rich-child-left-behind/?_php=true&_type=blogs&_r=0

Reinert, E. (2007). *How rich countries got rich and why poor countries stay poor.* New York: Public Affairs.

Ricardo, D. (1817). On the principles of political economy and taxation (3rd ed.). London: John Murray (1821).

Ricardo, D. (1971). *The works and correspondence of David Ricardo, Vol. II. Notes on Malthus's principles of political economy.* Cambridge: Cambridge University Press.

Richardson, H. W. (1969, October). The economic significance of the depression in Britain. *Journal of Contemporary History, 4*(4), 3–19.

Riddell, T., Shackelford, J., Schneider, G., & Stamos, S. (2011). *Economics: A tool for critically understanding society* (9th ed.,). New York: Addison-Wesley.

Robbins, L. (1932). *An essay on the nature and significance of economic science.* London: Macmillan.

Robeyns, I. (2013). Economics is a moral science. Post on blog: *Out of the Crooked Timber of Humanity no Straight Thing Was Ever Made.* Retrieved October 31, from http://crookedtimber.org/2013/10/31/economics-as-a-moral-science/

Robinson, J. (1962, September). Review of H.G. Johnson's money, trade and economic growth. *Economic Journal*, LXXII 287, 690–692.

Rochman, B. (2011). Unemployed men are more likely to divorce. *Time Magazine.* Retrieved July 11, from http://healthland.time.com/2011/07/11/unemployed-men-are-more-likely-to-divorce/

Roemer, J. E. (1988). *Free to lose: An introduction to Marxist philosophy.* Cambridge: Harvard University Press.

Roemer, J. E. (1994). *A future for socialism.* Cambridge: Harvard University Press.

Sackrey, C., Schneider, G., & Knoedler, J. (2013). *Introduction to political economy* (7th ed.,). Boston: Dollars and Sense.

Samuelson, P. (1966). A summing up. *The Quarterly Journal of Economics, 80*(4), 568–583.

Samuelson, P. (1971). Understanding the Marxian Notion of exploitation: A summary of the so-called transformation problem between Marxian values and competitive prices. *Journal of Economic Literature, 9*(2), 399–431.

Schiller, B. R. (2013a). *The macroeconomy today* (13th ed.,). New York: McGraw-Hill Irwin.

Schiller, B. R. (2013b). *The macroeconomy today* (13th ed.,). Burr Ridge: Irwin/McGraw-Hill.

Schumpeter, J. (1942). *Capitalism, socialism, and democracy.* New York: Harper & Row.

Schweickart, D. (1993). *Against capitalism: Studies in Marxism and social theory.* Cambridge University Press.

Schweickart, D. (2011). *After capitalism* (2nd ed.,). Lanham: Rowan & Littlefield.

Sen, A. (1987). *On ethics and economics.* Oxford: Blackwell Publishing.

Sigurjonsson, F. (2015). *Monetary reform: A better monetary system for Iceland*. Report commissioned by the Prime Minister of Iceland, March, Edition 1.0, Reykjavik, Iceland. Retrieved from http://www.forsaetisraduneyti.is/media/Skyrslur/monetary-reform.pdf

Simon, H. (1976). From substantive to procedural rationality. In S. J. Latsis (Ed.), *Method and appraisal in economics*. Cambridge: Cambridge University Press.

Singer, P. (1999). *Practical ethics*. Cambridge University Press.

Smith, A. (1759). The theory of moral sentiments (6th ed.). London: A. Millar. 1790.

Smith, A. (1776). An inquiry into the nature and causes of the wealth of nations. New York: Modern Library. Republished 1994.

Social Security. (2013a). *Social security programs throughout the world: The United States of America*. Social Security Administration (SSA) and The International Social Security Association (ISSA). Retrieved from http://www.ssa.gov/policy/docs/progdesc/ssptw/2012-2013/americas/united-states.pdf

Social Security. (2013b). *Social security programs throughout the world: Sweden*. Social Security Administration (SSA) and The International Social Security Association (ISSA). Retrieved from http://www.ssa.gov/policy/docs/progdesc/ssptw/2012-2013/europe/sweden.pdf

Sraffa, P. (1926). The law of returns under competitive conditions. *Economic Journal, 36*, 535–550.

Sraffa, P. (1960). *Production of commodities by means of commodities: Prelude to a critique of economic theory*. Cambridge: Cambridge University Press.

Steinberg, I. S. (1993). Economics: Value theory in the spirit of Bentham. In B. Parekh (Ed.), *Jeremy Bentham: Critical assessments*. New York: Routledge.

Stevenson, B., & Wolfers, J, (2008). *Economic growth and subjective well-being: Reassessing the Easterlin Paradox*. Institute for the Study of Labor (IZA), Discussion Paper No. 3654. Retrieved August 2008, from http://ftp.iza.org/dp3654.pdf

Stiglitz, J. (1996). *Whither socialism*. M.I.T. Press.

Stiglitz, J. (2002). *Globalization and its discontents*. New York: W. W. Norton.

Stiglitz, J. E., Sen, A., & Fitoussi, J.-P. (2009). *Report by the Stiglitz commission on the measurement of economic performance and social progress*. CMEPSP, Paris. Retrieved from http://www.stat.si/doc/drzstat/Stiglitz%20report.pdf

Stretton, H. (1999). *Economics: A new introduction*. New York: Pluto Press.

Swedish Association of Public Housing. (2015). *Public housing in Sweden*. Web publication accessed 8/31/15: http://www.sabo.se/om_sabo/english/Sidor/Publichousing.aspx

Swedish Institute. (2015). *10 things that make Sweden family friendly*. Web publication: https://sweden.se/society/10-things-that-make-sweden-family-friendly/. Dated 2013–2015. Accessed 8/30/2015.

Swedish Pensions Agency. (2015). *How you earn your retirement pension.* Web Publication accessed 8/31/2015: http://www.pensionsmyndigheten.se/HowYouEarnYourRetirementPension_en.html

Taleb, N. N. (2010). *The black swan: the impact of the highly improbable* (2nd ed.,). London: Penguin.

Tanfani, J. (2012). Richard Hart: Paul Ryan's political, economic mentor. *Los Angeles Times.* Retrieved August 15, from http://articles.latimes.com/2012/aug/15/news/la-pn-rich-hart-paul-ryans-political-mentor-20120815

Tassava, C. (2008). *The American Economy during World War II.* EH. Net Encyclopedia, edited by Robert Whaples. Retrieved February 10, from http://eh.net/encyclopedia/the-american-economy-during-world-war-ii/

Taylor, L. (2004a). *Reconstructing macroeconomics: Structuralist proposals and critiques of the mainstream.* Cambridge, MA: Harvard University Press.

Taylor, Q. P. (2004b, Winter). An original omission? Property in Rawls's political thought. *The Independent Review, VII*(3), 387–400.

Taylor, L. (2010). *Maynard's revenge: The collapse of free market economics.* Cambridge, MA: Harvard University Press.

Taylor, L. (2014, May). *The triumph of the Rentier? Thomas Piketty vs. Luigi Pasinetti and John Maynard Keynes.* Center for Economic Policy Analysis, New School for Social Research.

Thierer, A. (2010). Who'll really benefit from net neutrality regulation?, *CBS News.* Retrieved December 21, from http://www.cbsnews.com/news/opinion-wholl-really-benefit-from-net-neutrality-regulation/

Thrope, J. (2015). The next worry, a deflationary slump like Japan. *Financial Post.* Retrieved July 6, from http://www.financialpost.com/analysis/story.html?id=80453d8f-0110-4999-a295-c6f5469eb155

Tough, P. (2014). Who gets to graduate. *New York Times.* Retrieved May 15, from http://www.nytimes.com/2014/05/18/magazine/who-gets-to-graduate.html

Tuckness, A. (2012). Locke's political philosophy. In E. N. Zalta (Ed.), *The Stanford encyclopedia of philosophy* (Winter 2012 Edition). Retrieved from http://plato.stanford.edu/archives/win2012/entries/locke-political/

Varian, H. R. (1992). *Microeconomic analysis* (3rd ed.,). New York: W. W. Norton.

Varoufakis, Y. (2014). Egalitarianism's latest foe: a critical review of Thomas Piketty's Capital in the Twenty-First Century. *Real-World Economics Review, 69.* Retrieved from http://www.paecon.net/PAEReview/issue69/whole69.pdf

Veblen, T. (1899). *Theory of the leisure class: An economic study in the evolution of institutions.* New York: Macmillan.

Vernengo, M. (2000). What do undergrads really need to know about trade and finance. In R. Baiman, H. Boushey, & D. Saunders (Eds.), *Political economy and contemporary capitalism.* M.E. Sharpe: Armonk.

Visser, J. (2006). Union membership statistics in 24 countries. *Monthly Labor Review*, *1*. Retrieved from http://www.bls.gov/opub/mlr/2006/01/art-3full.pdf

Vogel, N. (2000). How California's consumers lost with electricity deregulation. *Los Angeles Times. Dec. 9.*

Vohs, K. D. (2013, August 30). The poor's poor mental power. Science, 341, 969–970.

von Bohm Bawek, E. (1884). *Capital and interest. Vol 1: History and critique of interest theories.* Republished 1958 by Libertarian Press.

Walras, L. (1877). *Elements of Pure Economics.* Reprint 1954 New York: Irwin.

Weeks, J. (2014). *Economics of the 1 %: How mainstream economics serves the rich, obscures reality and distorts policy.* London: Anthem Press.

Wen, Y., & Jing, W. (2014). *Withstanding great recession like China.* Research Division of the Federal Reserve Bank of St. Louis. Working Paper 2015–007. Retrieved March, from https://research.stlouisfed.org/wp/2014/2014-007.pdf

Whyte, W. F., & Whyte, K. K. (1991). *Making Mondragord: The growth and dynamics of the worker cooperative complex.* Ithaca: Cornell University Press.

Wiatrowski, W. J. (2012). The last private industry pension plans: a visual essay. *Monthly Labor Review.* Retrieved December, from http://www.bls.gov/opub/mlr/2012/12/art1full.pdf

Williams, J. C. (2012). Monetary policy, money, and inflation. *Federal Reserve Bank of San Francisco Economic Letter.* Retrieved July 9, from http://www.frbsf.org/economic-research/publications/economic-letter/2012/july/monetary-policy-money-inflation/

Wolff, E. N. (2010, March). *Recent trends in household wealth in the United States: Rising debt and the middle-class squeeze- an update to 2007.* Levy Institute of Economics Working Paper No. 589.

Wray, R. (2012). *Modern monetary theory: A primer on macroeconomics for Sovereign Monetary Systems.* New York: Palgrave Macmillan.

Wright, J. (2003). *The $300 billion question: How much do high-income countries subsidize agriculture?.* Center for Economic and Policy Research. Retrieved December, from http://www.cepr.net/publications/reports/the-300-billion-question-how-much-do-high-income-countries-subsidize-agriculture

INDEX[1]

[1] Note: Page numbers followed by 'f', 't' and 'n' refer to figures, tables and notes.

CPSIA information can be obtained
at www.ICGtesting.com
Printed in the USA
LVHW081556120921
697662LV00003B/455

9 781137 455581